A Ministry of Presence

A Ministry of Presence

Chaplaincy, Spiritual Care, and the Law

WINNIFRED FALLERS SULLIVAN

The University of Chicago Press
Chicago and London

Winnifred Fallers Sullivan is professor and chair of religious studies at Indiana University Bloomington, where she is also an affiliate professor at the Maurer School of Law.

The University of Chicago Press, Chicago 60637
The University of Chicago Press, Ltd., London
© 2014 by The University of Chicago
All rights reserved. Published 2014.
Printed in the United States of America

23 22 21 20 19 18 17 16 15 14   1 2 3 4 5

ISBN-13: 978-0-226-77975-1 (cloth)
ISBN-13: 978-0-226-14559-4 (e-book)
DOI: 10.7208/chicago/9780226145594.001.0001

Library of Congress Cataloging-in-Publication Data

Sullivan, Winnifred Fallers, 1950– author.
    A ministry of presence : chaplaincy, spiritual care, and the
law / Winnifred Fallers Sullivan.
        pages cm
    Includes bibliographical references and index.
    ISBN 978-0-226-77975-1 (cloth : alk. paper)—
    ISBN 978-0-226-14559-4 (e-book)   1. Chaplains—Legal status,
laws, etc.—United States. 2. Pastoral counseling—Law and legislation—
United States. 3. Religion and state—United States. 4. Religion and
law—United States.   I. Title.
    KF4868.C44S85 2014
    342.7308'52161—dc23
                                                                    2013043367

For George and Lloyd

CONTENTS

Where the theological rubber meets the road.

Professional religious work is usually thought of as work performed by clergy—ministers, rabbis, priests, imams, monks—laboring under the auspices of a particular religious sect and in accordance with its tenets, to perform religious duties, to care for the religious needs of their coreligionists, or to recruit new members to the community. Today, however, a significant amount of religious work is performed by chaplains who do not necessarily routinely publicly identify themselves with a particular religious community but who do their work rather within secular institutions caring for persons with whom they may not share a common religious creed or practice. Their clients are persons with whom they are temporarily brought together for other reasons—reasons such as war, sickness, crime, employment, education, or disaster—persons who may be of any religious affiliation or none. These professional encounters are spread across the secular landscape of contemporary life.

The ubiquity of chaplains today is largely invisible to most Americans; indeed, their place at all in the American religious landscape usually escapes notice except when their presence is specifically brought to mind in a particular setting, such as at the scene of the World Trade Center collapse or in hospice care. But chaplaincy is remarkably pervasive today, and not just in the United States; chaplains are present in the spaces of contemporary social encounter throughout much of the world.[1] The chaplain is, I will claim, a

1. It is extremely difficult to quantify and to give statistical backing to these statements. After working on this project for a number of years, I can only say that my reading and inquiring about chaplains during this research has persuaded me that there is both a real shift among clergy toward chaplaincy and away from congregational work as well as an increase in absolute numbers. See, e.g., David B. Plummer, "Chaplaincy: The Greatest Story Never Told," *Journal of Pastoral Care* 50 (Spring 1996): 1–12.

strangely necessary figure, religiously and legally speaking, in negotiating the public life of religion today.

It might seem surprising that a church office that originated in the Middle Ages has morphed into the twenty-first century's indispensable minister without portfolio—for that is what he has become: the minister who serves the spiritual needs of a large, diverse, and restless population. As I will explain further in the chapters that follow, while the role of the chaplain has a long history and has found a place in a number of different contexts, he is also very much the man of the hour. Today's chaplain is both heir to a complex past and brand new. The work that chaplains do, their training for that work, their responsiveness to the spiritual marketplace, and their regulation by the government deserve attention.

Chaplains serve throughout the myriad institutions of American contemporary life, public and private—governmental, nongovernmental, and quasi-governmental.[2] There are chaplains in airports, colleges and universities, fire departments, prisons, hospitals, the military, unions, and even businesses and workplaces.[3] The Seamen's Church Institute of Philadelphia has served as a chaplaincy to the port of Philadelphia since 1919. There are racetrack chaplaincies.[4] Even the Occupy movement has chaplains.[5] This book will consider those chaplains whose ministry takes place in secular rather than religious institutions. (The word "chaplain" is also used as an in-house designation by religious organizations themselves in a related but not entirely congruent use.[6])

2. I do not see bright lines to divide these denominations. Particularly since the widespread privatization of public services in the United States and the outsourcing of government work, the blurred line between public and private makes a sharp distinction inaccurate with respect to much of the work of chaplains as in other fields.

3. See, e.g., Mark Oppenheimer, "The Rise of the Corporate Chaplain," *Bloomberg Businessweek*, August 23, 2012, 58–61. On workplace spirituality outside the United States, see, e.g., Daromir Rudnyckyj, "Spiritual Economies: Islam and Neoliberalism in Contemporary Indonesia," *Cultural Anthropology* 24 (2009): 104–14. Princeton University has a center devoted to the study of religion and business, the Faith and Work Initiative. http://www.princeton.edu/faithandwork/ (accessed June 25, 2013).

4. See, e.g., Race Track Chaplaincy of America: Pennsylvania Division, Inc., http://www.rtca-pa.org/history.php (accessed January 26, 2013).

5. Mark Oppenheimer, "At 'Occupy' Protests, Bearing Christian Witness without Preaching," *New York Times*, November 11, 2011, A19.

6. For example, priest-chaplains exist in Catholic institutions such as Catholic colleges. The Church of Scientology uses "chaplain" to denominate some in-house counselors. See Stacey Solie, "For Scientologists Divorce Is No Simple Matter," *New York Times*, July 8, 2012, 8.

The chaplain is at once a distinctively Old World religious type, one originating in the late Roman Empire and featuring at critical points in European history and literature, as well as, in his present incarnation, the product of a distinctively modern settlement between church and state. The US chaplain, in particular, has come to instantiate the peculiar and shifting religious terrain framed by the religion clauses of the First Amendment to the US Constitution; she operates at the intersection of the sacred and the secular, a broker responsible for ministering to the wandering souls of a globalized economy and a public harrowed by a politics of fear—while also effectively sacralizing the institutions of the contemporary world.

The chapters of this book will consider the institution of the contemporary chaplaincy, its practices, its legal regulation, and its value as a site for understanding contemporary religion more generally. Before getting down to that work, though, this preface will briefly introduce the reader to one chaplain who provides what she—like other chaplains—calls "a ministry of presence" in a seemingly unlikely, but in many ways typical, chaplaincy, for the state of Maine: the Reverend Kate Braestrup.

Reverend Braestrup has been a government-paid chaplain to the game wardens of the state of Maine for almost ten years. In a 2006 interview with public radio, she explained her job, beginning with a day when the warden service was engaged in a hunt for a lost child. The child's anxious mother was surprised and delighted to find that she was there: "'It's so cool that the warden service *has* a chaplain,' Marian Moore said to me, just moments before the call came in that Alison, her lost child, had been found." Braestrup was also surprised and delighted:

> The first time I put on my uniform and looked in the mirror, I thought, *This is really cool.* I put my warden service ball cap on, adjusted the plastic tab on the back to account for my big fat head, and admired myself, made faces. But then I slid the little vinyl boomerang into my collar, the sliver of white that transforms my ordinary shirt into a clerical shirt. It was a startling moment, that first look in the glass. . . . The character I resemble most, I decided after some reflection, is Father Mulcahy from *M*A*S*H*. And why not? Like him, I am a sort of generic, ecumenical clergyperson representing the God that even atheists pray to in foxholes, an undemanding character.[7]

7. Kate Braestrup, "Presence in the Wild," chapter 11 from *Here If You Need Me*, http://being .publicradio.org/programs/braestrup/chapter11.shtml, 2 of 3, March 2, 2011, (accessed January 26, 2013).

Sixty years after the Korean War, more than forty years after *M*A*S*H* first played on TV, a Unitarian woman in a Roman collar describes Father Mulcahy's role as having served a universal and gender-neutral spirituality rather than the particular needs of Catholic soldiers needing an authorized dispenser of sacraments. In those sixty years, the role of the chaplain—both in the military and in other spaces—has shifted in ways only barely suggested by her wardrobe appropriation. Father Mulcahy may have ministered to all, but he did so as priest of a singularly bounded church; in 1950, it would have been unusual to describe a Catholic priest as "a generic, ecumenical clergyperson" representing an "undemanding God."

Braestrup continued her story, carefully distinguishing her work, that is, pastoral care and counseling—the work of chaplains—from that of mental health professionals:

> A law enforcement chaplain is charged with providing pastoral care, and that includes what is known as pastoral counseling. . . . Pastoral counseling isn't the same as therapy, though it may (I hope) prove therapeutic. I am not trained or credentialed for psychotherapy. . . . If a warden has the slightest indication of a mental health problem—clinical depression, let's say, or substance abuse—I refer him to a medical professional, emphasize the blessed efficacy of such interventions, and offer myself as glad company for the Journey.

Braestrup is trained and credentialed to offer "glad company for the Journey":

> As we encounter each other at search scenes and debriefings, over bleary-eyed breakfasts at a truck stop following a long night's search, and meet at promotion ceremonies and flag-waving parades; as I preside over funerals and weddings, welcome the birth of children, and sympathize at the death of friends, the relationship between chaplain and warden grows and deepens.
>
> "It's so cool that the warden service has a chaplain to keep us from freaking out," is what Marian Moore actually said in full.
>
> "Ah." I smiled. "I'm not really here to keep you from freaking out. I'm here to be with you while you freak out," or grieve or laugh or suffer or sing. It is a ministry of presence. It is showing up with a loving heart. And it is really, really cool.

Braestrup is not there, she says, to keep you from freaking out. She is there to be with you while you freak out. It is simply a "ministry of presence." But perhaps she understates her role. After all, the state does pay her because it believes she will help to keep the peace.

Braestrup gave National Public Radio audiences a further example of her work on the Maine coast, describing a morning spent riding with Rob Greenlaw, one of the wardens, on his beat:

> It was March, and the weather was warm enough to melt most of the snow. . . . We headed down Route 1 toward Nobleboro, then turned down one of the scrawny peninsulas that dangle off the mainland into Penobscot Bay. We were on a narrow, winding, two-lane road, chatting about this and that, when a car came screeching out of a driveway in front of us and took off, hitting sixty before Rob caught up to him, siren whooping and blue lights clacking and flashing along the front window of the truck.

As she explained, "Maine game wardens have the same statewide jurisdiction, the same arrest powers as Maine state troopers, and they are empowered to do traffic stops." Rob returned to the truck: "He says he peeled out of his driveway because he was late for work. I asked him if he'd had a fight with his girlfriend or something. . . . He said no, just late for work. He just does it that way sometimes. I told him he really oughta relax a little."

They move on to investigate a possible illegal killing of a moose and a coyote. Braestrup describes the scene:

> Farther down the road, Rob showed me a little patch of sumac and birch where someone had hauled a dead moose to use as bait for coyotes. Being in possession of a moose carcass, even assuming the guy didn't shoot the moose, is illegal, but the perpetrator would probably hold his hand over his heart and swear the moose just happened to drop dead of natural causes right at the bait site . . . Above the moose carcass, the corpse of a crow dangled in a sapling. "They hang up a dead one to scare the other crows away," Rob said. "Crows would eat the carcass before the coyotes came, and a big crowd of crows will bring the wardens anyway. We look for them —'deputy wardens,' we call 'em."

She then explains Rob's theory of the criminal personality:

> Rob wants to catch this coyote hunter. Rob knows who he is, can identify him by the wet prints of his truck tires on the road, and says he is "a mean guy." As with so many criminal offenders, those willing to commit one crime are generally willing to commit a raft of others, and in fact, this moose poacher

is well known to area wardens and troopers as a domestic violence, drug, and traffic offender. A scofflaw is a scofflaw. This is the warden's work: enforcing the traffic laws, protecting coyotes and moose, and partnering with state troopers with respect to a range of other offenses.

Braestrup's relationship to what she calls the wardens' work is ambiguous, as is the relationship of all chaplains to the work of the institutions in which they do their ministry. She is "present to" the wardens as they enforce the law; she ministers to the public with whom they come into contact. She is both "bridge builder" and "whistle-blower," as others have described the work of chaplains.[8]

In her book about her ministry, Braestrup explains why she decided to work in law enforcement:

> If you prefer applied and practical theology to the more abstract and vaporous varieties, it is difficult to find a more interesting and challenging ministry than a law enforcement chaplaincy.
>
> Law enforcement officers, like all human beings, are presented with grand questions about life's meaning and purpose. They consider the problem of evil, the suffering of innocents, the relationships between justice and mercy, power and responsibility, spirit and flesh. They ponder the impenetrable mystery of death. I was sure that working with cops would take me right up to where the theological rubber meets the road.[9]

"Where the theological rubber meets the road" is, for Braestrup, at the particular intersection of religion and the state that is found in law enforcement: "the problem of evil, the suffering of innocents, the relationships between justice and mercy, power and responsibility, spirit and flesh . . . the impenetrable mystery of death."

After the scofflaw, the moose, and the crow, Braestrup and Greenlaw encounter some children who try to sort out the differences between their respective jobs. The children decide that it comes down to the gun Greenlaw carries:

8. Julian Rivers, *The Law of Organized Religions: Between Establishment and Secularism* (Cambridge: Cambridge University Press, 2010), 207.

9. Kate Braestrup, *Here If You Need Me* (Boston: Little Brown, 2007), 60; see also Kate Braestrup, "Blessing the Moose: Praying for Good News, Planning for Bad; True Stories from the Chaplain of the Maine Warden Service," *Boston Globe*, September 23, 2007.

We drove a few miles and then stopped by the side of the road. Almost in-
stantly, we were surrounded by a group of small, grubby children. They clus-
tered eagerly around Rob.

"I know why you got a gun," one little boy said. "It's so if someone's bein'
stupid, then you can shoot 'im."

"Don't listen to him," his sister advised. "He's a silly monkey." No more
than nine, she carried on her hip a toddler in urgent need of a fresh diaper.

Another child looked up after examining the great seal of Maine on the
door of Rob's truck. "Did you arrest Paul for speeding?" he inquired.

"No," said Rob. "Should I have?"

"He drives like that all the time. He's my uncle, so I know."

"Uh-huh," said Rob. "I'll arrest him next time."

The children laughed uproariously at this, and the toddler bounced on the
little girl's hip and laughed too.

"Who are you?" the silly monkey asked me, pulling on my fingers.

"I'm the chaplain," I said.

"You ain't got a gun?"

"No, I don't."

"Oh," said the boy, immediately losing interest. He turned his attention
back to the quiet armed man. "What kinda guns you got?"

She concludes her account: "It is Warden Greenlaw's job to get out of his
truck and walk through the quiet woods as the maples swell and leaf, his job
to stand and gaze across a shining lake, the scent of moss rising, birdsong in
his ears. It is my job to go with him."

In this brief account, Braestrup displays her role as companion or go-
between, both affirming the law-and-order world of the warden and placing it in a larger framework, one that for her is defined in large part by the
natural world and an undemanding God. Greenlaw sees "the telltale signs
of illegal fishing." She sees "the quiet woods as the maples swell and leaf."
Their joint mission is to put these two pictures together.

Kate Braestrup is an ordained minister in the Unitarian Universalist
Church. She holds a master of divinity degree from Bangor Theological
Seminary and has a certification in clinical pastoral education. While some
chaplains are more forthcoming and specific in their professional self-
presentation about their particular religious orientations than she is—and
there are chaplains who identify with religious communities from across
the entire spectrum of American religion—Braestrup's carefully universalist
account of her work is very similar in tone and structure to many other de
scriptions of the work chaplains do in hospitals, in prisons, in the military,

in schools, in workplaces of various kinds, in hospice care. It is both natural and necessary work, as she—and her employers and her clients—understand it, work that acknowledges the essentially spiritual nature of the human person and her world, but which understands that work in an institutional context and defers to the client as director of his own Journey. When they consider its public meanings, chaplains understand what they do as constitutionally appropriate work for government, at each of its levels, and for the government's agents.[10]

What kind of religion is this seemingly slight and ephemeral practice, and how does it fit into the constitutional framework we set for legally managing religious life in the United States? Is it a conformist kind of religion that accepts law enforcement's categorization of people as law abiders or lawbreakers, or is it a place of resistance to the modern state, sometimes standing with the scofflaw and his Journey? Is the world being sacralized through these activities, or is religion being secularized? This book argues that contemporary spiritual practices in the United States, including those of chaplains, are as much the product of law as of the interesting and well-documented negotiations between religion and the rationalism of modern science. Religious and legal ideas, institutions, and practices combine to structure the place that Americans understand themselves to inhabit, religiously speaking; that is, the form and shape that the ministry of chaplains takes is indebted to a linked legal and religious history and shared subjectivity. This is true of ordinary everyday law and religion as well as that of the Constitution. There is no religion without law and no law without religion.[11] The chaplain and her work are very much a creature of that intersection.

It is a truism in the study of American religion that religion in the United States is the way it is because of constitutional disestablishment. That is its origin myth. Sociologically speaking, the free market in religion that is understood to characterize the United States is often described as being the direct result of the separation of church and state—a once-and-for-all libera-

---

10. Braestrup addresses her understanding of her work from a constitutional perspective in *Here If You Need Me*, 102–3, typically side-stepping any disabling legal conflict by characterizing her work as nonimpositional, but helpful, while stressing its significance.

11. Understood this way, religion is always "established" in some sense. Bernard Harcourt makes a related point in *The Illusion of Free Markets: Punishment and the Myth of Natural Order* (Cambridge, MA: Harvard University Press, 2011), 137–58. See also Winnifred Fallers Sullivan and Lori Beaman, eds., *Varieties of Religious Establishment* (London: Ashgate, 2013).

tion that allowed each to go its separate way.[12] I mean to resist that tidy story here. While there is indeed something distinctive about the way American religion is organized, in contrast to that of most other countries, religion continued after the founding to be significantly structured by law in both explicit and implicit ways, and American law continued to be indebted to religious imaginaries. Examining the role of the chaplain in American institutions today displays the idiosyncrasies of modern American religion in particularly revealing ways. American religion continues to idealize the free-church model while it is singularly bound by secular logics; it's ways reflect and express the pain and loneliness of contemporary life under the rule of law.

I will return to Kate Braestrup in the last chapter, considering in more depth the ways in which her ministry is characteristic of a certain American style of law and religion. In the following chapters, I will set US chaplaincy in its legal and historical contexts, showing how and why the ministry of presence she and others practice answers particular needs and expresses certain anxieties produced by the legal regulation of spirituality today.

12. For a careful history of the use of market metaphors to describe American religion, see Courtney Bender, "Pluralism and Secularism," in *Religion on the Edge: De-centering and Re-centering the Sociology of Religion*, ed. Courtney Bender, Wendy Cadge, Peggy Levitt, and David Smilde (New York: Oxford University Press, 2013), and "The Power of Pluralist Thinking," in *After Religious Freedom*, ed. Winnifred Fallers Sullivan, Elizabeth Shakman Hurd, Saba Mahmood, and Peter Danchin (Chicago: University of Chicago Press, forthcoming).

ACKNOWLEDGMENTS

I have worked on this book over a number of years. It is, in my mind, the fruit of a collaborative but dispersed effort—of crowdsourcing, if you will. I have learned much about US religion and about religion more generally from the published and unpublished work of many other writers and researchers, not all of whom I have cited. I am very grateful for this education. Characterizing US religion as a whole is a fraught project indeed. I have cited those most proximate to this project. I have also benefited from innumerable conversations with friends, colleagues, and gracious strangers. I am indebted to all of you.

I am grateful to the University at Buffalo Law School and the Institute for Advanced Study in Princeton for institutional support during the writing. I was also generously supported with fellowships from the Guggenheim Foundation and the American Council of Learned Societies.

I had valuable opportunities to present versions and parts of this project on a number of occasions: at the Institute for Advanced Study; the Law and Public Affairs program at Princeton; the Michigan Legal Theory Workshop; the Yale Colloquium on Religion and Politics; the Center for Religion and Conflict at Arizona State University; the Religion and Politics Seminar at Harvard; and Luther College; as well as in the Department of Religious Studies at Indiana University. I benefited from all of these conversations.

For help with understanding the day-to-day work of chaplains I am particularly indebted to Kevin Boyd, Wendy Cadge, Donald Doherty, George Fitchett, Kim Hansen, Kristen Leslie, Cynthia Lindner, Joan Miller, Christopher Swift, and Edward Waggoner.

Many conversations along the way helped me to sort out what I was trying to say. I owe much to Gil Anidjar, Dan Arnold, Dianne Avery, Lori Beaman, James Beckford, Courtney Bender, Anna Chave, David Engel,

Constance Furey, Peter Gottschalk, Carol Greenhouse, Beth Hurd, Stan Katz, Pamela Klassen, Fred Konefsky, Cécile Laborde, Tomoko Masuzawa, Melani McAlister, Peter Nguyen, Frank Reynolds, Ben Schonthal, Joan Scott, Donald Senior, Barry Sullivan, Mateo Taussig-Rubbo, and Kristen Tobey.

For reading the whole manuscript with care, I am indebted to Dianne Avery, Wendy Cadge, Constance Furey, Beth Hurd, Fred Konefsky, Barry Sullivan, Christopher Swift, Rachel Weil, Robert Yelle, and the anonymous reviewers, one of whom I especially thank for having the generosity to deliver a message of skeptical enthusiasm at a critical moment. I am also immensely grateful to Alan Thomas for his patient support. For able editorial assistance, I thank Kerilyn Harkaway-Krieger.

US Law and Religion Today

In the United States, American religion is often described as being distinctively free—unfettered by law—uniquely so for the first time, perhaps, in human history. Americans got it right, we believe. Religion should not be ruled by the state. Yet, at the same time, of course, as everyone also understands, American law and American religion never were separate. They were always mixed up in each other's affairs. Public morality perhaps requires such a mutuality. Yet, for a long time it was thought by many that this entanglement was simply the result of unfinished business—that we just needed to work harder to separate them, to keep both religion and government free. Today a new accommodation is under consideration—perhaps a new realism.

It is not just in the United States, of course, that the intersection of law and religion is newly salient. The mutual articulation of religion and government is being reconsidered today almost everywhere. Religion and government are also themselves each being transformed in the twenty-first century. How legal and constitutional commitments to religious freedom might be realized in this unfolding picture is unclear and highly contested. Among other questions is the pressing concern as to whether religious freedom pertains primarily to the integrity of an individual conscience, often in opposition to the state or other institutions, or whether religious freedom pertains rather to groups, groups dependent for their continuation and their capacity for self-government on partnerships, or accommodations, between would-be sovereign states and robust multiple "autonomous" religious— and often transnational—organizations. These two alternatives are founded in a particular understanding of religion, an understanding that itself is being questioned. Does such a distinction between the individual and the communal make sense under the rubric of religion? Does religious history or our understanding of how persons are formed support such a clean dichotomy? Are not individual consciences always shaped in some sense in community, and are communities less bounded and coherent than their propaganda would suggest? The new salience of religion for law also raises the question, again, as to whether religion—or spirituality—is natural to humans and to human society? Was secularization a delusion? If religion is natural, does government have an obligation to acknowledge, even enable, "religious freedom" through the positive support of religious ways of life?

Americans have a distinctive way of talking about these questions. Americans made the unusual decision some two centuries ago to unite a right to the free exercise of religion with a prohibition against an establishment of religion. Those twin commitments, expressed in the First Amendment to the US Constitution, have always been understood to embody a tension, but they have arguably entered a new social and jurisprudential accommodation in the last several decades as the result of larger legal and social changes, most especially privatization of governmental functions, but also in the wake of further transformations in the ways in which Americans are religious and in which they understand religion. This new accommodation appears to be at once formally shifting responsibility for the ordinary regulation of religion from the courts to the political branches and opening a larger space for the independence of religious bodies in the disciplining of their own members. Disestablishment, one might say, has once again produced a new establishment.[1] Increasingly eschewing a continued need to strongly separate religion from other spheres of public life, government is once more openly recognizing Americans as religious, or as spiritual, and incorporating that recognition into its work.

This book is about a religious practice that sits at the intersection of democratic governance and the multiplicity of religious ways of life in the United States today. It is about the spiritual care delivered by governmental and quasi-governmental chaplaincies—as well as chaplaincies within private but regulated industries such as hospitals and schools—a religious practice that interestingly epitomizes many of the ambiguities inherent in

---

1. Historians David Sehat and Samuel Moyn, among others, have shown the ways in which American government and American religion have worked in tandem to support various American political projects, undercutting claims that American religion is uniquely free of government support or influence. David Sehat, *The Myth of American Religious Freedom* (New York: Oxford University Press, 2011); Samuel Moyn, "From Communist to Muslim: Religious Liberty in European Human Rights Law," *South Atlantic Quarterly* 113 (Winter 2014). See also Elizabeth Shakman Hurd, *Politics of Secularism in International Relations* (Princeton, NJ: Princeton University Press, 2007).

imagining religion under the modern rule of law. Chaplaincies both normalize religion through the situating of religious work alongside that of other modern bureaucracies and set it apart through the multiple allegiances of the chaplain herself and the client; it is an unstable encounter between strangers, strangers stranded in the gaps created by modern life. Chaplains trained by religious communities minister to a clientele often unmarked at that moment by any specific religious identity, and they do so on behalf of a secular institution bound, at least theoretically, to rational epistemologies. Chaplaincies are, one might say, a placeholder for the sovereign exception, with all of the troubling references implied by those curious words.[2] The chaplain has, without paradox, become a priest of the secular.

The chaplain, as provider of spiritual care, attempts to integrate universalist and particularist understandings of the flourishing of human beings under the banner of religious freedom. A constitutional order that, for many avid secularists, seems a guarantee to keep religion out, appears, for many religious practitioners today, a license to promote religion—and spirituality—given certain parameters of tolerance and noncoercion. Spiritual care, as a practice, tries to finesse the differences through attention to a universal and natural aspect of human beings, their spiritual nature.

For Americans, though, the question immediately presents itself. Is that legal? Is it legal in the United States for a chaplain paid for by government to provide spiritual care to game wardens, and other government employees as well as to the public, with the understanding that the chaplain's work serves a universal—and even, perhaps, a civic—need? Is that what the founders had in mind? US courts and administrative agencies have, in the last few decades, over the protests of both secularists and separationists, found the delivery of spiritual care to be within the constitutional competence of government, and, indeed, to be mandated in some cases by the Constitution. Religious freedom, legally speaking, now increasingly means government providing opportunities for Americans to encounter their religious selves and realize their religious commitments. This book describes the convergence of changes to both law and religion that makes this finding unsurprising. This introductory chapter further introduces the character of the chaplain and situates the study of chaplaincy within the broader fields of American religion and law, as well as of religious and legal studies today.

---

2. The "sovereign exception" is taken from the work of Carl Schmitt although the words have taken on new meanings as they have spread across academic and political contexts in recent years as efforts are made to describe the gaps left by the enlightenment project.

I take my examples primarily from the United States because that is where my training and expertise lie, but I will give comparative examples from time to time, in the text and in the notes. Spiritual care by chaplains is not limited to the United States.[3] Religious practice and its legal regulation are only understood when seen in the richness of their long mutually involved history and their transnational manifestations today.

The Chaplain

Chaplains have been present in Christian societies for more than fifteen hundred years. Today there are chaplains in non-Christian ones as well. Their precise origins are incompletely understood, and aspects of their role surely must both exceed and predate Christianity, but the role becomes necessary in a new way after the Constantinian revolution and the formal need for Christian ministers to serve as representatives of the church in secular contexts, caring for Christian soldiers and others, and monitoring and blessing the operations of the political authorities. The first Christian chaplains that we know of are military chaplains working for the Frankish kingdoms. But they quickly appear in other secular institutions. They eventually serve in hospitals, aristocratic households, schools, and prisons. By the early modern period, they are also employed by private secular enterprises. The East India Company, for example, employed hundreds of chaplains. Many of those were promised shares in the company as a part of their pay for preaching sermons and tending to the moral character of the employees. Chaplains were understood to be critical to ensuring the company's success, together with that of the empire, as a political, commercial, and spiritual enterprise.[4]

The chaplain is also a modern literary character, appearing in countless operas, novels, plays, movies, and TV series; while occasionally heroic, he is often an ambiguous, even menacing, character, hobbled by his dual allegiance. Toward the end of Franz Kafka's *The Trial*, Joseph K. encounters

3. Adam Lyons, for example, a PhD student in Harvard University's Committee for the Study of Religion, is engaged in a study both of the mostly Buddhist chaplains introduced into prisons in Japan during the Meiji period and of Japanese prison chaplaincy today. Chaplaincy studies is also emerging formally as an academic discipline, both in the United States and elsewhere. See, for example, the program at Cardiff University in Wales. Cardiff School of History, Archaeology and Religion, "Chaplaincy Studies (MTh)," Cardiff University, http://www.cardiff .ac.uk/share/degreeprogrammes/religion/postgraduate/taughtpostgraduate/mthprogrammes /chaplaincystudies/chaplaincy-studies-mth.html (accessed January 26, 2013).

4. Daniel O'Connor, *The Chaplains of the East India Company 1601–1858* (New York: Continuum, 2012).

the chaplain of the prison. As the chaplain takes his leave, K. addresses him, complaining of his treatment:

> "You were so friendly to me earlier on," said K., "and you explained every-thing, but now you abandon me as if I were nothing to you." "You have to go," said the priest. "Well, yes," said K., "you need to understand that." "First, you need to understand who I am," said the priest. "You're the prison chap-lain," said K., and went closer to the priest, it was not so important for him to go straight back to the bank as he had made out, he could very well stay where he was. "So that means I belong to the court," said the priest. "So why would I want anything from you? The court doesn't want anything from you. It accepts you when you come and it lets you go when you leave."[5]

K. is both attracted and repelled by the priest. K has to go and yet he tries to speak to the chaplain as one who has been a guide for him, as someone in-dependent of the place they are in; the chaplain corrects him, emphasizing that it is K. who is leaving and that he, the chaplain, "belongs to the court." The figure of the chaplain in *The Trial* calls attention to, indeed, is insepa-rable from, the law as experienced by Joseph K., a law that is fragmentary, unknowable, and dangerously informal, even for those experts who are its intimates. His encounter with the chaplain is of a piece with the novel's larger mood, which almost gags the reader with the indifference and lack of decency in the law, perhaps of modern life more generally.[6]

Closer to home, and even less forgiving to the figure of the chaplain is Herman Melville's *Billy Budd* in which the ship's chaplain, "the minister of Christ, tho' receiving his stipend from Mars," as Melville describes him, vis-its Billy and sets out to "bring home to him the thought of salvation and a Saviour" before his execution. After describing the unsatisfactory encounter, Melville turns to the reader:

> Marvel not that having been made acquainted with the young sailor's essen-tial innocence (an irruption of heretic thought hard to suppress) the worthy man lifted not a finger to avert the doom of such a martyr to martial dis-cipline. So to do would not only have been as idle as invoking the desert, but would also have been an audacious transgression of the bounds of his

---

5. Franz Kafka, *The Trial*, trans. Willa and Edwin Muir (New York: Alfred A. Knopf, 1937), 278.

6 My reading of *The Trial* is indebted to Robert P. Burns. His book on *The Trial* is forthcom-ing from the University of Chicago Press.

function, one as exactly prescribed to him by military law as that of the boat-swain or any other naval officer. Bluntly put, a chaplain is the minister of the Prince of Peace serving in the host of the God of War—Mars. As such, he is as incongruous as a musket would be on the altar at Christmas. Why then is he there? Because he indirectly subserves the purpose attested by the cannon; because too he lends the sanction of the religion of the meek to that which practically is the abrogation of everything but brute Force.[7]

In Melville's telling—as in Kafka's—the powerful hierarchical structure of the law and of the chaplain's role in that hierarchy renders him practically impotent, even complicit.[8]

Later American wars also produced such chaplains. Writing for the *Army and Navy Chaplain* immediately after Pearl Harbor, then retired Chaplain Julian Yates explained to his fellow chaplains why there was no contradiction between Christianity and war:

Probably the best text on American ideology is found in the Bill of Rights. . . . In the literature of government that is the grandest and most significant docu-ment ever penned by mortal man . . . Study it along with your Bible. . . . Christ never condemned the life and activities of the soldier. To the extent that you are an effective propagandist for militant righteousness you are speeding the triumph of American arms.[9]

No minister of the religion of the meek, the chaplain is here propagandist for US military righteousness and a virile Christianity.

Yet the chaplain also figures in history and literature as the heroic refusenik, identifying with and standing for the prisoner, the soldier, the patient, the student, the employee, against the institutions that threaten to encompass or overwhelm him. A slim volume called *Chaplain on the Water-front* recounts the efforts of Father Saunders, chaplain to the longshoremen on the Brooklyn waterfront in the 1940s:

At a time when, literally, the entire public damned all longshoremen as hood-lums, Father Saunders kept a steadfast faith in their innate goodness . . . he

7. Herman Melville, *Billy Budd, Sailor (An Inside Narrative)* (Chicago: University of Chicago Press, 1962); for a discussion of Melville's view of the law, see Alfred S. Konefsky, "The Acciden-tal Legal Historian: Herman Melville and the History of American Law," *Buffalo Law Review* 52 (2005): 1179–1276.

8. See Konefsky, "The Accidental Legal Historian," 1270.

9. Julian E. Yates, "Armed for Combat," *Army and Navy Chaplain* 12, no. 3 (1942): 4–6.

has been unpaid mediator in labor disputes, has comforted and befriended hundreds of waterfront families in trouble, has inspired a highly successful grass-roots harbor organization . . . and has worked closely with one of the most powerful and controversial leaders of the dock workers' union.[10]

Father Saunders is in the heroic mode, like Father Duffy. The most highly decorated of American military chaplains ever was Fr. Eamon Duffy of the Fighting Sixty-Ninth, whose sacrificial service in the Spanish-American War and in France in World War II and after led to the placing of his statue in Times Square in New York. He was friend and advisor to Al Smith.

For some, that heroic time has passed. As one university chaplain commented, "The work of the chaplain is no longer to be the lightning-rod, the conscience of the university, but to facilitate the many ways students express themselves spiritually or religiously."[11] Neither wholly apologist for an oppressor nor reliably friend of the oppressed, the chaplain today usually has a more muted and ambiguous role.

American Spirituality

While it is notoriously difficult to generalize about American religion because of its extreme variety and diffuse governance, at the beginning of the twenty-first century some new trends are being noted. Often cited is the fact that a growing number of Americans, when asked by social science surveyors, identify themselves as "spiritual, not religious." It is not entirely clear what they mean by this, but they seem mostly to mean, at a minimum, that they honor or participate in the idea that human life has a spiritual dimension, while rejecting what they denominate "organized religion."

This piece of news from social surveys, along with the increased frequency of "none," in answer to questions of religious affiliation, can sometimes be read to overwhelm the much stronger evidence that many more Americans identify as both religious and spiritual. The conviction that humans are naturally spiritual is something that churched and unchurched Americans have in common.[12] Spirituality as a practice alongside formal

10. Van McNair Jr., *Chaplain on the Waterfront: The Story of Father Saunders* (New York: Seabury Press, 1963), 20–21.

11. Ian Oliver, pastor of the University Church and senior associate chaplain, Yale University, personal communication.

12. For a compact summary of survey data about trends in American religion, see Mark Chaves, *American Religion: Contemporary Trends* (Princeton, NJ: Princeton University Press, 2011). Chaves sees a slight but unmistakable decline in religious attachment and participation

religion has a long American history.[13] That history has included a wide spectrum of Americans from experimenters with Ouija boards and Eastern imports to readers of Rumi's poetry and charismatic Catholics. Distrust of organized religion also has a long American history.[14] Americans like to mix and match their religion. They like to be in charge of their own religious lives. The eclecticism and do-it-yourself quality of contemporary religious life in the United States is difficult to overstate.

Specifying with particularity what the many who self-identify as "spiritual not religious" have in common, what they mean by this self-designation, and how many of them there are, has proved difficult. The phrase seems to reflect a double gesture, an affirmation of religious interest, maybe even commitment, with a simultaneous distancing from current religious options. Rejection of organized religion may signify distaste for hierarchy, or dogma, or the symbiotic corruptions of church or state, but there is evidence that the designation "spiritual not religious" may also represent a move toward a new inclusiveness—an openness to new collectivities and even that *desideratum* of many sociologists, political scientists, and liberal theorists, engagement, even while affirming religious individualism and multiplicity.

Listening to the way the word is used by Americans today, "spirituality" appears less an alternative religious practice—what is sometimes derisively viewed as the vague, eclectic, self-absorbed embrace of various forms of mysticism once termed New Age—and more an attitude, one that is descriptively adopted to express a belief in the natural universality of religion and a resistance to top-down religious authoritarianism: an intuition and set of actions that resist institutionalization. "Not religious," in American parlance, also means not "sectarian." Spirituality denotes something humans have in common. That is particularly the case in legal contexts where a reference to a universal "spirituality" is adopted to solve the legal problem

---

in the United States over the last several decades. For another recent sociological effort to draw a portrait of US religion today, see Robert D. Putnam and David E. Campbell, *American Grace: How American Religion Divides and Unites Us* (New York: Simon & Schuster, 2012). See also the regular reports of the Pew Research Center: http://www.pewforum.org/ (accessed September 30, 2013).

13. See, e.g., Leigh Eric Schmidt, *Restless Souls: The Making of American Spirituality* (San Francisco: Harper, 2005). Schmidt describes spirituality as a practice of the religious left. That seems less and less the case, if it was ever so.

14. Beginning, perhaps, with the more radical of the Puritans. See the work of Roger Williams and his *The Hireling Ministry None of Christ's* (London, 1652), in particular.

of establishment, religious discrimination, or the privileging of one group over others.[15]

While the terms "spiritual" and "spirituality" suffer today from overuse, appropriation, and commodification by marketers of books and CDs and other products, they also have a long history in the Christian tradition. The words "spiritual" and "spirituality" speak to theological elaborations of the work of the Holy Spirit as well as to a long history of both monastic and lay devotional practices. In the United States, a very specific history of spirituality brings together transcendentalists, spiritualists, William James, importers of Asian religions, New Age enthusiasts, and a remarkable group of experimenters and do-it-yourselfers.[16] It also reflects a distinctive American engagement with psychology.[17]And, as Bender has recently argued, contrary to popular belief, those who claim this identity are not asocial, idiosyncratic, and ahistorical.[18] It is often assumed that spiritual folks are not socially responsible and don't have a politics, a legacy in part of the impact of such works as Robert Bellah's *Habits of the Heart* and its dismissal of Sheilaism, but it is also a result of a polemic against spirituality by clergy and other defenders of the social importance of institutional religion.

Bender argues that contemporary "metaphysicals," as she terms them, are very much connected to communities and to history, and that their invisibility to the received story of American religion is the result of the logic of secularism, academic and political. "Spirituality," she says, "emerges over and over in our collective imagination as free floating and individualistic. Spirituality appears to be a condition of modern life: it has no organization, no clear shape. Studying spirituality thus appears akin to shoveling fog."[19] On the contrary, speaking authoritatively on the basis of her own ethnographic research among those who claim the identity, she says, "We can no longer conscientiously reassert these positions or the problematic logics that continue to reinforce them. Instead we must approach spirituality and 'the spiritual' in America as deeply entangled in various religious and secular histories, social structures, and cultural practices." I will argue here that

15. As Courtney Bender and Omar McRoberts have argued in a recent paper, spirituality has a very wide semantic range today. "Mapping a Field: Why and How to Study Spirituality," published on the Social Science Research Council website (October 2012), http://blogs.ssrc .org/tif/wp-content/uploads/2010/05/Why-and-How-to-Study-Spirtuality.pdf (accessed January 26, 2013).

16. See Schmidt, *Restless Souls.*

17. Christopher G. White, *Unsettled Minds: Psychology and the American Search for Spiritual Assurance, 1830–1940* (Berkeley: University of California Press, 2009).

18. Courtney Bender, *The New Metaphysicals* (Chicago: University of Chicago Press, 2010).

19. Ibid., 182.

law is one of those entanglements and chaplains are among its ministers. In other words, contrary to the assertions of Martin Marty, among others, spirituality does make hospice calls.[20]

Ironically, perhaps, throughout Christian history, rejection of church authority does not end religious practice but rather enables other forms of religious life. One of those forms has been that fostered by secular government, disappointing those who understand churches and other religious institutions to be salutary mediating institutions between the individual and the modern state.[21] The wide embrace of spirituality as a common religious practice reflects, in part, the fact that skepticism about what is termed organized religion has a respectable American pedigree inside and outside the church.[22] Organized religion, one might say, is for Americans closely identified with Old World "established" religion; it is what one might call the evil twin of religious freedom.[23] While, to be sure, different Americans might have somewhat different objects in mind when they reject organized religion and embrace spirituality, reflecting their own ecclesiologies, organized religion has long been understood by many in the United States

20. See the following excerpt from an interview with Marty: "On being spiritual but not religious: I appreciate the spiritual search of the non-churched, non-synagogued people as being full of imagination, discovery, and satisfaction of the individual. But I once saw a bumpersticker that said: 'Spirituality doesn't make hospice calls.' Spirituality remains, normally, individualistic. You may gather for a retreat, and then you disperse. You may gather at the coffee shop or the bookstore, and then you disperse. The people who are handling the homeless and dealing with addiction and trying to improve senior care and who care about the training of the young— they have to bond together. If they don't do it in old-fashioned churches, they'll do it in new-fashioned churches. But I don't think it adds up to much unless there is some development of community." Bob Abernethy, "Martin Marty: Extended Interview," *Religion and Ethics News-weekly*, May 9, 2002. http://www.pbs.org/wnet/religionandethics/2002/05/03/may-3-2002 -martin-marty-extended-interview/11648/ (accessed September 30, 2013).

21. For a description of the effect that Protestant devolution of authority onto the state has on the law of marriage, see Mary Anne Case, "The Peculiar Stake U.S. Protestants Have in the Question of State Recognition of Same-Sex Marriage," in *After Secular Law*, ed. Winnifred Fallers Sullivan, Robert A. Yelle, and Mateo Taussig-Rubbo (Stanford, CA: Stanford University Press, 2011), 302–21. See also Greg Johnson, "Varieties of Native Hawaiian Establishment: Recognized Voices, Routinized Charisma, and Church Desecration," in *Varieties of Religious Establishment*.

22. This suspicion is related to but interestingly different from the anticlericalism of European and postcolonial countries. Anticlericalism is more characteristic of countries with a history of strong church-state collaboration, such as France. For a comparison of countries with different church-state histories and the effect on the political salience of religion, see José Casanova, *Public Religions in the Modern World* (Chicago: University of Chicago Press, 1995).

23. For a very useful and comprehensive report on the present state of church-state law in England, historically speaking the quintessential established church for Americans, see Julian Rivers, *The Law of Organized Religions*.

across the religious spectrum to be dangerously hierarchical, authoritarian, corrupt, and bound to outdated orthodoxies. Spirituality, in contrast, is democratic, innocent of political partisanship, and open to the sacred in its many incarnations. It is not necessarily non-Christian or personal and self-centered. And, speaking from the outside, it is in fact neither apolitical nor independent of government and law.

In myriad contexts today, American government speaks of its citizens as being naturally spiritual and in need of spiritual care. The US Army recently created some controversy by announcing that soldiers would be tested for spiritual fitness, part of a larger army initiative to tune up its fighting force. Soldiers, it was said, need to be spiritually healthy in order to engage in warfare.[24] The accrediting authority for American hospitals (which performs its work under the auspices of federal, state, and local regulation) requires that all hospitals provide spiritual care.[25] Veterans Administration (VA) hospitals require all patients to be given a spiritual assessment on admission and require that spiritual care be included in a patient's treatment if indicated. Workplace spirituality is a burgeoning field of activity, one that seems to be escaping laws prohibiting religious discrimination in employment. Transit lounges in airports, train stations, and bus terminals provide worship services and opportunities for spiritual reflection. College chaplaincies are being reinvented as custodians and facilitators of a universal human need, rather than outposts of particular church ministries. Spiritual care is being built into emergency preparedness as chaplains standby ready to be deployed in cases of natural disaster or terrorist attack.

American religion is not all about finding a common spirituality, of course. Americans are often critical of each other's religion. The sorting out of good religion and bad religion, and good religious folks from bad religious folks, and people "of faith" from people "not of faith" is a perennial project in the United States, one that is produced in part by the disestablished market in religion, as well as apparently mandated by religious teaching, but it is also authorized and structured by the religion clauses of the First Amendment, which themselves institutionalize such a dualism. "Congress shall make no law respecting an establishment of religion or prohibiting

24. The spirituality of the warrior is an old theme of course. The War on Terror is only the most recent occasion for such talk. See Jonathan Ebel, *Faith in the Fight: Religion and the American Soldier in the Great War* (Princeton, NJ: Princeton University Press, 2010).

25. The Joint Commission, an independent accrediting organization, monitors the work of hospitals and other health-care providers. www.jointcommission.org (accessed June 26, 2013).

the free exercise thereof." Bad religion is established religion. Good religion is free religion. That dualism is now being worked out globally as the politics of religious freedom has gone viral.[26] But, in general for Americans, religion is better than nonreligion, and governmentally endorsed spirituality is increasingly understood to be good religion. American religion is, as Sidney Mead wrote some fifty years ago, distinctively voluntary, fissiparous, denominational, moralistic, and nationalist.[27] But the language and practices of spirituality are making paths across the divisions produced by those structural conditions in interestingly new ways today.

Legalizing Spirituality

US law is struggling to adapt itself to a new religious politics and to redefine religious freedom under the Constitution. The messy visibility and ubiquity of religion and religious diversity today is making strong demands on government in the United States and elsewhere. Disestablishment has never meant complete separation or privatization. But for the last half of the twentieth century, disestablishment was understood by the courts and others to mean a striving to keep government and religion out of each other's business—a project known in the popular constitutional mind as "separation of church and state." In the last couple of decades, however, significant decisions by the Court in the religion area are closing the book on that fifty-year experiment.[28] Recent decisions suggest a new era of First Amendment interpretation, one in which the Supreme Court understands the religion clauses to authorize both a real involvement of religion in the domains of government and a legitimate interest of the government in promoting religious life.

Any American effort at the rearticulation of law concerning religion participates, of course, in wider global shifts in the legal management of religion. Notwithstanding an American exceptionalism that resists the overt application of international norms to American life, the United States is becoming more like, rather than more unlike, most countries in this re-

---

26. See Winnifred Fallers Sullivan, Elizabeth Shakman Hurd, Saba Mahmood, and Peter Danchin, eds., *After Religious Freedom* (Chicago: University of Chicago Press, forthcoming).

27. Sidney Mead, *The Lively Experiment: The Shaping of Christianity in America* (New York: Harper & Row, 1963).

28. For a description of US litigation about religion in the second half of the twentieth-century, see Sarah Barringer Gordon, *The Spirit of the Law: Religious Voices and the Constitution in Modern America* (Cambridge, MA: Harvard University Press, 2010).

spect.[29] All increasingly accept religious pluralism as natural and religious freedom as normatively to be desired and all resist a secularist elimination of all public expression of what is conceived to be a universal aspect of the human person. The tidiness of separation and privatization makes no sense anthropologically and sociologically, and perhaps theologically, for many people today.

This book aims to intervene in several contemporary conversations about the legal regulation of religion today. It asks lawyers and other public policy makers interested in religion to pay more attention to new forms of religion—or spirituality—beyond conventional churches and proper noun religions, and it asks religious folks and religion scholars to attend more carefully to the ways in which ordinary religion is not free but is shaped by ordinary law. Law on the ground, that is, below the level of the Court. To focus this intervention I use the role of law in shaping a widespread contemporary practice of multifaith spirituality—what is called a ministry of presence—a pervasive practice of chaplains today, one that is offered by chaplains of diverse religious affiliations, or no religious affiliation, to people in a variety of settings other than the regular weekly congregation.

For the most part, chaplaincies have been studied in their distinctive and separate institutional settings, that is, different scholars have studied chaplaincies in particular venues, such as hospitals, prisons, the armed services, law enforcement, and so on. There is some evidence that chaplains themselves understand the work they do in each of these settings to be quite different from each other. While these institutions do indeed have their own histories, cultures, and social purposes, this study considers chaplaincy practices across these many settings as exhibiting common religio-legal characteristics. These characteristics are not entirely new, but they have been newly enabled by the privatization, or devolution, of government services, the broad dismantling of top-down religious authority, and the legal recognition of a naturalization of spirituality understood as an aspect of what it means to be human. This naturalization has deep roots in a variety of religious universalisms while being motivated at the same time by newer trends in evolutionary psychology and the press of developments in biotechnology, among other things.

In other words, the language of universal spirituality is making it possible for law to grasp the whole sprawling complexity and persistence of

---

29. The outliers are now those that would continue to insist on a secular nationalism, most notably France, what is left of Kemalist Turkey, and some lingering forms of state-enforced atheism.

American religious life. And one place where this is apparent is in the regulation of the growing number of chaplaincies that are appearing across the United States. These chaplaincies offer spiritual care to Americans in a range of secular institutional settings. The care they offer is increasingly understood to be authorized, even mandated, by the free exercise clause of the First Amendment. The spiritual religion practiced by chaplains is, at least aspirationally, inclusivist, therapeutic, and self-consciously constitutional. As we will see, it is legally defined and managed, and it serves secular purposes, including patriotic ones; it is also deeply ambiguous in its metaphysical assumptions and its regulatory purposes. Chaplains are shape-shifters, slipping between and among traditions, political and religious authorities, and theories of the human person. (While there is overlap with Foucault's notion of pastoral care, as I will discuss, Anglo-American-style spiritual care, in my view, lacks the church-and-statism of Foucauldian pastoral care.)

The actual practice of spiritual care brings together the chaplain, the client, and the secular institution in a collaborative performance of religious and legal displacement. The chaplain works outside of the immediate hierarchical discipline of his sending religious body, the client is away from her congregation or may have none, and the secular host, whether governmental or nongovernmental, has an opportunity to spiritualize its mission in ways that cannot easily do directly itself.[30] The structure of the performative encounter is, among other things, a result of, or a place for, the working out of changes in the legal management of religion. That encounter is more complex than might be imagined at first blush, not easily reduced either to an exercise of state power or to a by-product of neoliberalism. The role of each participant, and the religion each participant engages in, is legally regulated, even perhaps legally produced. The chaplain is trained and disciplined by degree- and certificate-granting bodies. Her employment is highly regulated by federal, state, and local authorities, as well as by religious tradition, formal and informal. The secular institution in which she works is also highly regulated. The client brings with her legal rights and expectations. The practice of spiritual care by chaplains is thus normatively constrained in ways that are not entirely acknowledged by a culture that celebrates religious freedom as absolute and envisions true religion as antinomian in character.

30. Or perhaps to outsource spirituality. See Mateo Taussig-Rubbo, "Outsourcing Sacrifice: the Labor of Private Military Contractors," *Yale Journal of Law & the Humanities* 21 (1): 105–70.

A Legal Anthropology of Religion

Most countries have government offices or ministries that formally identify and manage religion—a ministry of religious affairs. These offices may not be any more or less accurate in assessing human religiosity than the informal and dispersed ways of the United States, but they have the advantage of administratively locating authority to make pronouncements on the subject. As Daniel Boyarin says with respect to defining Christianity and Judaism in the first centuries of the common era, "There is no nontheological or nonanachronistic way at all to distinguish Christianity from Judaism until institutions are in place that make and enforce this distinction."[31] That continues to be the case today. How to isolate and define religion for law—how to articulate a legal anthropology of religion—without official bodies to undertake the task has always been a problem in the United States.

In the United States, there has been, instead, since the early nineteenth century, a mix of more or less explicitly scientific and religious anthropologies present in the public space—in the media, in political discourses, and in law, especially family law,[32] but also in public school classrooms. One of my goals here is to disturb some of the comfortable, confident, a priori ways in which law talks about religion in the United States—ways embodied in words the courts use like "church," "faith," "belief," "practice," "sect," "cult," "freedom," "establishment," "world religions," "Christianity," "monotheism"—ways that prevent American law from seeing actual religion and the remarkable changes that are taking place in the ways religion today is imagined, organized, and governed.[33]

By a legal anthropology of religion, I mean in quite a mundane methodological way to suggest a desire to think inductively from the evidence of the nature of religious life today as presented in a variety of legal settings. I mean to insist on the ways in which the prevalence of the secular rule of law itself acts as a disciplining force on religious life, not simply because of the monopoly of force claimed by the modern state but also because of

31. Daniel Boyarin, "Rethinking Jewish Christianity: An Argument for Dismantling a Dubious Category (to Which Is Appended a Correction of My Border Lines)," *Jewish Quarterly Review* 99 (2009): 28.

32. For a critique of family law as a legal invention, see Saba Mahmood, "Sectarian Conflict and Family Law in Egypt," *American Ethnologist* 39 (2012): 54–62.

33. A startling example of this failure can be seen in Chief Justice Roberts's ahistorical use of the category of "the church" in his opinion for the Court in Hosanna-Tabor v. EEOC, 132 S. Ct. 694 (2012). See Winnifred Fallers Sullivan, "The Church," *The Immanent Frame*, January 31, 2012, http://blogs.ssrc.org/tif/2012/01/31/the-church/ (accessed January 26, 2013).

the structuring effect of law's assumptions.[34] At the same time, of course, religion exercises constraints on law's empire. That happens implicitly, but also, secular law must—to some extent—take religion as it finds it. This double constraint means understanding that modern disestablishment and separation do not create a religion without law or a law without religion, but a religion with law in a particular way—a new distribution of the tasks of law and religion. It means resisting the modern myth that true religion is free religion. Religious lives are changing very rapidly today. What might we see if we do not assume that what we will see is a church and a courthouse on a split screen? Rather than accepting legal representations tied to long-dominant religious forms, rather than looking in the obvious places and listening to the obvious persons, what can be seen out of the corner of one's eye?

My interest is to better understand the religious and legal anthropologies that inform the present practices of law and government in the United States in their regulation of religion. To use anthropology in this way is in part to deliberately finesse or sidestep the science versus religion or faith versus reason problem.[35] It is intentionally to leave ambiguous and unsettled how and where to locate explanations for human consciousness and all that that entails, looking rather at the places where that search is being made operational and trying to see inductively how Americans locate and imagine how to begin to answer the question the Baltimore Catechism asked more than a century ago: "Who made us?"[36] The return of religion today, among other things, arguably stands in for and enables ideas and practices focused on the nature of the human person—resisting an imposed disenchantment, while naming and claiming the universality of the spiritual, in the interest of a political theology.[37]

We live in a period in which a set of fairly recent social shifts is profoundly affecting how law governs religion. Above all, decisions about religious life have largely migrated, particularly in historically hierarchical churches, from institutional authorities to individuals and communities.[38]

34. See Benjamin Berger, "Law's Aesthetics," in *Varieties of Religious Establishment* (London: Ashgate 2013); Paul W. Kahn, *The Cultural Study of Law: Reconstructing Legal Scholarship.* (Chicago: University Of Chicago Press, 2000).

35. See Robert Wuthnow, *The God Problem: Expressing Faith and Being Reasonable* (Berkeley: University of California Press, 2012).

36. *A Catechism of Christian Doctrine, Prepared and Enjoined by Order of the Third Council of Baltimore* (1865).

37. See Faisal Devji, *The Terrorist in Search of the Humanity: Militant Islam and Global Politics* (New York: Columbia University Press, 2008).

38. See, e.g., Robert Hefner, "Religious Resurgence in Contemporary Asia: Southeast Asian

Across the religious spectrum, Americans are making decisions about what counts as authoritative for their lives. Even quite conservative religious persons are mixing and matching religious practices and ideas. Law and government are both taking up the slack and scrambling to keep up. To summarize then, this book makes the argument that after the late twentieth-century abandonment of church/state separationism in the United States, religion can be seen to be predominantly subject to legal regulation today through public-private partnerships such as chaplaincies that effectively normalize religion as an aspect of human life. Understood to be fundamentally spiritual in her anthropology, the citizen is being provided with spiritual care in her workplace and other secular settings away from the conventional spaces of churches and temples. Decisions of the US Supreme Court in the last couple of decades have shifted the Court's interpretation of the religion clauses of the First Amendment away from the high separationism of the middle part of the twentieth century toward a jurisprudence that increasingly sees religion as being neither particularly threatening nor particularly in need of protection. Parallel with this shift in the Court's decisions have been changes in US religious life, changes that reveal a religious field that is fragmented, decentralized, and syncretic, a field in which authority is increasingly exercised in a bottom-up rather than top-down manner. The coming together of these two trends results in the current framework of private-public partnerships that regulate American religious life horizontally—a regulatory formation one might call spiritual governance.

While this new situation resembles in some ways what is sometimes called the de facto Protestant establishment of the United States in the nineteenth and early twentieth centuries, and the spread of chaplaincy finds interesting parallels in earlier parachurch efforts in the United States such as the nineteenth century Sunday school movement, it is significantly different both in the way it is legally managed and in its religious content and style. Both the legal framework of religious life and the spectrum of religious possibility in the United States have changed. But significant early themes continue to play themselves out.

The next chapter, on spiritual governance in the United States today, discusses practices of spiritual assessment used by chaplains in their work and describes a recent court case that unsuccessfully challenged the constitutionality of the spiritual care offered by the Veterans Administration. This chapter sets up the legal and religious issues of the book. Chapters 2 and 3 focus

<hr>

Perspectives on Capitalism, the State, and the New Piety," *Journal of Asian Studies* 69, no. 4 (November 2010): 1031–47.

on the chaplain, his history, the principle settings in which chaplains find themselves today—the military, the hospital, and the prison—and on the credentialing of chaplains through government regulation of the master of divinity (MDiv) degree, clinical pastoral education (CPE) certification, and ecclesiastical endorsements. Chapter 4 is an extended discussion of how law constitutes spirituality today in the United States. Chapter 5 then turns to the elusive phenomenology of the ministry of presence, the quintessential spiritual care practice of the chaplain. Finally, in the afterword I consider broader contexts for this new universalism.

I will use both spirituality and religion interchangeably to denominate the religiousness of human beings in accord with an increasingly dominant practice in the United States. I do not mean by this to do more than refer descriptively to the eclectic range of cultural manifestations that fall within this set of rubrics for Americans and to take note of this semantic practice. I make no normative judgment as to what law—or the academy—should regard as religious or spiritual, or what law—or the academy—should regulate under these signs.

ONE

Spiritual Governance

Military chaplaincies, health-care chaplaincies, and others often use the image of the shepherd or the symbol of the shepherd's crook to convey the role of the chaplain. What is this image intended to convey about the chaplain's job? How did the chaplain become a shepherd? Or, perhaps, how did the shepherd become a chaplain? Chapter 2 will look at the history and professional role of the chaplain in more detail. In this chapter, I consider emerging practices of spiritual assessment in the United States that resonate in some ways with Michel Foucault's description of the administration of pastoral power yet partake of a distinctively American cast.[1] Foucault's analysis of the importance of the image and role of the shepherd in the Christian West in what Foucault terms the governing of men, rather than of territory, has a clear correspondence with the purposes of spiritual assessment today and surely the ubiquity of the image today reflects the historical shifts of which he speaks.

Contrasting Greek ideas of governing with Hebrew ones, Foucault explained that Hebrew ideas were founded in the image of the shepherd. "The shepherd," he says

> is someone who feeds and who feeds directly, or at any rate, he is someone who feeds the flock by first leading it to good pastures, and then by making sure that the animals eat and are properly fed. Pastoral power is a power of care. It looks after the flock, it looks after the individuals of the flock, it sees to

1. Michel Foucault, *Security, Territory, Population: Lectures at the Collège de France, 1977–78,* trans. Graham Burchell (New York: Picador, 2007).

it that the sheep do not suffer, it goes in search of those who have strayed off course, and it treats those that are injured.[2]

Such care in ancient Israel was associated with God. It was Christians, according to Foucault, who, over the course of the Middle Ages, made pastoral care an instrument of government:

> The pastoral theme in Christianity gave rise to an immense institutional network that we find nowhere else. . . . The God of the Hebrews is indeed a pastor God, but there were no pastors within the political and social regime of the Hebrews . . . the pastorate in Christianity gave rise to a dense, complicated, and closely woven institutional network that claimed to be, and was, in fact, coextensive with the entire Church, and so with Christianity, with the entire Christianity.[3]

It was through practices of care—and through the promotion of self-examination—Foucault says, that Christianity effected the suffocating governmentality it engendered and which became important in early modern Europe in the formation of the state and of the citizen's relationship to the state:

> The Christian pastorate is . . . absolutely innovative in establishing a structure, a technique of, at once, power, investigation, self-examination, and the examination of others, by which a certain inner truth of the hidden soul, becomes the element through which the pastor's power is exercised, by which obedience is practiced. By which the relationship of complete obedience is assured, and through which, precisely, the economy of merits and faults passes.[4]

For Foucault, then, the Christian pastorate was a distinctive historical institution that evolved in Europe from the second to the eighteenth century and which, on the model of the shepherd, undertook care for the salvation of all persons, one by one. It accomplished this in part through the practice of confession.[5] As he describes it, in the early modern period this form of pastoral governance then shifted from the church to the state, in the process

2. Ibid., 127.
3. Ibid., 164.
4. Ibid., 183.
5. Ibid., 184–85. See also John Bossy, "The Social History of Confession in the Age of the Reformation," *Transactions of the Royal Historical Society*, 5th ser., 25 (1975): 21–38.

lending its techniques of individual self-discipline and care to the ends of the state.

The US state, perhaps the Anglo-American state more generally, including the wider diaspora of colonial and postcolonial administrations, and the Anglo-American churches as well, exercises power in a different way from that of the European state.[6] Foucault speaks of the role of the minister, in both senses of the word, as a broker between religion and government in modern Europe:

> In modern Europe . . . the fundamental problem is undoubtedly not the Pope and the Emperor, but rather that mixed figure, or the two figures who in our language, and also in others, share one and the same name of the minister. The minister, with all the ambiguity of the word, is perhaps the real problem and where the relationship between religion and politics, between government and the pastorate, is really situated.[7]

For Foucault, the modern European state through its parliamentary ministers employs the techniques of pastoral power inherited from the church and embodied in its image of the shepherd.

Members of Congress in the United States are not ministers in this sense—although they, too, may be the "real problem." The US form of popular sovereignty and associationalism is understood to disperse the European-style paternalism of the welfare state. But there is a sense in which the logic of pastoral power is structured into American consciousness in a parallel way, as Alexis de Tocqueville famously observed, through the dominance in the United States of Christian forms of self-knowing and monitoring, Protestant and Catholic, avoiding the heavier hand of the state-established church, even in its welfare-state guise. These forms are taught today through Christian self-help literature and other media, as well as in twelve-step programs and their ilk. It is the very "strategic flexibility" of American Christianity that is its strength, as historian Tracy Fessenden says.[8] I want to suggest, however, that there is a sense in which the doubling effect

---

6. See Jean Baubérot and Séverine Mathieu, *Religion, modernité et culture au Royaume-Uni et en France, 1800–1914* (Paris: Seuil Points Histoire, 2002); William Novak, "The American Law of Association: The Legal-Political Construction of Civil Society," *Studies in American Political Development* 15 (Fall 2001): 163–88, and "The Myth of the 'Weak' American State," *American Historical Review* (2008): 752–72.

7. Foucault, *Security, Territory, Population,* 191–92.

8. Tracy Fessenden, *Culture and Redemption: Religion, the Secular, and American Religion* (Princeton, NJ: Princeton University Press, 2007).

of the two forms of pastoral power, in Foucault's sense, continues to play a role in, among other places, the work of the chaplain and her practices of spiritual care.

This chapter will look first at efforts to measure spiritual health in a new program in the army and, second, at an unsuccessful challenge to similar efforts in health care brought in a lawsuit against the Veterans Administration. These sorts of efforts, and the epistemologies underlying them, frame and legitimate much of the work of chaplains today. They reflect a shift for both the army and the health-care system away from an understanding of and interaction with religion founded in the institutional identities of discrete religious organizations, that is, the Protestant churches, the Catholic Church, and various American Jewish associations, toward a more universal, dispersed, and naturalized understanding of human religiosity, one that reflects aspects of the obsessive attention to and auditing of individual care delineated by Foucault. This book is about chaplains. But before getting to the work they do and how that work is legally managed, this chapter will further elaborate the spiritual services world in which they work.

Spiritual Fitness

Because religion, or spirituality, is today understood by many in the United States to be both natural and necessary to human health, it is also understood as subject to the same forms of empirical measurement as other aspects of human well-being. The passion for quantification, efficient use of resources, and evidence-based care that is evident throughout American government, business, social service delivery, education, law enforcement, military readiness, and health care today is evident in the administration of spiritual care as well.[9] Tools are being developed to measure the spiritual health of Americans and the value of spiritual interventions to the productivity, overall health, and morality of Americans. The results of these efforts are a curious set of mash-ups from the history of religion, philosophy, pop psychology, and, increasingly, biochemistry and neuroscience. Empiricism

9. For a discussion of nineteenth-century precursors to this very American approach to spiritual health, see John Lardas Modern, *Secularism in Antebellum America* (Chicago: University of Chicago Press, 2011). Closely related to the measuring of spiritual health is the collection of social data on religion. Because the US census does not collect data on religion, that effort has been taken up by various private groups including the Pew Research Center, NORC at the University of Chicago, and the World Values Survey, all of which generate sociological data about American religion. See also Chaves, *Contemporary Trends*, and Putnam and Campbell, *American Grace*.

also characterizes American law today. Legalism is closely tied to scientism, economic theories of the human, and "data-driven decision-making." Confidence in empirical work on spirituality also underwrites the constitutionality of faith-based government and legitimates the work of chaplains. Quantification implies neutrality and secularity as well as an efficient use of resources.

Several years ago, anxious atheists, ever vigilant to spot threats to the presumed and necessary secularity of American government, learned, to their horror, that the army had instituted a spiritual fitness test for all soldiers.[10] The spiritual fitness test was part of a larger comprehensive fitness test instituted by the army to assess the overall readiness of the US Army for the wars of the twenty-first century, what the army calls Total Army Fitness. In connection with this campaign, the US Army Office of the Surgeon General, the Army National Guard, and the Office of the Chief, Army Reserve provided the hooah4health.com website (initially open to the public but now password protected) as a public service to provide soldiers with information about the army's health fitness program.

Emphasizing that spiritual fitness is a facet of good health, the new army website informed service personnel thus:

Spiritual Fitness

The third element of HOOAH4HEALTH deals with spiritual fitness. This subject means many things to many people. The goal of this module is to explore another facet of health and wellness. Health surveys conducted by the U.S. Army Center for Health Promotion and Preventive Medicine and the Army Reserve Component indicate that spiritual matters rank within the top five health concerns of those surveyed. Some of the resources you will find here include hyperlinks to the Army Chaplain's office, a wide array of links to support systems, discussions relating to Family and friendship, and various suggestions for spirit enhancement. Visit us regularly and provide your perspective on matters of the spirit.

Notwithstanding its inviting openness to various perspectives on spiritual health, hooah4health.com affirmed and legitimated the secular scientific nature of its concern with what it called the cognitive, experiential, and

10. See Freedom from Religion Foundation, "FFRF Calls for Halt to Army 'Spiritual Fitness' Survey" (December 29, 2010), http://www.ffrf.org/news/releases/ffrf-calls-for-halt-to-army -spiritual-fitness-survey/ (accessed January 27, 2013).

behavioral dimensions of spiritual health, quoting from two researchers on the medical value of spirituality:

> The cognitive or philosophic aspects include the search for meaning, purpose and truth in life and the beliefs and values by which an individual lives. The experiential and emotional aspects involve feelings of hope, love, connection, inner peace, comfort and support. These are reflected in the quality of an individual's inner resources, the ability to give and receive spiritual love, and the types of relationships and connections that exist with the self, the community, the environment, and the transcendent (e.g., power greater than self, a value system, God, cosmic consciousness). The behavior aspects of spirituality involve the way a person externally manifests individual spiritual beliefs and inner spiritual state.[11]

Spiritual health is constituted by linking "meaning, purpose and truth in life" with "feelings of hope, love, connection, inner peace, comfort and support" and "an individual's inner resources, the ability to give and receive spiritual love, and the types of relationships and connections that exist with the self, the community, the environment, and the transcendent." Together these rubrics cover a spectrum of conventional Christian themes, themes that have over time been universalized and secularized through the use of abstract language and scientistic framing.

To assist the soldier who accessed the site, "Spirit Resources" were listed on a drop-down menu. They included "Spiritual Fitness: What Is It, Can We Train It, and, If So, How?," "The Official Song of the U.S. Army," "Decision-Making Skills," "Herbs," "Humor," "The Combat Medic Prayer," "Pets and Well-Being," "Relaxation," "The Road to Resilience," "Self-Esteem," "On the Spirit of Competition: Sports Tips and Trivia," "Time Out," "Army Values," "The Vegetable Garden," "Volunteerism," "12 Signs of Health," "Consideration of Others Handbook," and "May Is National Military Appreciation Month."[12] There was something for everyone and a virtual table of contents for today's highly presentist therapeutic culture and spiritual self-help style.

"HOOAH Salutes Our Soldiers" illustrates spiritual fitness through a display of iconic American war photography, beginning with the planting

---

11. Quoting from Gowri Anandarajah and Ellen Hight, "Spirituality and Medical Practice: Using the HOPE Questions as a Practical Tool for Spiritual Assessment," *American Family Physician* 63, no. 1 (2001): 81–88.

12. May is historically the month of Mary in the liturgical churches.

of the flag at Iwo Jima, selected from "The 100 Greatest Military Photos PowerPoint presentation," including photos from all American wars since the Civil War, available for download. "Spiritual Fitness: What Is It, Can We Train It, and, If So, How?" features an interview conducted by an army chaplain describing what he calls "the deep spiritual bankruptcy" of American soldiers today, a spiritual bankruptcy reflected in stories of their misbehavior: "another revenge killing, another senseless rape or murder of innocents; another immoral act from an American warrior who swore to uphold the Army Values."[13] The spiritual bankruptcy of soldiers is described as beginning "long before the soldier enters the Army" reflecting a broader malaise in American society as a whole.

The website also offered a transcript of a conversation among army chaplains about spiritual fitness, religion, and army values. One of the chaplains sees spiritual fitness as "the development of those personal qualities needed to sustain a person in a time of stress, hardship and tragedy," another "as something to do with self discipline." He goes on to add, "Soldiers that had just come back from combat . . . viewed Iraq as the Wild, Wild West: 'If they don't look like me I can shoot them and there will be no consequences.'" Spiritual fitness separates soldiers from outlaws. All three chaplains featured on the Hoohah website struggled to distinguish spiritual fitness from religion (understood to be potentially divisive and perhaps constitutionally suspect) but concluded in the end that the distinction didn't really matter. One said: "As long as you get to the end result, the direction in which you get there is pretty much irrelevant. . . . They may not profess a belief in God but within their mentality they have a line they're not going to cross whether they call it religion or atheism. I don't believe in God but I'm not going to cross that line . . . you cannot completely divorce religion when teaching it; you have to show there are many paths to get there." For these American military chaplains, spiritual fitness was religion defined in terms of its ends with the legally problematic bits removed, particularly sectarianism and evangelization, both of which they explicitly reject.

In contrast to the mid-twentieth century, when the army was regarded as a place of immorality in need of redemption, and evangelical chaplains flocked to the military to bring it religion, many in the army today see it as a place of better values than the world from which new recruits come. One of the chaplains explained: "We're going to have to be involved at the very

13. M. Sgt. Eric B. Pilgrim, "Spiritual Fitness: What Is It, Can We Train It, and If So, How?," http://www.hooah4usa.com/spirit/FHPspirit.htm (accessed January 27, 2013).

bottom, so that the initial entry of men and women from the American culture—the video culture, the video game culture, the violence culture— are all introduced to this idea that good Soldiers are Soldiers who maintain hope, who maintain serenity, who seek to respect life and are responsible." The army needs spiritual fitness because "spiritual fitness is a basic upon which the Army Values flourish. It's like a tree with fruit. The fruit of spiritual fitness ought to be selfless service, ought to be loyalty and ought to be personal courage." The army and the army chaplaincy understand themselves to be modeling and teaching values that the rest of the culture has lost. They are mounting a rescue operation, not just for the Iraqis and the Afghans, but for Americans as well, and spiritual fitness is basic to that effort.[14]

Sociologist Kim Hansen, author of a new ethnography of the US military chaplaincy, also observed and described this attitude. He quotes a Muslim chaplain in the navy whom he interviewed:

> Many chaplains described sailors and marines as coming into the military with hardly any sense of morality at all but with plenty of emotional scars and "baggage" from domestic violence, premarital sex, and substance abuse. By contrast, those who have been in the military for a while are assumed to be superior to their civilian counterparts. According to Chaplain Hamoud, "military service members are a cut above the society in terms of their physical training, in terms of their personal conduct, in terms of their social behavior. The military has done sexual harassment training, has conducted drug awareness classes, zero tolerance, suicide awareness, smoking reduction, so all these things help make a better person."[15]

It is a question of training and education, physical and spiritual.

The army's new spiritual fitness program is explicitly founded in positive psychology, a newish branch of psychology focused on human flourishing. Among other advisors to the army in the development of the program was

14. This vision is interestingly similar to that of prison reformers, who also have often understood themselves to be creating better places than those from which the inmates come, and better values from which the whole society could benefit. See, e.g., Winnifred Fallers Sullivan, *Prison Religion: Faith-Based Reform and the Constitution* (Princeton, NJ: Princeton University Press, 2011).

15. Kim Philip Hansen, *Military Chaplains and Religious Diversity* (New York: Palgrave Macmillan, 2012), 18–19. Hansen's work is an ethnographic study of military chaplains in the United States, particularly in the navy, focusing on the tension between universalist and particularist identities and approaches in the chaplaincy.

Martin Seligman, a psychologist at the University of Pennsylvania and the author of *Flourish*, a theory of human happiness based in an appropriation of stoic philosophy.[16] In a recent article, Kenneth Pargament and Partrick Sweeney, the two "positive" psychologists who were the actual authors of the army's program, described the development of the program.[17] They start by emphasizing that spiritual fitness is not founded in a particular ontology but is, rather, universal and adaptable to an individual's own position on these matters:

> The spiritual fitness component of the CSF [Comprehensive Soldier Fitness] program is not based on a particular stance or position on the ontological truth or validity of philosophical, nonreligious, or religious frameworks of belief and practice. Department of Defense leaders are not in a privileged position to answer ontological questions about God's existence or the truth of religious claims. However, they can facilitate the search for truth, self-knowledge, purpose, and direction in life as group members define it. In this project, we define *spirit* as the essential core of the individual, the deepest part of the self, and one's evolving human essence.[18]

According to the army, while spirit is the essential core, each person has to find the truth for himself. Spirituality, the promotion of spiritual fitness, is religion without ontology, or perhaps more accurately, religion with a universalist and naturalistic ontology that is deliberately obscured by the disclaimer.

The Department of Defense does not answer ontological questions because answers to those questions are multiple, but it does train for spiritual fitness because the spirit is universal and natural. Citing Christian theologians Rudolf Otto and Paul Tillich, Pargament and Sweeney explain: "the human spirit is more than a set of fixed traits and characteristics; it is an animating impulse—a vital, motivating force that is directed to realizing higher order goals, dreams, and aspirations that grow out of the essential self. In this sense, the human spirit organizes people's lives and propels people forward."[19] The army training program aims to harness the human spirit. First, the soldier must come to an awareness of his spiritual core; next,

---

16. Martin Seligman, *Flourish: A Visionary New Understanding of Happiness and Well-Being* (New York: Free Press, 2011).

17. Kenneth Pargament and Patrick Sweeney, "Building Spiritual Fitness in the Army: An Innovative Approach to a Vital Aspect of Human Development," *American Psychologist* 66 (January 2011): 58–64.

18. Ibid., 58.

19. Ibid.

the soldier develops his spirit; and, third, he builds connections with others and builds social awareness.[20]

All army personnel are required to take the Comprehensive Fitness Test. The Global Assessment Tool, an online questionnaire, explains:

> You will be assessed on your emotional, spiritual, social, and family fitness. The spiritual dimension on the GAT pertain to the domain of the Human Spirit: they are not "religious" in nature. The comprehensive Soldier Fitness Program defines spiritual fitness as strengthening a set of beliefs, principles, or values that sustain a person beyond family, institutional, and societal sources of support. Also, spiritual fitness provides a person a sense of purpose, meaning, and the strength to persevere and prevail when faced with significant challenges and responsibilities. It promotes general well-being, enhances self-confidence, and increases personal effectiveness.

Five of the questions address spirituality directly, asking the solider to respond as to whether each of a set of statements reflects how she actually lives her life: "I am a spiritual person," "My life has meaning," "I believe that in some way my life is closely connected to all humanity and all the world," "The job I am doing in the military has lasting meaning," "I believe there is a purpose for my life." The answers to these questions are scored. A low score leads to referral for remediation.[21]

The 2010 program was not the army's first foray into spiritual fitness. A pamphlet describing its earlier 1987 Fit to Win Spiritual Fitness program, in addition to stressing the importance of "stress management" and "total wellness," used a nautical metaphor from the work of English literary critic and Christian apologist C. S. Lewis, author of the *Chronicles of Narnia* series, to describe the interdependence of human life and the need for values. "Spiritual fitness," the 1987 program announced "is the development

---

20. "Building on the Army's model of the human spirit, our team of psychologists has designed three tiers of education modules to facilitate the spiritual resilience of soldiers. The intent of the first tier is to enhance soldier's self-awareness of their spiritual core, including their essential values and beliefs, purpose, and meaning, and also to introduce them to the human spirit model. The intent of the second tier is to provide Army personnel access to spiritual resources, to facilitate the development of the human spirit and to help them anticipate and deal with struggles of the spirit that they may encounter in their military service. The third tier is designed to assist soldiers in building greater social awareness to foster a sense of deep connectedness with other people and the world." Ibid., 62.

21. These documents were posted on their website by the Military Association of Atheists and Freethinkers. Interestingly, MAAF does not oppose the chaplaincy but only wishes it to live up to its commitment to universality and nondiscrimination. www.maaf.info (accessed June 26, 2013).

of those personal qualities needed to sustain a person in times of stress, hardship, and tragedy. These qualities come from religious, philosophical, or human values and form the basis for character, disposition, decision-making, and integrity." The program went on to illustrate the relationship between values and spiritual health with a quote from Lewis:

> You can get the idea if you think of us as a fleet of ships sailing in formation. The voyage will be a success only, in the first place, if the ships do not collide and get in one another's way, and, secondly, if each ship is seaworthy and has her engines in good order . . . And however well the fleet sailed, its voyage would be a failure if it were meant to reach New York and actually arrived at Calcutta.[22]

Earlier campaigns for spiritual fitness share much with today's, notwithstanding the opacity of Lewis's nautical and imperialist references. In 1987, as today, the personnel tasked with building spiritual resilience was the chaplain. The military chaplain's raison d'être has always been the creation of a healthy soldier fit for service, seaworthy and with her engines in good order, ready to sail in formation, and headed in the right direction.

The army's new spiritual fitness program is a part of its larger effort to modernize the army after the invasions of Afghanistan and Iraq. In 2009, the army published its campaign plan listing overall objectives for updating the army's readiness and "restoring balance." Doing its part, and anxious to prove its value in the new millennium, the army chaplaincy produced its own extraordinarily ambitious Army Chaplaincy Strategic Plan, 2009–14 in order to implement the objectives of the new army campaign.[23] Focused on its mission to serve "God and Country" (the motto of the army chaplaincy is *Pro Deo et Patria*), and its vision of "spiritual leadership for the Army Family" and the well-being of the warriors they serve, the chaplaincy eagerly detailed how each overall army campaign objective would be served by a newly tuned-up chaplaincy.

The chaplaincy's strategic plan repeatedly insists on the spiritual fitness of the warrior as its goal. Aligning the chaplaincy's objectives with those announced in the army's overall campaign, the chaplaincy explains how those objectives will be furthered by the work of the Unit Ministry Teams

22. See "Spiritual Fitness," a 1987 pamphlet published by the Department of the Army. Department of the Army Pamphlet 600-63-12.

23. US Army Chaplain Corps, "The Army Chaplaincy Strategic Plan 2009–2014," http://www.chapnet.army.mil/pdf/strategic_map.pdf (accessed January 27, 2013).

(UMTs) to improve the spiritual resilience and fitness of every soldier. Evident throughout is a distillation and tight interweaving of familiar American religious styles and commitments—to religious freedom, to diversity, to country, to family, and to self-improvement. The soldier is envisioned as the very embodiment of what William James named the healthy-minded style of the religious individual.[24]

For each overall army campaign objective, the chaplaincy announces corresponding objectives for itself. Thus, for "Army Campaign Objective 1: Man the Army & Preserve the All-Volunteer Force," among the chaplaincy's objectives is to "Honor the Sacred Privilege of Serving 'For God and Country.'" The chaplaincy is well equipped for this mission, it announces, because "in no other environment do so many ministers of diverse faith groups come together in such varied ways to accomplish one mission . . . To bring God to Soldiers and Soldiers to God." To further "Army Campaign Objective 3: Support Current Global Operations with Ready Land-power," the chaplaincy committed itself to "Provide Spiritually-based Religious Support to The Army." As it further explained, "spiritually-based support is at the heart of our responsibilities to ensure the 'free exercise' of religion for America's Soldiers and their Families."

For "Army Campaign Objective 4: Train the Army for Full Spectrum Operations," a corresponding chaplaincy objective is to "Expand UMT Training in Cultural Awareness and the Impact of Religion on Operations." Cultural awareness is necessary because "in the current operational environment, our UMTs are deployed around the globe." This situation requires new training for chaplains in ministering to local populations, as well as to soldiers:

> Chaplains and Chaplain Assistants must be prepared to provide the operational capability of engaging in religious leader liaison activities with host nation religious leaders. The Chaplaincy will continue to evaluate, develop and field resources which will enable us to utilize the world religions expertise available in the Chaplain Corps and the civilian sector to better equip our UMTs. We will ensure that they have the training, requisite skill sets, and tools necessary to analyze the religious and worldview dimensions of culture and advise the Commander of their impact on operations.

A well-rounded army chaplain is someone who is a battle staff officer, spiritual leader, manager, diplomat, and shepherd:

24. William James, *Varieties of Religious Experience: A Study in Human Nature* (New York: Longmans, Green & Co., 1902).

Chaplains and Chaplain Assistants must be multi-skilled, spiritually fit, agile, adaptive, innovative, self-aware, and mission focused Spiritual Leaders. . . . We will prepare Chaplains and Chaplain Assistants to serve as a *Battle Staff* officer or NCO who advises the Commander and participates in staff processes; a *Spiritual Leader* who conducts services and ceremonies in any environment, who provides or performs the rites, sacraments, religious education, or counseling that our Soldiers and Families need; a *Manager* of people and resources who ensures full ministry team coverage, can capably work religious support logistics, and is a trainer of excellence; a *Diplomat* who is proficient in their ability to dialogue on world religions and culture, and when appropriate function as a religious leader liaison with NGOs or local leaders; and a *Shepherd* who combines all these competencies with a primary focus of caring for the souls of Soldiers and their Families.

The spiritually fit soldier is someone whose "inner life" has been strengthened "through culturally relevant, engaging, and innovative worship, religious education, moral leadership training, and pastoral care."

Finally, for "Army Campaign Objective 7: Transform the Operating Force," the chaplaincy commits to "develop and maintain the Chaplaincy Automated Religious Support System (CARSS), a state-of-the-art, agile, always-on, global religious support network" in order to "Leverage Technology to Support and Sustain the Spiritual Fitness of Commanders and Soldiers."

The Chaplaincy Strategic Plan concludes with an acronym diagramming what it terms Sacred Values:

Spirituality	Seek to know God and yourself at the deepest level
Accountability	Hold yourself and others to the moral and spiritual high ground in every area of life
Compassion	Love in word and deed
Religious Leadership	Model spiritual truths wisely and courageously
Excellence	Do your best for God's glory
Diversity	Respect the differences of others

Above this diagram is a photo of American soldiers in camouflage sitting on the ground before a chaplain, also in camouflage, holding a shepherd's crook, the very embodiment of pastoral power and care.[25]

25. One of the symbols of Pharaoh's power was also the shepherd's crook. Foucault, *Security, Territory, Population*, 124.

Tightly bound together in this strategic plan are the army's need for a certain kind of soldier, theories of behavior modification, a vision for an ideal society, and a long history of American religion. All of these are further made possible by a perceived constitutional need to enable the free exercise of religion, as we will explore in more detail in chapter 4. The army's new commitment to spiritual fitness necessitates relentless self-measurement and assessment in this area, as in every other contemporary American endeavor founded in evidence-based research.

Measuring spiritual fitness is not a new American religious phenomenon. Beginning with the Puritans, whose personal conversion narratives were vetted by town officials to determine their fitness for membership and eligibility to vote in the Puritan communities of New England, through the various revivalist obsessions with taking spiritual temperatures and then the nineteenth-century spiritualists' enthusiasm for the latest psychological measurements, from phrenology to muscular Christianity, to contemporary scientific studies of the effect of spiritual practices on physical health and happiness, many American religious persons, liberal and conservative, have had a zeal for spiritual assessment and improvement.[26] The army here seems to be successor to Edwin Starbuck and William James, late nineteenth-century explorers into the psychology of religious experience.

While many today who name themselves as spiritual do so in contradistinction to something they seem to call organized religion, as we have seen, spiritualists and spirituality have a long history in the United States as an affirmative identity, one rooted in evolving ideas about psychology and the natural and involved at various points in organizing itself for a range of purposes. Importantly, the language of spirituality or the spiritual has allowed chaplains and others to generalize across and bridge differences among religious traditions. This enabling capacity of the language of spirituality to move beyond pluralism is at least as significant for the courts as its connection to a genealogy of spiritual experimentation in the United States.

Army chaplains are adapting to a world of natural religiosity with all of its inclusive vagueness, the legitimating and presumed universality of science, and the accommodation of diversity demanded by a commitment to nondiscrimination and religious freedom in a world of religious multiplicity. How this effort is actually being implemented and how it is being

26. Valuable studies of this history include Ann Taves, *Fits, Trances and Visions: Experiencing Religion and Explaining Experience from Wesley to James* (Princeton, NJ: Princeton University Press, 1999); Christopher G. White, *Unsettled Minds;* and Modern, *Secularism in Antebellum America.*

received by the rest of the army is not completely understood. There is a long history of evangelization in the military services and clearly the valuing of this work differs across different commands; there is much skepticism and cynicism about these efforts in the army, as elsewhere. There are also chaplains who resist the generalizing language of spirituality, insisting on the particularity, even exclusivity, of their teaching.[27] But concern for the spiritual fitness of Americans is not just the army's.

Resisting Spiritual Fitness

Universal spirituality as a political and religious program is a problem for the right and for the left: for the right because it violates specific religious commandments, for the left because it rejects the secular as the universal standard for modern rationality and morality. As "spirituality" is more and more accepted today in the United States as a fundamental and necessary aspect of human anthropology, and therefore properly the object of solicitude on the part of those anxious to promote good public health, efforts to measure an individual's spiritual well-being, even fitness, have multiplied in health care as well as in the army. Employers also concern themselves with spiritual fitness.

The assessment of spiritual health within health-care organizations is authorized today by the standards mandated by the Joint Commission (formerly the Joint Commission on the Accreditation of Health Organizations, the JCAHO). The Joint Commission is the largest, but not the only, private accrediting organization for health-care facilities in the United States. A majority of states will reimburse only Joint Commission–accredited facilities under Medicare.[28] The Affordable Care Act also mandates accreditation. These accrediting standards concerning spiritual health are not entirely new. They find their origins in changes to nursing diagnostic standards made decades earlier, changes that focused on a need to address what nurses critical of a scientistic medical culture termed "spiritual concerns, spiritual distress and spiritual despair."[29]

Not everyone agrees, however. Increased attention to the need to foster spiritual health on the part of health-care organizations has brought

27. See Hansen, *Military Chaplains and Religious Diversity.*

28. See Timothy Stoltzfus Jost, "Medicare and the Joint Commission on Accreditation of Healthcare Organizations: A Healthy Relationship?," *Law and Contemporary Problems* 57 (1994): 15–45.

29. See Wendy Cadge, *Paging God: Religion in the Halls of Medicine* (Chicago: University of Chicago Press, 2012), 39.

backlash from rights advocacy groups. The Freedom from Religion Foundation,[30] also active in monitoring the army's spiritual fitness efforts, is a Wisconsin organization dedicated to promoting free thought and litigating to protect the separation of church and state. FFRF is not persuaded that spirituality is a constitutionally appropriate form of religion for the government to promote in its hospitals. FFRF is as vigilant in challenging programs of spiritual health as it is in challenging religious symbols on public land. Their spirited but largely unsuccessful opposition to both, founded in what might be understood to be an outdated separationist First Amendment jurisprudence, demonstrates the persistence of a hard-edged refusal of some on the left to accept the pervasive religiosity of American life.[31]

FFRF is familiar to many through its bus ads and billboards promoting atheism. For example, a sign bearing the words "Sleep in on Sundays" has appeared on the sides of buses around the country in recent years.[32] The manifesto on the FFRF website explains its conviction that freethinking has driven human progress:

> The history of Western civilization shows us that most social and moral progress has been brought about by persons free from religion. In modern times the first to speak out for prison reform, for humane treatment of the mentally ill, for abolition of capital punishment, for women's right to vote, for death with dignity for the terminally ill, and for the right to choose contraception, sterilization and abortion have been freethinkers, just as they were the first to call for an end to slavery. The Foundation works as an umbrella for those who are free from religion and are committed to the cherished principle of separation of state and church.

Paralleling other triumphal modern narratives of the necessary link between secularization and the rise of human rights, FFRF sees social progress as resulting from the liberation of humankind from religious dogma and authority. Advocates for religion, of course, cite the very same markers of

---

30. www.ffrf.org (accessed June 26, 2013).

31. It is not just the left that worries about spiritual practices in hospitals. Candy Gunther Brown argues that the mainstreaming of alternative medicine has been the result of a stealth campaign to disguise the metaphysical underpinnings of these practices for the purposes of concealing their non-Christian origins and deceiving conservative Christians into accepting them. She also argues that these practices are constitutionally suspect. Candy Gunther Brown, *Healing Gods* (Oxford: Oxford University Press, 2013).

32. http://www.ffrf.org/press/high-resolution-images/ (accessed July 9, 2013).

social progress—prison reform, humane treatment of the mentally ill, abolition of capital punishment, women's right to vote, death with dignity for the terminally ill, opposition to slavery, and reproductive rights—as having originated with religious activists. One might write the same paragraph beginning "The history of Western civilization shows us that most social and moral progress has been brought about by persons of faith . . ." An honest and responsible appraisal of the historical record would suggest that the bumpy road to an uneven achievement of these social changes, just as to opposition to them, has been accomplished with the participation of both self-styled freethinkers and self-identified religiously motivated persons; sorting out leadership in these areas as religious or secular would be difficult, if not impossible, on any objective criteria.

FFRF is an energetic litigator, vigilant in outing religion in government. It has sued to challenge Ten Commandments displays; the Internal Revenue Service (IRS) parsonage exemption; Governor Rick Perry's prayer rally; the promotion of faith-based initiatives; national and state days of prayer; recitation of the Pledge of Allegiance in schools; release time credits; public display of crosses, statues of Jesus, and crèches on publicly owned property; prayer and Bible instruction in public schools; Good Friday holidays; and the teaching of creationism, among other suspect practices. It also targets government chaplaincies.

In 2005, FFRF brought a taxpayer action in the US District Court for the Western District of Wisconsin challenging the constitutionality of the administration of the hospital chaplaincy of the US Department of Veterans Affairs.[33] Among the long catalog of concerns listed in its Complaint, FFRF alleged that

> as part of the evaluation of each patient's health care needs, the VA requires that a spiritual and pastoral care screening assessment be provided to each patient as part of the interdisciplinary admissions process; VA chaplains then are to determine the "need" for any pastoral care interventions deemed necessary if "spiritual injury or sickness" is assessed by the chaplain.[34]

And, further, that

---

33. Freedom from Religion Foundation v. Nicholson, 469 F. Supp. 2d 609 (W.D. Wis. 2007), *vacated and remanded*, 536 F.3d 730 (7th Cir. 2008).

34. Complaint, Freedom from Religion Foundation v. Nicholson (W.D. Wis. 2007), No. 06-C-212-S.

the integration of religion and spirituality into the medical services provided
by the VA is intended to promote religion and belief, rather than to accommodate free exercise rights of veterans who are otherwise limited by their
hospitalization from freely exercising religious choices.[35]

The relief sought was an order enjoining the VA from future violations of
the First Amendment and

> for an order requiring the defendants to establish rules, regulations, prohibi-
> tions, standards and oversight to ensure that future disbursements are not
> made and/or used to fund activities that include religion as a substantive
> integral component of the VA's medical treatment protocols.[36]

The FFRF was careful in its Complaint to draw a bright line between what
it understands to be constitutionally permitted, perhaps even required, that
is, facilitating the free exercise rights of veterans who may not otherwise
have access to religious services, and what is not, that is, the full integration
of religion, or what it calls "pastoral care" in the Complaint, into medical
care. What is apparent from the subsequent litigation is that the bright line
drawn by FFRF between the free exercise of religion and the providing of
spiritual care is losing plausibility to many in the United States, perhaps
especially to many judges, who are persuaded that fostering spirituality may
be a path to many sorts of fitness, including for those leaving prisons, as
well as to those, like the army, who are eager to restore spiritual values to
American life, as well as toward realizing religious freedom.

The defendant in *FFRF v. Nicholson*, the US Department of Veterans Affairs (the VA), is an executive agency of the US government. The department
is charged with responsibility, among other things, for providing health
care to veterans of the armed forces as well as to their eligible family members and survivors. The Veterans Health Administration has a congressional
mandate to "provide a complete medical and hospital service for the medical care and treatment of veterans."[37] In 2005, at the time the FFRF suit was
filed, the VA operated 154 medical centers, 1,300 other "sites of care,"
136 nursing homes, 43 residential rehabilitation treatment programs, and
88 comprehensive home-care programs in the United States; over five mil-
lion people received health care in VA facilities that year. Projected numbers

35. Ibid.
36. Ibid.
37. Freedom from Religion Foundation v. Nicholson, 563 F.3d 730 (7th Cir. 2008).

of patient visits and health-care expenditures have only increased since then, particularly as the result of casualties from two wars, casualties that present new and challenging mental and medical health-care needs, and also because of the priority President Obama has given to veterans' health care. The VA also provides spiritual care to these patients, care that is administered by the National Chaplain Center of the VA in Hampton, Virginia.

The VA's approach to medical care does not just affect service personnel and their families. The VA also manages the largest medical education and health professions training program in the United States. Each year, about ninety thousand health professionals are trained in VA medical centers. Indeed, more than half of the physicians practicing in the United States have received part of their clinical training in the VA health-care system.

The VA chaplaincy traces its beginnings to the Homes for Disabled Soldiers established by President Abraham Lincoln during the Civil War. Chaplains in those early days were paid a salary of "$1500 per year and forage for one horse."[38] Formal existence of the VA chaplaincy as a fully institutionalized national service begins, however, only after World War II with the appointment of the first chief of chaplaincy services and the ambition to provide full-time chaplains for all VA hospitals. Today, the VA chaplaincy does not just serve in VA institutions; first initiated in response to an airplane crash in 1996, since 9/11 the VA chaplaincy is now fully integrated into the nation's first responder system. (The Aviation Disaster Family Assistance Act of 1996, a landmark law setting the standard for federal responses to disaster, is explicit about victims' right to care that considers each person's uniqueness and respects spiritual values.[39]) VA chaplains trained as emergency responders by the Red Cross and the Department of Homeland Security are now enrolled in a computer database allowing them to be electronically and geographically deployed in the event of a national disaster.[40]

38. US Department of Veteran Affairs, "History of VA Chaplaincy," available at http://www.va.gov/CHAPLAIN/components/History_of_VA_Chaplaincy.asp (accessed January 19, 2013). The Civil War marks many shifts in American religious practice and in the practices of American government.

39. 49 U.S.C. 1136 and 41113.

40. Telephone interview by author with Don Doherty, education specialist at the National Chaplain Training Center in Hampton, Virginia, March 2, 2011. Doherty subsequently provided the author with a copy of a PowerPoint presentation used to train chaplains in such work. The Billy Graham Evangelistic Association has its own rapid deployment chaplaincy, described as follows: "To meet the critical need for emotional and spiritual care following disasters, the Rapid Response Team (RRT) currently has chaplains in the United States, the US Territory of Puerto Rico, Australia, Canada and the United Kingdom. These approved volunteer chaplains are carefully selected and prepared to demonstrate the compassion of Jesus Christ, and appropriately share God's hope through the One who 'heals the brokenhearted and binds up

Trained to identify signs of spiritual stress, among their tasks is offering a "ministry of presence."[41]

As the district court told the story in its Memorandum and Order in the *Nicholson* case, the VA chaplaincy has evolved since its founding from a focus that was once what the court calls "sacramental" to a focus that it now terms "clinical."[42] These terms have very specific meanings in this context. According to the VA's official history, "The national Chaplaincy was originally organizationally assigned to the Office of Special Services, which also included the departments of Recreation, Canteen, Athletics and Patient Welfare." What the *Nicholson* court refers to as "sacramental" denominates this now older system of supplying opportunities to patients to access religious services on a piecemeal demand basis, as an auxiliary to medical care, by analogy with sports and snacks.[43] FFRF wishes the VA to return to this sacramental order with its carefully policed distinction between religion and health care. Already attenuated, of course, is any explicit link to a Christian understanding of sacrament and the significance of that understanding for both Reformation-era theological disputes and earlier Protestant versus Catholic battles in the United States. Interestingly, it is now the secularists who seek to maintain the old sacramental order.[44]

The new "clinical" chaplaincy has a different role and a different purpose. The chaplain has now become a member of the medical team. As the Wisconsin court explained, in order "to effectively implement its clinical chaplaincy program, the VA Chaplain Service was recently reorganized under the Medicine and Surgery Strategic Healthcare Group. The purpose of this reorganization was to recognize VA's chaplaincy as a clinical, direct patient care discipline." Religion, in the words of FFRF, had become a "health benefit." Indeed, every new patient must now be given an initial spiritual

---

their wounds,' Psalm 147:3." http://www.billygraham.org/rrt_index.asp (accessed December 1, 2012).

41. Per Doherty's PowerPoint presentation.

42. 469 F. Supp. 2d at 612.

43. Wendy Cadge calls this practice one in which "traditional chaplains . . . conducted rituals." Cadge, *Paging God*, 36.

44. What constitutes a sacrament and whether sacraments are biblically warranted have been live questions between Catholics and Protestants and among Protestants until recently. In Catholic theology, a sacrament is a canonically regulated occasion for the mediated transmission of grace within what is known as the Sacramental Economy. Seven sacraments are canonically ordained: baptism, Eucharist, confirmation, marriage, confession, holy orders, and anointing of the sick. Other minor rites are known as sacramentals. The sacramental order bound Christians in the Latin West before the Reformation to a liturgical calendar and ritual order administered by the church. *Catechism of the Catholic Church*, http://www.vatican.va/archive/ENG0015/__P2U.HTM (accessed June 27, 2013).

screening and assessment upon admission and recommendations must be made concerning his spiritual care. With religion universalized as spirituality, the VA no longer waits for the patient to request care. Spiritual care is no longer separated. No longer the facilitator of divine communication through a sacramental intervention institutionalized through the authority of a church or synagogue, the VA chaplain now assesses and ministers to every patient's spiritual needs as a routine and ongoing aspect of the patient's overall medical care.

The district court explained this evolution in the VA chaplaincy:

> In the early beginnings, the primary focus of the VA chaplain was sacramental in nature and involved caring for seriously ill and dying patients, leading worship, and administering the sacraments. However, during the past ten years the VA chaplaincy has developed a more clinical focus . . . today's clinical chaplains draw from both the behavioral sciences and theological reflection in understanding the human condition . . . the VA believes that the spiritual dimension of health must be integrated into all aspects of patient care, research, emergency preparedness, and health care education.[45]

The court concluded with a description of the new role:

> a "clinical chaplain" is an individual who: (1) meets all VA qualifications for chaplain, (2) provides spiritual and pastoral care characterized by in-depth assessment, evaluation, and treatment of patients, (3) has a high degree of integration into the total care and treatment program of a health care facility; and (4) has close working relationships with staff members of other professional health care disciplines.[46]

Emphasizing the professional clinical training of chaplains, the court further explained that what chaplains do is spiritual, not religious because "a chaplain trained in CPE avoids initiating or guiding religious instruction . . . VA pastoral care is religious in content only if that is the wish of a given patient . . . providing pastoral care need not involve religion at all . . . spirituality is not necessarily religious because it concerns the meaning of life on a more general level."[47] What was seen as a sacralizing move by FFRF, the integration of chaplains into the clinical health-care team, is seen as a

45. 469 F. Supp. 2d at 612.
46. Ibid.
47. Ibid. at 612–13.

secularizing move by the court. FFRF sees no distinction between the language of religion and the language of spirituality while the court sees the distinction as crucial.

The difference in perspective between FFRF and the court illustrates the irresistible doubling effect and irresolvability of the totalizing discourse of secularism, making the legal and constitutional designation almost entirely arbitrary. Any practice can be moved from the unconstitutional to the constitutional column simply by being renamed. Whether it is a good idea for such care to be mandated is left aside. Indeed the question is obscured by the skirmish as to whether it is religious or not. The district court's view of spiritual assessment and treatment in the *Nicholson* case is one founded in what is understood to be a benign and generalized spirituality, not in religion. The secularized training of the chaplains and the voluntary nature of the interaction is understood by the court to insulate the VA from any danger of imposition: "VA chaplains do not incorporate religious content into either their pastoral care or spiritual counseling unless that is the patient's wish . . . VA chaplains provide spiritual and pastoral care to both religious and non-religious patients but only if they desire such services."[48] Slipping between the universal language of pastoral care and spirituality, on the one hand, and the particularity of religion, on the other, the court mimics the training and ethics of the modern chaplain, as will be further described in chapter 3.

Spiritual diagnosis and assessment in modern clinical health settings, as with the army, is usually accomplished through a formal questionnaire designed to evaluate and quantify the state of an individual's spiritual health. Such assessments are founded in new holistic medical anthropologies developed in the last several decades that seek, on the one hand, to move beyond narrow scientistic understandings of sickness and health and, on the other, to naturalize religion, removing it from the purview of religious and political authorities. Assessment tools are produced by psychologists interested in religion and spirituality and by theologians interested in psychology. Many are copyrighted and commercially marketed.[49]

Nurses were critical to the introduction of spirituality into health care. As sociologist Wendy Cadge explains, after a period of informal use of spir-

48. Ibid. at 621.

49. For one account of and comparison of spiritual assessment tools by an academic expert in pastoral care, see George Fitchett, *Assessing Spiritual Needs: A Guide for Caregivers* (Minneapolis: Augsburg Fortress, 1993). George Fitchett is associate professor and director of research and spiritual assessment in the Department of Religion, Health, and Human Values at Rush-Presbyterian-St. Luke's Medical Center, Chicago.

itual assessment tools by nurses, "The North American Nursing Diagnostic Association (NANDA) approved spiritual concerns, spiritual distress and spiritual despair as nursing diagnoses in 1978 and then combined them into one category of spiritual distress."[50] She adds that "spiritual distress is today defined as 'impaired ability to experience and integrate meaning and purpose in life through connectedness with self, others, art, music, literature, nature and/or a power greater than one-self.'"[51] But physicians also got involved, as Cadge explains, developing their own assessment tools: "With names like SPIRITual History, FICA, FAITH and HOPE, these assessments asked questions about sources of Hope, Organized religion, Personal spirituality and practices, and Effects on medical care and end of life issues." Physicians also added spirituality to the training of doctors: "With the support of the National Institute for Healthcare Research and the John Templeton Foundation, the American Association of Medical Colleges also published a report in 1999 detailing the importance of spiritual and cultural concerns in medical education."[52]

One spiritual history tool uses the acronym FACT to assist the physician who is taking the history to ask about "F—Faith or Beliefs; A—Availability, Accessibility, Applicability; C—Coping or Comfort; and T—Treatment Plan." The tool's designers caution that "faith is already a FACT affecting the lives and healthcare choices for many patients and most already utilize faith-based practices as complementary treatment modalities: healthcare professionals need to assess how it impacts their treatment choices." They add that "a spiritual history is not about what a person believes; it is about how their faith or belief functions as a coping mechanism." Finally, they warn the doctor to "respect the privacy of patients with regard to their spirituality; do not impose your own beliefs" and to "make referrals to professional chaplains, spiritual counselors and community resources as appropriate."[53]

At the hospital administration level, in its guidelines for self-evaluation, the Joint Commission reminds hospitals that it "requires organizations to include a spiritual assessment as part of the overall assessment of a patient to determine how the Patient's spiritual outlook can affect his or her care, treatment, and services."[54] In a sidebar, the Joint Commission explains that

50. Cadge, *Paging God*, 39.

51. Ibid.

52. Ibid.

53. Mark LaRocca-Pitts, "In FACT Chaplains Have a Spiritual Assessment Tool," *Australian Journal of Pastoral Care and Health* 3 (2009): 8–15.

54. Joint Commission on Accreditation of Healthcare Organizations, *The Source* 3, no. 2 (February 2005): 6.

spirituality is important to a patient's health and that studies show that patients want their health-care providers to discuss spirituality with them:

Why Assess Spirituality?

Spirituality is an often overlooked, yet still important element of patient assessment and care. Addressing and supporting patients' spirituality can not only make their health care experiences more positive, but in many cases can promote health, decrease depression, help patients cope with a difficult illness, and even improve outcomes for some patients. In addition to the potential medical benefits, patients want their health care providers to discuss spirituality with them. In one study, a majority of patients indicated that they would like their physicians to ask whether patients have spiritual or religious beliefs that would influence their medical decisions if they became gravely ill. Another study found that 40% of patients felt that physicians should discuss pertinent religious issues with their patients, however only 11% of physicians frequently or always did.[55]

Reflecting a continuing ambivalence about whether religion is a "coping mechanism" or actually affects "outcomes," a focus on patient spiritual care is the result of a long historical process, initiated in large part by nurses, which was intended to refocus medical care on the whole person and acknowledge the pervasively religious and cultural context for sickness in the United States.

The spiritual assessment tools used by the VA are, as FFRF says in their brief on appeal, "structured to measure information about Organized Religious Activity, Non-organized religious activity, and Intrinsic Religious Values, which together provide . . . a Total Religious Index."[56] A low Total Religious Index, or spiritual assessment score, on a VA assessment results in referral to a chaplain and the creation of a spiritual treatment plan. Spiritual healing is then integrated into treatment in a variety of ways.

Defending its new chaplaincy and assessment practices in the *Nicholson* case, the VA argued that what plaintiffs derided as a violation of the establishment clause, that is, a government funded "faith-based" treatment, is constitutionally permissible as long as it is noncoercive.[57] No one argued

---

55. Ibid.

56. Brief of Appellants, *Nicholson*, at 10.

57. In the last seventy years since the establishment clause of the First Amendment was incorporated through the Fourteenth Amendment and applied to the states, the Court has developed a series of tests and standards for evaluating the presence of an establishment clause

in *Nicholson* that the VA program is formally coercive. One may refuse both spiritual assessment and spiritual care. Indeed, one may refuse any care. But the VA, and many others within the larger health-care community, are making a stronger claim than simply that spiritual care is constitutional as long as it is optional. They are asserting that spiritual assessment and care are fundamentally not religious and that they are necessary to good health care. (Depending how one evaluates the evidence concerning the importance of spiritual health to overall health, one might ask if it would not be a rational extension of such a position to charge atheists higher insurance rates.)

The Freedom from Religion Foundation argues, on the other hand, that routinely to assess and treat every VA patient's spiritual health is itself to establish religion. To assume that every patient's health has a spiritual aspect is, they say, to promote religion over nonreligion, an activity that the Supreme Court has repeatedly spoken of as prohibited to government. To do so is to discriminate against atheists and to suggest that religion is a positively good—or necessary—thing, rather than being simply an optional or "recreational" thing. The VA, FFRF complained, had "undertaken to diagnose spiritual injury and to offer religious cures."[58] The VA, they said, had crossed the constitutional line by incorporating religion into the delivery of all VA health-care services.

Actual administration of VA medical facilities is quite decentralized so, as the court in *Nicholson* acknowledged, the practice of spiritual assessment and treatment in those facilities may vary from place to place. The form that spiritual assessment and spiritual care take in a VA hospital in Alabama might look quite different from the form it takes in Maine or California. The court in the *Nicholson* case offered several examples from the record of spiritual treatment given in VA hospitals from around the country, starting

---

violation. The dominant but often criticized test is the *Lemon* test, originating in the Court's opinion in Lemon v. Kurtzman, 403 U.S. 602 (1971), asking whether a particular practice has the purpose or effect of advancing religion. In her concurring opinion in Lynch v. Donnelly, 465 U.S. 668 (1984), Justice O'Connor proposed a standard founded in an assessment of whether a particular government practice might be perceived as an endorsement of religion by government. Justices critical of the Court's establishment clause jurisprudence have argued that what must be shown is more than simple favoritism on the part of government. Government action must be shown to be coercive to rise to the level of a constitutional violation, that is, government must be involved in active proselytizing or other coercion. Otherwise both the display of religious symbols and the enabling of religious activity by government is regarded as simply a permissible acknowledgment of the religiosity of Americans. Justice Thomas has argued that incorporation was a mistake and the Court should leave all such issues to the states. Cutter v. Wilkinson, 544 U.S. 709 (2005).

58. Brief of Appellants and Appendix, *Nicholson*, at 17.

with Dayton, Ohio, where a mixing of Christian practice and behavioral psychology reflected the contemporary training of chaplains.

The Dayton chaplain used Fowler's *Stages of Faith Development,* a classic in the psychology of religion, with the religious prayer form of lament to structure her work with patients with posttraumatic stress disorder. (Fowler developed a theory of six stages that all people go through as their faith matures, a theory based in the work of psychologists Jean Piaget and Lawrence Kohlberg.[59]) As the court explained, Dayton Chaplain Dietsch uses "poetry, meaningful quotes, children's stories, film clips, and music to evoke memory and experiences, illustrating the various stages [of faith]."[60] Chaplain Dietsch also "introduces the veterans to the Lament as a form of prayer . . . and then invites the veterans to contribute to a group Lament."[61] (Lament is a genre of mourning significant for Jews and Christians because of the reference to the biblical books of Lamentations and Psalms, but such prayers exist in many traditions.)

One can see in the treatments administered by chaplains an accumulating set of practices that excerpt and generalize from a wide range of sources, scriptural and otherwise. (This range reflects the widespread eclecticism of seminary training and the influence of psychology on that training in the last century, as will be further discussed in chapter 3.) Another example the court described came from Sheridan, Virginia, where the VA Medical Center provides a drug and alcohol treatment program entitled the Spiritual Recovery Support Group, a program that was described by the court as a form of applied grace: "SRSG is used as an attempt to bring the spiritual components of faith and God's grace to bear on treatment and enhance the health care recovery of veterans."[62] SRSG works, the court explained, because when "God's gift of spiritual faith and grace is applied, it is good medicine. . . . SRSG incorporates the idea that God sees the veterans of infinite worth and value and that God wants them to treat themselves with 'His grace and mercy as His precious child.'"[63] Explicitly Christian in many ways, SRSG also echoes language in evangelical self-help literature, a literature that also combines Christian theology with the language of therapy.[64]

59. James W. Fowler, *Stages of Faith: The Psychology of Human Development and the Quest for Meaning* (San Francisco: Harper & Row, 1981).
60. 469 F. Supp. 2d at 615.
61. Ibid. Capitalizing "Lament" subtly references its biblical origins.
62. Ibid. at 615–16.
63. Ibid.
64. Evangelical and liberal Christians have both absorbed psychology into their theologies of pastoral care, although with somewhat different emphases. For a history of these differences, see Susan E. Myers-Shirk, *Helping the Good Shepherd: Pastoral Counselors in a Psychotherapeutic*

Evidence was also introduced in the *Nicholson* case concerning treatment for spiritual distress in VA hospitals in Gainesville, Florida, and Detroit, Michigan, each of which offers substance abuse programs based in twelve-step spirituality. As the court explained, "The focus of the program is on recovery spirituality which does possess a religious component. However, defendants assert it 'has more to do with the mind-body-spirit connection of how the patient's own internal values and core beliefs affect self-esteem, relationships with others, and his/her Higher Power.'"[65] Like the Virginia program, the practical spirituality of the Gainesville program is founded in a combination of religion and behavioral psychology translated into a universal language that rids it of any constitutionally suspect connection with religion.

In Detroit, too, dependency was approached through an integration of spirituality "so treatment can be approached from a holistic perspective."[66] The court explained the Detroit chaplain's role: "A treatment plan begins with a diagnosis. From the diagnosis, the chaplain will identify the patient's short-term inpatient goals, goals which usually involve: (1) spiritual introspection, (2) relapse insight; and (3) learning the Twelve Steps of Alcoholics Anonymous. A veteran is provided ten days to complete the short-term goals and a treatment review is conducted after approximately nine days."[67]

FFRF lost its case against the VA. Since the decision in *Nicholson*, however, the Veterans Health Administration has instituted some reforms, standardizing and further universalizing its spiritual assessment program, carefully adhering to perceived constitutional norms and, likely, also, to advice of counsel. Spiritual assessment and spiritual care are now described in generously broad and apparently intentionally and deliberately secularizing language: "VHA spiritual and pastoral care is the total program of assessment and care, administered and overseen by chaplains, which identifies patients' religious and spiritual needs and desires, addresses spiritual injuries, and enhances patients' spiritual health, utilizing the full spectrum of

---

Culture: 1925–1975 (Baltimore: Johns Hopkins University Press, 2009). See also Sullivan, *Prison Religion*, for a discussion of the use of this literature in the prison context.

65. 469 F. Supp. 2d at 616.

66. Ibid.

67. Ibid. In spite of continuing efforts by Alcoholics Anonymous and others to distinguish the spirituality of twelve-step programs from religiously based recovery programs, courts have from time to time held that compulsory attendance at AA may be prohibited by the establishment clause. See Warner v. Orange County Dept. of Probation, 115 F.3d 1068 (2d Cir. 1997), *aff'd.* Warner v. Orange County Dept. of Probation, 173 F.3d 120 (2d Cir. 1999), *cert. denied sub nom* Orange County Dept. of Probation v. Warner, 528 U.S. 1003, 120 S. Ct. 495, 145 L. Ed. 2d 382 (1999); Kerr v. Farrey, 95 F.3d 472 (7th Cir. 1996).

interventions."[68] Terms are carefully and universally defined. The chaplain is explicitly understood to have no specific religious identity or purpose.

The glossary in the new VHA handbook now includes a definition of "spiritual," carefully attempting to correlate semantic references to a whole history of natural philosophy:

> e. *Spiritual.* "Spiritual" has to do with that which is related to the "Spirit of Life." Spirituality may be used in a general sense to refer to that which gives meaning and purpose in life, or the term may be used more specifically to refer to the practice of a philosophy, religion, or way of living. The word "spiritual" is derived from the old Latin word "spiritus" The English words "inspire," meaning to breathe in and "expire" meaning to breathe out, come from the same Latin root. The concept of breathing captures the meaning of the word "spiritual" in relation to that which is or is not "life giving." Therefore, spirituality may positively or negatively affect one's overall health and quality of life.

"Meaning and purpose," "philosophy, religion, or way of living," "life giving" support, and the tentative and qualified "*may* affect" signal the uneasy issue of causation in this area. "Pastoral" is also defined:

> f. *Pastoral.* "Pastoral" is an adjective derived from the image of the shepherd and is used to describe a relationship characterized by expressions of compassionate care, including spiritual counseling, guidance, consolation, empathetic listening, and encouragement. Describing care as pastoral may refer to the motivation or attitude of the caregiver. In VA, pastoral care refers to care provided by a chaplain, professionally-educated and endorsed by a particular faith tradition to provide such care.[69]

Again we see the generalizing language, here of care and compassion, combined with the incongruous image of the shepherd, an image that in the United States can only be legible to most Americans through the Bible. There are few other shepherds in the imagination and collective memory of most Americans.

Spiritual assessment is carefully explained in the new VA guidelines, emphasizing the control the VA will now exercise over these processes. "Only NCC-approved spiritual assessment instruments or procedures are to be used." Again the VA is clear that spirituality is about beliefs and practices:

68. VHA Handbook 1111.02 (2008).
69. Ibid.

"Spiritual assessment should, at a minimum, determine the patient's denomination, beliefs, and what spiritual practices are important to the patient." But the VA is somewhat less certain about the relevance of those beliefs and practices to their medical care: "This information would assist in determining the impact of spirituality, if any, on the care and services being provided and identifies if any further assessment is needed." What follows are a list of questions a spiritual assessment might include:

(a)   Who or what provides the patient with strength and hope?
(b)   Does the patient use prayer in the patient's life?
(c)   How does the patient express the patient's spirituality?
(d)   How would the patient describe the patient's philosophy of life?
(e)   What type of spiritual or religious support does the patient desire?
(f)   What is the name of the patient's clergy, minister, chaplain, pastor, priest, rabbi, imam, or traditional practitioner, if any?
(g)   What does suffering mean to the patient?
(h)   What does dying mean to the patient?
(i)   What are the patient's spiritual goals?
(j)   Is there a role of church or synagogue (religious worship) in the patient's life?
(k)   How does faith help the patient cope with illness?
(l)   How does the patient keep going day after day?
(m)   What helps the patient get through this health care experience?
(n)   How has illness affected the patient and the patient's family?[70]

There is a plaintive solicitude in the VA's effort to include every possible way of seeing the patient as other than an object of scientistic medical interest and intervention. Who are these people in these beds? What are their lives like? The very language of this handbook seems to struggle with the gap between what hospitals do and the lives of their patients, ranging from specific references to rabbis and imams to the despairing existential cry, "How does the patient keep going day after day?"

In January 2007, the Wisconsin federal district court granted the VA's motion for summary judgment in the *Nicholson* case, finding that no hearing on the facts was required because, as a matter of law, the VA's administration of the spiritual assessment and treatment programs did not violate the Constitution: "The undisputed facts of this action establish that none of the aspects of VA's chaplaincy program being challenged by plaintiffs

70. Ibid.

violate the Establishment Clause."[71] Rehearsing a range of interpretive theories of the establishment clause, the court found in the end that the VA's
new integrated chaplaincy program did not constitute an establishment of
religion because the VA's purpose, the delivery of health care, and the effect of the program (i.e., enhanced spiritual health) are secular goals with
secular effects.[72] Further, there was not an impermissible level of entanglement between church and state in the administration of the program, and,
perhaps most importantly, all religious activity was entirely voluntary on
the part of the patient.[73]

The court also noted that the monitoring of the VA desired by FFRF might
actually lead to more government involvement with religion:

> Interestingly, it is the relief requested by plaintiffs that would actually lead to
> excessive entanglement between government and religion. Plaintiffs request
> an order requiring defendants to establish rules, regulations, prohibitions,
> standards and oversight to ensure that future disbursements are not made
> and/or used to fund activities that include religion as a substantive integral
> component of the VA's medical treatment protocols. Such pervasive monitor-
> ing would excessively entangle the government with religion and would run
> afoul of the Establishment Clause.[74]

While courts routinely warn against the dangers of such monitoring, in a
sense it is just such monitoring that has been put into place by the VA, as
well as by the army, although, because of the collapse of organized religion
such monitoring has shifted to the individual believer, not to the activity of
churches. The court sees government entanglement with religious institutions as problematic but not entanglement with the spiritual life of persons.
Spiritual care monitors persons not religious institutions.

The VA chaplaincy was defended by the government and understood
by the court to be "spiritual not religious." Religion in the form of pastoral care had successfully disestablished itself, shedding its problematic
religious features, making itself universal, benign, and of public value. Distinguishing the school prayer cases as involving the coercion of children, a

71. 469 F. Supp. 2d at 623.
72. The secular purpose test is widely criticized. See Andrew Koppelman, "Secular Purpose,"
Virginia Law Review 88 (2002): 87–166. See also Justin Latterell, "Secular Purpose Tests, 1815–
2012: The Moral Logics of Separating Civil and Religious Law in U.S. Courts" (dissertation in
progress, Emory University).
73. 469 F. Supp. 2d at 623.
74. Ibid.

distinctively and historically recognized vulnerable population, the *Nichol-son* court found no establishment clause violation by the VA because there was no coercive government indoctrination. Each VA patient is legally free to direct her own spiritual care. Yet, carefully supported by association with the Joint Commission accreditation process and bolstered by scientific evidence, the court's opinion is at the same time a full-throated endorsement of the human as naturally spiritual and in need of spiritual care: "research studies have shown 'that when outpatients have access to quality spiritual and pastoral care significant improvement in quality of life, reduced inpatient admissions and costs savings result.'"[75] Religion is no longer seen as divisive. Here, as elsewhere, the American judiciary, in raising the bar for finding an establishment clause violation, leaves behind the anti-Catholic legacy of separationism. American religion continues successfully to both disestablish and reestablish itself.

It is not just VA hospitals. Decades of criticism of mainstream medical care, advocacy for holistic health and alternative therapies, cultural and contextual theories of health-care delivery, and changes in the understanding of mental illness have together transformed ideas about, and the delivery of, health care. The integration of liberal theologies and modern psychologies has a long history. Historian Pamela Klassen in her recent book on healing and liberal Protestantism speaks of the "holistic trinity"—mind, body, and spirit—that came to take the place of the Christian trinity for some reform-minded liberals over the course of the late nineteenth and early twentieth centuries.[76] Others have since taken up the cause, including many nonliberals.

While FFRF and others find use of the word "spirituality" to justify government intervention to be a form of stealth establishment of religion, or even as evidence of a disguised proselytization, it is, I suggest, a more complex semantic phenomenon, one that does not easily map on to the ways in which separationist academics—or lawyers and judges—use these words.[77] One might see the use of the term "spirituality" as a real effort to generalize helpfully about religion in a country of diverse traditions, one in which

75. Ibid. at 615.

76. Pamela Klassen, *Spirits of Protestantism: Medicine, Healing, and Liberal Christianity* (Berkeley: University of California Press, 2011).

77. Some also argue that the semantic extension of spirituality is a product of neoliberalism, a form of religious commodification that is politically quietest. See, e.g., Jeremy Carrette and Richard King, *Selling Spirituality: The Silent Takeover of Religion* (New York: Routledge, 2005). Candy Brown sees such projects as an effort deliberately to hoodwink conservative Christians and the courts into seeing alternative medical treatment as secular. Brown, *Healing Gods*.

most people believe both that humans are naturally spiritual and that the varieties of religions ought to be respected and put to good use. Separation makes no sense in this anthropology.

The actual practice in most US hospitals is a combination of what the Wisconsin court in the *Nicholson* case distinguishes as the sacramental and the clinical. Highly specialized hospital chaplains with extensive clinical training, representatives of religious communities on hospital staffs, and visiting religious leaders and counselors from the community, some with no training in pastoral care, all participate in delivering spiritual care to patients today in the United States. In many hospitals, chaplains are asked to do the hard work no one wants to do, like counseling patients and families on end-of-life decisions. As Wendy Cadge explains, the work done by hospital chaplaincies in the United States varies widely depending on the location, the kind of hospital, its patient population, and its history. Aspiration to the positive role of hospital chaplains often outstrips the reality.

Conclusion

Military and hospital chaplaincies each have their own particular demands when it comes to spiritual assessment and healing. Military chaplains serve in a volunteer army that has a new relationship to the nation in a time of continuing and unpopular wars while they also operate in the poisonous religious political landscape of the War on Terror. Hospital chaplains work in a market-driven environment of increasingly high-tech science and technology in the midst of a national crisis in health care.[78] Each experiences the intimate and immediate face of death and dying and the insistent presence of difficult moral decisions. But they share much with other forms of chaplaincy today. The diversity of their clientele, the ambiguity of lines of authority, the transience of the encounter, and, above all, the pressure to work in a radically undefined setting religiously speaking, and a rapidly deconstructing religious field—while justifying that work using the seductively scientistic language of spiritual assessment and care—characterizes the work that chaplains do in every place. Chaplains are at a particularly interesting and focused interface between church, state, society, and a rapidly changing religious terrain. Chapter 2 looks more closely at those who do this work.

78. For thoughtful reflection on the popularity of spirituality in hospital settings today, see Christopher Swift, *Hospital Chaplaincy in the Twenty-First Century: The Crisis of Spiritual Care on the NHS* (Farnham, England: Ashgate, 2009), 139–43. Swift argues that "chaplains are there to make the question of god inescapable." Ibid., 157.

One might understand the indispensability and effectiveness of chaplaincy in the United States today as a form of governmentality that is at once secular and religious, both a secular transformation of early modern concerns with individual salvation and an instance of the peculiarly naive American reimagining of the church as free. Indeed, government chaplaincy, as it has evolved in the United States, is almost a parody of Foucauldian pastoral power, employing, as it does, attenuated Christian forms of care and discipline for each citizen and attention to analyzing and assessing spiritual injuries. Its individuation, its submission of will, its hidden truth, and its sacrificial nature, are startlingly religious in their phenomenology. Spiritual assessment resembles the many such techniques that preceded it, but none so much as the individuating practices of spiritual direction and early modern confession of which Foucault speaks. Assessing spirituality and spiritual fitness scientizes them and fits them for hospitals and other social service providers. Assessing spirituality also fits religion for the positivism of American law. Yet, while assessing and healing the spirit in the United States does partake of the same obsessive individuation and care of which Foucault speaks, it also has a ragged anarchic quality, so inclusive and eclectic as also to generate a kind of liberation—what Foucault called "revolts of conduct" against pastoral power—and what Americans call disestablishment.

TWO

The Chaplain

While spiritual care in the broadest sense is provided by a range of professionals, quasi-professionals, and amateurs in the United States today, including more or less officially designated priests, ministers, rabbis, gurus, monastics, pastoral counselors, spiritual directors, and shamans, in the last few decades there is a sense in which the chaplain is emerging as an indispensable person for the administration of spiritual care. She is the religious professional best suited to public ministry in the twenty-first century—the one best able to broker between the institutions of the secular, religious hierarchies and the presumed universal spiritual nature of the individual. Beholden primarily neither to a local congregation nor to a religious canon and hierarchy in the chain-of-command model of ministry, chaplains meet both a more diverse and often constantly changing clientele and are freer from strictures to orthodoxy in doctrine and practice than other religious specialists. They are committed to the mission of and usually paid by the secular institutions in which they work, whether that be a school, prison, branch of the armed services, business, hospital, park service, or other special purpose facility. Licensed to preach by once-well-defined religious hierarchies but finding their calling as clinicians for the religiosity of human beings in general, chaplains offer themselves as spiritual ministers without portfolio while still being bound by webs of authority, sacred and secular, past and present, that are not always fully acknowledged.

In other words, the work of the chaplain reifies an ongoing indeterminacy about where to locate religious work in the late modern period. The chaplain fills the gap between the individual conscience or religious sensibility and the no-longer-stable possibility of religious community. The rise of the secular professions and the transfer of much work that was formerly done by the churches to other institutions, among other social shifts, has led to chaplains going where people are—aspiring to deliver spiritual care wherever it is needed—and seeking to reinvent themselves as a profession distinct from traditional clergy. The decrease in prestige and remuneration for pastoral clergy and the decline in the size of congregations have also made secular employment more attractive.[1] Freed from the need to create entrepreneurially her own audience, a chaplain may draw a regular salary and hold other benefits while ministering to patients, soldiers, prisoners, disaster victims, workers, and students, on the one hand, and sanctifying the mission of doctors, generals, prison guards, business owners, and university administrations, on the other. All chaplains are also captured to some degree by the structures and rationalities of secularization, however that process is understood.[2]

The proliferation and ubiquity of chaplains today, in spite of all of the challenges they face in doing their work, suggests that even if you formally disaggregate religion and state, thereby formally privatizing religion, and even if most of life looks awfully secular, the state and its proxies have leftover business that needs to be done; ministering to the irreducibly religious part of being human is still arguably a part of a state's job and necessary for its stability. It cannot rely on voluntary local congregations to do that work. For their part, in a profession characterized by expert training and knowledge, licensing, associations that police their members, and a code of ethics, chaplains are working hard to establish themselves as offering just this kind of public good, finding ways to insert themselves into the late modern division of labor.[3] They are arguing that they, and they alone, are professionally competent to offer constitutionally compliant spiritual care in a multifaith secular setting.

Yet there is a lingering sense among some that the strenuous effort at professionalization and qualification for secular employment has robbed this ministry of its capacity to heal. Historically a consecrated officeholder in the high-liturgical traditions, but today mostly purveying a highly psychologized low-church piety, the chaplain may in time be on his way to

1. E. Brooks Holifield, *God's Ambassadors: A History of the Christian Clergy in America* (Grand Rapids, MI: Eerdmans, 2007), and Chaves, *Contemporary Trends*.

2. Paul J. DiMaggio and Walter W. Powell, "The Iron Cage Revisited: Institutional Isomorphism and Collective Rationality in Organizational Fields," *American Sociological Review* 48 (1983): 147–60.

3. Andrew Abbott, *The System of Professions: An Essay on the Division of Expert Labor* (Chicago: University of Chicago Press, 1988); Raymond DeVries, Nancy Berlinger, and Wendy Cadge, "Lost in Translation: The Chaplain's Role in Health Care," *Hastings Report*, November–December 2008.

becoming simply another member of the workforce, an employee and an aspiring independent professional, just at the time when the professions are perceived to be in decline and the religion that is his stock in trade is losing its coherence.[4]

Even if it is more the case today, however, the authority of chaplains has always been unstable, even deliberately so; because of their assignments away from their religious homes and their aspiration to minister to all comers, as well as the ambiguous position they hold in their workplaces, they have always been marginal to both the secular institutions they temporarily inhabit and to their religious organizations.[5] Chaplains take pastoral responsibility for those within the purview of the secular state and its private partners on behalf of unnamed gods while representing and negotiating on behalf of the state to their charges and to external constituents, at times even claiming the role of ombudsman, moral conscience or whistle-blower.

This chapter will outline the history of the legal and social doubleness or in-betweenness of chaplains, their presence in various US institutions, and their efforts to constitute themselves as professionals. The persistent ambiguity of the job is an old story. Histories of chaplaincy and world literature are replete with stories of kings, generals, and other captains of our fate demanding religious blessings on their military and other adventures from a chaplain who only sometimes attempted to maintain his independence and a moral stance on war and other social issues, not to mention his religious obligations. But the radically multifaith and egalitarian setting is new, theologically, sociologically, and legally.

History of the Chaplain

The chaplain is, of course, only one of many types of religious specialization. The governing of religious communities and the performing of religious work has taken a variety of forms and has intersected with government in manifold ways throughout human history. The successive emergence of, or success of, one form over another in the last half millennium or so can be

---

4. Terence Halliday, "Knowledge Mandates: Collective Influence by Scientific, Normative and Syncretic Professions," *British Journal of Sociology* 36, no. 3 (1985): 477–95.

5. This ambiguity attracts a certain personality. In a personal conversation, Kevin Boyd, CPE Supervisor, Chaplaincy Services and Pastoral Education, University of Virginia Health System, offered that chaplains are often misfits within their own communities, something he took to be a positive. Christopher Swift also talks about the kinds of people attracted to chaplaincy. Swift, *Hospital Chaplaincy*, 173. See also Hansen, *Military Chaplains and Religious Diversity*, 151.

seen to illustrate an ongoing set of negotiations among the types expressly authorized in a particular tradition, responses to the growth and development of the modern state as the indispensable political form, the shifting differentiation of society into different spheres, the development of market capitalism, migrations of religious forms across the globe, and the changing role of religion in mediating between gods, states, and people.

Before coming to the chaplain herself, a brief review of religious specialization and leadership in the United States more generally will set the chaplain in a larger context. Various efforts have been made by scholars to organize and categorize the types of religious specialization: founder, prophet, saint, scholar, ascetic, conjurer, judge, ecstatic. The United States has seen all of these figures and more. E. Brooks Holifield, historian of the clergy in the United States, uses Max Weber's three ideal types of authority, the charisma of office, the charisma of personality, and rational authority, to structure his history of Protestant clergy in the United States. But he also borrows from theologian Avery Dulles's various models for the Roman Catholic priesthood to consider the minister's sacramental powers and theology of servanthood.[6] Stepping back from the limiting focus on ideal types and specific functions, Bruce Lincoln has sought to understand how religious authority works by considering the circumstances under which any person in any social situation can speak or act with consequence.[7] Without an established church to structure formally its bureaucratic religious authority, the United States has seen a proliferation of possibilities, charismatic and routinized, in this as in other arenas.

American religious specialists have exercised traditional authority, charismatic authority, and rational authority; they have performed the role of founder, prophet, priest, advocate for the poor and the oppressed, champion of justice, and evangelist. They have celebrated, consecrated, preached, confessed, warned, advised; they have baptized, married, and buried countless Americans. Given the importance of the word to the dominantly protestant form of American public religion, however, they have mainly preached, seeking to speak the discourses of power, religious and political. But they have done all of this work in the shadow of the formal legal disestablishment of religion and conscious of the competition among religious options produced by that disestablishment. They have also invented their roles in

6. Holifield, *God's Ambassadors*, 337.
7. Bruce Lincoln, *Authority: Construction and Corrosion* (Chicago: University of Chicago Press, 1994).

a democratic and populist America alongside the invention of the other professions.

In the United States, congregation-based leadership is the most familiar form of religious specialization, although it is by no means the only form that religious leadership takes. A unified history, even of only Christian clergy in the United States, is a complex story moving from the colonial mix of French and Spanish Catholic missions, New England Puritans, Dutch ministers, and Church of England priests, through revival and immigration, to the multiple self-proclaimed crises of the churches in the twentieth century.[8] It is a story of continued movements of fragmentation and reform as well as periodic attempts at unification of purpose.[9] As American law found its voice, it, too, tracked these changes. Mark de Wolfe Howe, constitutional historian, wrote that US law favored the congregational form in the antebellum period, the national churches after the civil war, and finally came to address the transnational churches in the twentieth.[10] Federalism complicated the picture as different states developed different laws governing the incorporation of religious polities and the regulation of their various ministries.[11] Legally and historically speaking, courts have interacted with the multiple ecclesiologies of American Christians in many ways, perhaps most frequently in the context of church property disputes, but the dominant form of religious authority, whether Christian or not, has continued to be that of congregational leadership.

Founded in the free-church ecclesiology of the Anabaptist tradition, congregational leadership envisions a religious leader or pastor "called," or chosen, by an individual congregation, a role that has come to be understood as private, notwithstanding its many obvious public effects, and as distinctively separate from political leadership. The congregational leader may be trained by and represent a larger religious community and its orthodoxy to the congregation, but she also represents the congregation to its various publics, while ministering to the needs of the local members. The tension among the demands of these various constituencies is real but is, for the most part, centered in and rooted in the needs of the local living occupants

8. See Holifield, *God's Ambassadors*.

9. Ibid., 69

10. Mark deWolfe Howe, *The Garden and the Wilderness: Religion and Government in American Constitutional History*. (Chicago: University of Chicago Press, 1965).

11. For a comprehensive effort to describe US law pertaining to religious organizations, see James Seritella et al., eds., *Religious Organizations in the United States: A Study of Identity, Liberty, and the Law* (Durham, NC: Carolina Academic Press, 2004).

of the pews. The fastest growing form of church in the United States today is the independent congregation.[12]

Non-Christian religious groups have, to be sure, brought their own forms of religious specialization to the United States, but most have largely adapted to fit the spaces created by early settlement between churches and the states. Enduring forms of Native religious leadership fit uneasily within these types. Law scrambles to keep up with the diversity both of religious organization and of personnel.[13]

The congregation in the US model is understood, then, to be a group of like-minded individuals who associate together for religious worship, fellowship, and mutual aid, a group who calls, hires—and fires—a leader for themselves. A particular congregation may or may not be organization-ally related to other congregations and may or may not require candidates to have formal academic training.[14] Many American religious communities are organized this way, including many that are not Christian. This form of religious organization is grounded in a separatist religio-political ideol-ogy that understands religious people to be a group gathered together apart from, and for a separate purpose from, even perhaps in opposition to, the state and the common life of the larger political community, even while it may be understood to serve that larger public in some ways. Congregational leaders are not licensed by government in the United States. Although a kind of state recognition of such a role may be inferred from various tax privileges given to ministers, including, for example, a tax exemption for "parsonages," anyone is free to associate together for a religious purpose and to exercise religious leadership in the United States.

The free-church model is primarily Protestant in origins. With respect to providing regular pastoral care to laypersons, the Roman Catholic Church has a geographically based leadership founded in the theory of the apostolic

12. Chaves, *Contemporary Trends.*

13. One place where one can trace these changes is with respect to the expanding availabil-ity in evidence law of the priest-penitent privilege, allowing either or both religious counselor and penitent to refuse to testify in court, and to prevent others from testifying, concerning their private conversation. Such a privilege was successfully invoked by O. J. Simpson in his trial for murder to block revelation in court of a conversation with his friend and former teammate, Rosie Grier. Grier, who had become a pastor after retiring from football, visited the jail where Simpson was being held during trial. Their conversation was recorded by a guard.

14. While many American religious congregations have formal organizational ties through denominational bodies or through episcopacies, parachurch organizations such as the American Bible Society have throughout US history also brought together congregants and congregations in shared projects across denominational boundaries, such as in the production and distribu-tion of Bibles and Sunday school materials, political causes such as the abolition of slavery and prohibition, and various missionary activities, among many others.

succession of bishops, a scheme that provides hierarchically led religious leadership to all Catholic populations of the world under the authority of the pope, the bishop of Rome. Bishops rule over geographic areas and are responsible for supervising the religious life of Catholics within that territory, including the assigning of priests to parishes to celebrate the sacraments and care for the spiritual needs of the faithful. Hence the iconic account of mid-twentieth-century US Catholicism in which urban Catholics located themselves in conversation by referring to their parishes, not to the city neighborhoods. This is the reigning Catholic model. Nevertheless, there have been significant efforts in the United States since the early republic, and elsewhere at various times in church history, to institute local lay leadership and control of Catholic parishes, and an increasing number of Catholics today choose their own parish, refusing to be confined by Vatican geography.[15]

Outside of Protestant Christianity, religious specialists have served purposes quite distinct from the preaching and teaching role envisioned for most Protestant pastors. Rabbis and imams provide advice on how religious law is to be interpreted; priests supply sacraments; Buddhist monks acquire merit and provide occasions for lay good works; shamans travel through the spirit realm. These religious leaders and specialists may be more or less directly involved on a regular basis with the lives of ordinary members of the community at various points in their professional lives.[16] While religious leadership has gradually been formally separated from government in most countries beginning in the early modern period, the evolving role of the clergy in the new nation-states since that time has arguably been profoundly tied to the need for the imposition of social discipline. In the United States and elsewhere, the social task of congregational clergy today, as it has been throughout the early modern period, mostly eagerly embraced by that clergy, could be described as serving the modern state by producing good workers and good citizens through moral education, with occasional forays into advocacy for social justice and foreign missionizing.[17]

15. For accounts of the effect of American democracy on American Catholicism, see Jay Dolan, *In Search of an American Catholicism: A History of Religion and Culture in Tension* (Oxford: Oxford University Press, 2003), and John McGreevy, *Catholicism and American Freedom: A History* (New York: Norton, 2004).

16. See Sophie Gilliat-Ray, *Religion in Higher Education: The Politics of the Multi-faith Campus* (Burlington, VT: Ashgate, 2000) for a discussion of the "approximation" of roles that is occurring as non-Christian chaplains, particularly imams, are adapting to the British context and taking on responsibilities for individual pastoral care on a Protestant model in a variety of British institutions.

17. Holifield, *God's Ambassadors*.

Chaplains are different. Chaplains have always had a role distinct from that of congregational clergy. Chaplains work in and directly for the institutions of the state and other secular bodies. The formal role of the military chaplain in the Latin church is usually traced to the rules prescribed by the Frankish church for participation of bishops and priests in war.[18] The first chaplains in the Western church named as such, the *cappellani*, were those who had charge of the sacred relic of the cloak of Martin of Tours, fourth-century soldier-saint and patron saint of soldiers in war ever since. Martin of Tours is said to have divided his cloak with a poor person and later had a vision of Christ wearing his half cloak.

With the gradual conversion of the Roman Empire and the shift from penance as a once-in-a-lifetime rite to its repeatability as a technology of ongoing moral discipline, the need for priests in the military became acute. While there had always been Christian soldiers in the Roman armies, in the mid-eighth century, bishops began to issue specific instructions for the religious care of soldiers and to define the role of the military chaplain. Among other duties, including celebrating Mass, hearing confessions, preaching, and praying for victory, it was the chaplain's duty to carry relics into war as totems, a role that was given particular prominence in the Crusades of the twelfth century.

The first appearance of chaplains then in the Western churches is usually cited as occurring in the military, but the continuing bureaucratic institutionalization of the Roman Church in the medieval period, the reception of Roman law into both church and state, and struggles between the church and the emerging states with the prolonged investiture controversy led to the development of many new specialized roles for clergy inside and outside the church. The chaplain became the medieval Latin denomination of the priest who said the divine office (the prescribed liturgy) in a chapel, as opposed to a church, often as an advisor attached to an aristocratic household. Other medieval institutions also had chapels and chaplains. Christopher Swift traces the history of the hospital chaplaincy in England to the foundation of medieval hospitals in the eleventh century and then to their refounding in the seventeenth century.[19] Under canon law today, Roman

18. David S. Bachrach, "The Medieval Military Chaplain and His Duties," in *The Sword of the Lord: Military Chaplains from the First to the Twenty-First Century*, ed. Doris L. Bergen (Notre Dame, IN: University of Notre Dame Press, 2004).

19. Swift, *Hospital Chaplaincy*; see also William Gibson, *A Social History of the Domestic Chaplain: 1530–1840* (London: Leicester University Press, 1997).

Catholic and Anglican, a chaplain may be attached to any one of a number of secular institutions.[20]

The Reformation changed the understanding and institutions of religious specialization in the Christian churches. Martin Luther criticized the exceptional role of the priesthood and of vowed monastic life, arguing that biblical authority warranted instead a belief in the priesthood of all believers. Lutheran and Calvinist Protestant churches did not eliminate clerical roles, but the monastic virtues were rejected in favor of a married clergy who lived in the world. Other Protestants would, however, radically further de-emphasize the authority and consecrated work of the clergy, sometimes eliminating the role altogether, as with Quakers, for example. But even with the decline of the medieval church-state accommodations and their successors in the nation-states of Europe, chaplains continued to be necessary. In all European countries and beyond, chaplains are found in many secular institutions and represent many religious communities inside and outside of the Christian churches.

With the expansion of the British Empire, chaplains did not serve solely in the armed forces, prisons, hospitals, royal households, and colonial administrations, but also in the commercial companies that extended imperial power. The East India Company and other chartered commercial ventures hired their own chaplains, as has been mentioned.[21] At its height in the seventeenth and eighteenth centuries, the company generated half of the world's trade and employed a third of the British workforce. It also employed hundreds of chaplains all over the world. Chaplains were stationed on its ships and in its garrisons and factories, chaplains who worked to civilize and Christianize both the company's employees and those they

20. Catholic chaplaincies may also be established by laypersons as a form of charity or simply as a way to ensure the performance of masses in that family's memory. There is a curious 1929 US Supreme Court case about a chaplaincy, certiorari to the Supreme Court of the Philippines, then an American possession: Gonzales v. Roman Catholic Archbishop of Manila, 280 U.S. 1 (1929). *Gonzales* holds that the petitioner, heir to a collative chaplaincy bestowed on his family a century earlier, has no right to occupy the position over the objection by the church that he lacks the qualifications. For a brief history of the chaplaincy in the Roman Church and an explanation of the nature of a collative chaplaincy, see William H. Fanning, "Chaplain," in *Catholic Encyclopedia,* ed. Robert C. Broderick (New York: Thomas Nelson, 1990).

21. See Daniel O'Connor, *The Chaplains of the East India Company, 1601–1858.* A foreword by Gordon Brown, former prime minister of Great Britain, explains his interest in the topic by reference to his concern with ethics in economic life, implying that the role of chaplains in business enterprises is to make them ethical.

encountered. As the chronicler of the East India chaplains explains about the company records, "the documents are shot through with a sense of divine presence, providence, judgement, in every aspect of the Company's operations."[22] Applicants for the position of chaplain were required to preach a sermon to the company's directors. Their duties included regular reading of the divine word and preaching as well as teaching "the principle means which draweth all Christians to conformity and submission to such as are set over them."[23] Their pay included shares in the company.

What would now be called workplace chaplains are becoming more common today as well. As *New York Times* religion reporter Mark Oppenheimer reports, "Workplace chaplains . . . can be found at more than 1,000 companies in the U.S. and Canada. These chaplains are a rising regiment of corporate America's human-resources army, as employers have found that a pastoral touch is often more appealing to workers than an impersonal hotline of the sort included in many benefits packages."[24] Reporting on a study by David Miller and Faith Ngunjiri of Princeton University's Faith & Work Initiative, Oppenheimer interviewed chaplains at a range of companies, large and small, from a local auto dealer to Walmart, describing how companies see chaplains as ministering holistically to people on the job while reporting to the bosses about what is making workers dissatisfied: "chaplains are supposed to help companies avoid conflict and keep everyone happy . . . The chaplains help productivity."[25]

Chaplains today are the recognizable successors to the medieval and early modern versions in that they minister to the inhabitants of secular institutions to which they are also responsible, but they and their clients are becoming a more varied group. Chaplains in the United States and elsewhere may identify with any historic religious community or with none. There are chaplains associated with many different American religious communities, including Buddhism, Islam, Judaism, and others. The US Army hired its first world religions chaplain with great fanfare in 2010 and its first Hindu chaplain in 2011.[26] Harvard hired its first humanist chaplain in the

22. Ibid., 20.
23. Ibid.
24. Mark Oppenheimer, "The Rise of the Corporate Chaplain."
25. Their employment is also understood to reduce liability. Lake Lambert III, *Spirituality, Inc.: Religion in the American Workplace* (New York: New York University Press, 2009), 150.
26. See Timothy K. Bedsole Sr., "The World Religions Chaplain: A Practitioner's Perspective," *Review of Faith & International Affairs* 7, no. 4 (2009): 63–69.

1980s.[27] Stanford hired an avowedly atheist chaplain in 2012.[28] Yet all of these non-Christian chaplains are often explicitly understood according to a Christian template.

Kim Hansen, writing about the military chaplaincy in the United States, explains why Muslims are more tolerated than Wiccans in the navy. He quotes one of his ethnographic chaplain-informants, implying that imams are simply more recognizable to their Christian counterparts than wiccans: "My Muslim lay reader . . . He sounds like one of the Christians we had—'I'm just a Bible-believing Christian.' Well, he's a Koran-believing Muslim."[29] As Hansen explains, "The chaplains' ability to make such direct comparisons between Muslims and members of their own faith is yet another advantage Muslims have over Wiccans." In other words, "the Muslims have a book. They acknowledge Jesus as a prophet. They are patriarchal."[30] Wiccans don't have a book, acknowledge Jesus, or organize themselves in a patriarchal manner.

While chaplains find their origins in the complex and diverse religious specializations that characterized the religious bureaucracy of the medieval church, their persistence, even resurgence today, attests to their continuing appeal as an interface between the impersonal secular institutions of the contemporary world and a human imagined as religious or spiritual. Their particular appeal today in the United States might also be attributed to the dislocations at a time of high mobility and economic downturn, increasing diversity, globalization, and the politics of religious freedom. Chaplains serve the times and places in which participation in common local public worship is undesirable, impracticable, or even impossible. In addition to the special purpose of the aristocratic household and the hospital, chaplains have since medieval times also included clergy, and, increasingly today, specially trained laypersons, assigned to minister to Christians, and others, who are away from their regular congregation for any of a range of reasons,

27. Harvard's humanist chaplain describes himself as the chaplain for "humanist, atheist, agnostic, and the non-religious at Harvard." See Greg M. Epstein, "Military Needs Chaplains for Humanists, Atheists," *Washington Post*, July 25, 2008, http://newsweek.washingtonpost.com /onfaith/panelists/greg_m_epstein/2008/07/us_military_needs_chaplains_fo.html (accessed January 29, 2013). Other schools, including Rutgers and Columbia, have humanist chaplains as well.

28. Nanette Asimov, "Stanford Gets a Chaplain for Atheists," *San Francisco Chronicle*, December 22, 2012, www.sfgate.com/news/article/Stanford-gets-a-chaplain-for-atheists-4139991 .php (accessed January 29, 2013).

29. Hansen, *Military Chaplains and Religious Diversity*, 113.

30. Ibid.

in the military, in prisons, in legislatures, on the sea, in schools, on sports teams, on oil rigs, and in many other vocationally defined settings.

In countries with centralized church or other religious administrations that coordinate with the government, such as in England, for example, government-supported seminaries and churches continue to provide and train chaplains for such institutional settings—and those chaplains are responsible for administering religious services both for members of the national church and for nonmembers.[31] In the United States, because there is no licensed religious authority or established church whose function it is to train and provide chaplains for government bodies, chaplains have an eclectic history, more attested to in the military and prison context, but in the United States, too, chaplains have played a role in a range of social service institutions and today are increasingly hired by governmental and quasi-governmental authorities to serve various populations that are understood to be in temporary need of pastoral care away from their home communities. Millions of Americans now receive their primary pastoral care from such chaplains. And those chaplains come from a wide array of religious backgrounds. Their variety and quasi-official status make them more difficult to study because of the decentralization of authority.

Different Institutions, Different Histories, Same Ministry

For a variety of reasons over the course of the twentieth century, but particularly since the 1960s, the task of the chaplain in the United States has become increasingly homogenized, first across the Protestant churches, and then more recently across all religious communities, as well as across the secular settings in which they do their work. After several centuries in which American Christians were profoundly split over the need for an educated clergy, and while many, perhaps most, congregational leaders in the United States still have no formal theological education, education for the ministry in the United States has become more common, more professionalized, and more standardized across the Christian denominations and beyond. Increased demand for credentials has led to a proliferation of specialized degrees and licensing of religious professionals across a very wide range from yoga teachers to military chaplains. Many of these degrees and certi-

31. See, e.g., for a description of the ways the Church of England accommodates the religious needs of Muslim prisoners in Her Majesty's prisons, James Beckford and Sophie Gilliat-Ray, *Religion in Prison: Equal Rites in a Multi Faith Society* (Cambridge: Cambridge University Press, 1998), and Sophie Gilliat-Ray, "Being There: Shadowing a British Muslim Hospital Chaplain," *Qualitative Research* 11, no. 5 (2011): 413–32.

fications are available through distance learning arrangements. While congregational work continues to be the expressed preferred vocational goal of most seminarians and divinity school students, an increasing number look to exercise their functions in more specialized and secure institutional settings, including government, where they minister to a ready-made clientele. They call what they do "a ministry of presence."

The credentialing of chaplains and the nature of their ministry will be discussed in chapters 3 and 5. Here, I will briefly describe the particular chaplaincies of the major institutions in which they function: the hospital, the prison, and the military.[32] While now thought of as the secular institutions of the modern state, each of these institutions has a profoundly religious past. The history of the chaplain is coincident with the long history of secularization. There is a sense in which all chaplains in all settings share the experience of serving at a juncture of rapidly changing religious ways of life distinct from what most congregational pastors encounter. But each institutional situation also presents its own opportunities and challenges for the chaplain.

Military Chaplains

Military chaplaincy has a long history, a history told by different people in different ways. The specific role of the medieval military chaplain is attached to a particular theological and ecclesiological history within the medieval church—but the function of the holy man in war has a much longer history. Priests and oracles have surely always accompanied military commanders, both to ensure success and to bless the endeavor. Perhaps also to offer counsel. As conventionally told by many in the US military, however, the story of the American military chaplaincy reflects a curiously vernacular appropriation and editing of church history. Ministry to military personnel, according to these accounts, begins with the Old Testament, then skips to a brief mention of Martin of Tours, and then to George Washington and the American Revolution.[33] Perhaps rejecting medieval church practices as

32. On university chaplains, Ian Oliver, "In Coffin's Pulpit: Re-envisioning Protestant Religious Culture, in *College & University Chaplaincy in the 21st Century*, ed. Lucy Forster-Smith (Woodstock, VT: Skylight Paths Publishing, 2013).

33. See, e.g., Michael T. Jones, "The Air Force Chaplain: Clergy or Officer?" (research report submitted to the faculty in fulfillment of the curriculum requirement, USAF Air War College, 1996); Robert Nay, "The Operational, Social, and Religious Influences upon the *Army Chaplain Field Manual*, 1926–1952" (master of military art and science thesis, US Army Command and General Staff College, 2008).

papist innovations, or perhaps less interested in history and more interested in authorizing associations recognizable to Americans, many American Protestants trace the origins of the military chaplain to the priests who served the kings in Old Testament wars, omitting the medieval developments and pushing the legitimating origins of the chaplaincy first to ancient Israel and then forward to the Revolutionary War.

Two recent theses on chaplaincies written in the military academies illustrate this pattern, although with different Old Testament precedents. Michael Jones of the Air War College emphasizes the dual role of the American chaplain: "Are chaplains first clergy or officers? The answer can be given now and it is chaplains are both clergy and officers first." He begins with Moses:

Some 3500 years ago, Moses wrote the following in Deuteronomy 20:1–4:

"When you go to war against your enemies and see horses and chariots and an army greater than yours, do not be afraid of them, because the Lord your God, who brought you up out of Egypt, will be with you. When you are about to go into battle, *the priest shall come forward and address the army. He shall say: 'Hear, O Israel, today you are going into battle against your enemies. Do not be faint-hearted or afraid; do not be terrified or give way to panic before them. For the Lord your God is the one who goes with you to fight for you against your enemies to give you victory.'*"

Jones reads this passage as follows: "Moses recognized the importance of the impact of spiritual leaders on the morale of the armies." Moses says that it is the chaplain's job to say that God will be with you and not with your enemies.

Robert Nay of the General Staff College begins his thesis on army chaplain manuals with verses from 2 Samuel and 2 Kings. From Samuel: "When they came to the threshing floor of Nacon, Uzzah reached out and took hold of the ark of God, because the oxen stumbled. The LORD's anger burned against Uzzah because of his irreverent act; therefore God struck him down and he died there beside the ark of God."[34] From Kings: "Great is the LORD's anger that burns against us because our fathers have not obeyed the words of this book; they have not acted in accordance with all that is written there concerning us."[35] A much harsher lesson, God here punishes

---

34. 2 Samuel 6:6–7 (New International Version).
35. 2 Kings 22:8, 22:10–13 (New International Version).

the priests for irreverence. Nay goes on to explain how these verses author-ize the need for disciplining military chaplains today:

> In the Old Testament God gave the Israelites written instructions on how the Israelites were to worship him and how the priests should conduct them-selves. Any violation of this received punishment from God. The reason for this punishment was not to amuse God but to instill the seriousness of the responsibility of entrusting God's people to the priest.

Nay exhorts chaplains to remember that "the United States Army chaplains are God's priests, prophets and servants here on earth. God and the United States entrust chaplains to take care of the spiritual needs of soldiers as-signed to their units."[36] For Nay, chaplaincy is about the spiritual needs of the soldiers, not about prevailing over their enemies. But both Jones and Nay find their authority in the Old Testament. Both engage in a familiar American biblical style of picking bible verses suitable to the need. We see here both the priestly and the pastoral role of the chaplain.

Chaplains have been present in the US military since the Revolution-ary War, serving much the same roles that the chaplains of earlier armies performed, supporting the mission and morale of the troops, delivering pastoral care to soldiers and their families, and leading worship services, although their full professionalization and formal integration into the military chain of command does not come until the twentieth century.[37] Today there are approximately three thousand active-duty and two thou-sand reserve chaplains in the US armed forces.[38] US military chaplains were also involved in evangelizing the west: "With America's westward expan-sion, Army chaplains manning territorial posts 'were often called upon to

36. Nay, "The Operational, Social, and Religious Influences upon the *Army Chaplain Field Manual, 1926–1952*," 1–2.

37. For a summary history of chaplains in the US military, see Hansen, *Military Chaplains and Religious Diversity*, 14–16, and Israel Drazin and Cecil B. Curry, *For God and Country: The History of a Constitutional Challenge to the Army Chaplaincy* (Hoboken, NJ: KTAV Publishing House, 1995), 1–26. See also Ronit Y. Stahl, "God, War, and Politics: The American Military Chaplaincy and the Making of Modern American Religion" (PhD diss., University of Michigan, 2014). The Civil War was an important moment of consolidation for US Army chaplaincy, but the chap-laincy declined after the Civil War and was not restored to its former glory until World War I. Richard Budd, *Serving Two Masters: The Development of American Military Chaplaincy, 1860–1920* (Lincoln: University of Nebraska Press, 2002). For a history of the post–Vietnam War chap-laincy, see John W. Brinsfield Jr., *Encouraging Faith, Supporting Soldiers: The United States Army Chaplaincy 1975–1995*, pts. 1 and 2 (Washington, DC: Office of the Chief of Chaplains, Depart-ment of the Army, 1997)

38. Hansen, *Military Chaplains and Religious Diversity*, 16.

perform duties as librarian, post gardener, commissary and bakery manager, post treasurer, and defense counsel.' They supervised and taught at the post schools for children. Some chaplains ministered to Native Americans, 'baptized them and even lobbied in Washington for them.'"[39] Military chaplains have been involved in humanitarian work in all of America's wars.

The army chaplaincy has only gradually diversified religiously. President Lincoln commissioned the first Jewish chaplain in 1862. Smaller Christian communities, such as the Orthodox, were only gradually institutionalized in the military. The first Muslim chaplains were appointed to the army in 1993.[40] A Buddhist endorsing organization was registered in 1987 after a long struggle. Buddhist Military Sangha, an online resource for Buddhists in the military, explains the efforts to establish a Buddhist chaplaincy during World War II, when many Japanese Americans joined the US Army: "The Buddhist Missions of North America (the precursor of the Buddhist Churches of America) petitioned the then-War Department to commission a Buddhist chaplain, but this request was denied, as Buddhism was not recognized as a legitimate religion, and was confused with State Shinto, the religion of wartime Japan." The policy changed in the late 1980s: "Finally, in 1987, through lobbying by WWII and Korean War Buddhist Veterans, and Rev. Haruo Yamaoka, then the Abbot (*Socho*) of the Buddhist Churches of America, the BCA was granted endorser status."[41] The article goes on to delineate the now conventional credentials necessary for chaplaincy service, the MDiv degree, CPE credits, and ecclesiastical endorsement, and to describe how would-be Buddhist chaplains can acquire such credentials.

From the beginning, the presence and role of chaplains in the US military has not been entirely uncontroversial, either constitutionally or theologically speaking, notwithstanding the example of Moses and the Israelites. James Madison, for example, opposed the establishment of military (and legislative) chaplaincies on theological and constitutional grounds, and constitutional objections have been raised periodically ever since.[42] Min-

---

39. Paul McLaughlin, "The Chaplain's Evolving Role in Peace and Humanitarian Relief Operations," *Peaceworks* 46 (Washington, DC: US Institute of Peace, September 2002): 13.

40. Emilie Kraft Bindon, "Entangled Choices: Selecting Chaplains for the United States Armed Forces," *Alabama Law Review* 56 (2004): 249.

41. Jeanette Yuinen Shin, blog post on Buddhist Military Sangha, an online resource for Buddhists in the military, July 31, 2007, http://buddhistmilitarysangha.blogspot.com/2007/07/buddhist-chaplaincy-in-us-armed-forces.html (accessed January 30, 2013). Buddhist Churches of America is an association of Japanese Buddhist temples that was founded at the beginning of the twentieth century. The designation "church" was a deliberate effort at making themselves legible to Americans.

42. James Madison wrote about military chaplains in 1817: "Look thro' the armies & navies

isters from some pacifist denominations have refused to serve at all, and some chaplains have resisted particular assignments, as, for example, being assigned recreation duties. Some have refused to show movies to their troops, a task often given to chaplains in the twentieth century, or have refused to implement certain social policies such as "don't ask, don't tell," or, in turn, the repeal of that policy. There are heroic accounts of the courage and sacrifice of chaplains in all of America's wars, the most famous being the "four chaplains" of WWII,[43] but broader theological and social issues have played out in the history of the military chaplaincies, including the rise and fall of Sabbath regulations, temperance restrictions, racial discrimination, and changing sexual mores.

Among other ways in which the US military recognizes the peculiar role of the chaplain is through the careful defining of their officer status. Chaplains in the US armed services today are uniformed noncombatant commissioned officers. They have rank but are without command and have usually been unarmed. Today, US chaplains are accompanied by a chaplain's assistant who provides armed protection. (The Geneva convention specifies that chaplains are noncombatants, but different countries have different ways of defining the chaplain's role within the military establishment.[44] For example, chaplains in the Royal Navy of the United Kingdom assume the

---

of the world, and say whether in the appointment of their ministers of religion, the spiritual interest of the flocks or the temporal interest of the Shepherds, be most in view: whether here, as elsewhere the political care of religion is not a nominal more than a real aid. If the spirit of armies be devout, the spirit out of the armies will never be less so; and a failure of religious instruction & exhortation from a voluntary source within or without, will rarely happen: and if such be not the spirit of armies, the official services of their Teachers are not likely to produce it. It is more likely to flow from the labours of a spontaneous zeal. The armies of the Puritans had their appointed Chaplains; but without these there would have been no lack of public devotion in that devout age. The case of navies with insulated crews may be less within the scope of these reflections. But it is not entirely so. The chance of a devout officer, might be of as much worth to religion, as the service of an ordinary chaplain." Madison also opposed legislative chaplains, saying, "If Religion consist in voluntary acts of individuals, singly, or voluntarily associated, and it be proper that public functionaries, as well as their Constituents shd discharge their religious duties, let them like their Constituents, do so at their own expence." James Madison, "Detached Memoranda," ca. 1817, *The Founders' Constitution*, Vol. 5, Amendment I (Religion), Document 64 (Chicago: University of Chicago Press, 1987).

43. The four chaplains went down with the USAT *Dorchester* in 1943, giving their places to other civilian and military personnel. They were Methodist minister George L. Fox, Rabbi Alexander D. Goode, Catholic priest John P. Washington, and Reformed minister Clark V. Poling. Goode, Poling, and Washington met at the Army Chaplains School at Harvard University. See Kevin Schulz, *Tri-Faith America: How Catholics and Jews Held Postwar America to Its Protestant Promise* (Oxford: Oxford University Press, 2013) for a description and analysis of the story of the Four Chaplains.

44. Art 43.2 of Protocol I, 8 June 1977.

rank of the person they are counseling.[45]) The particular combination of marks of integration yet difference is defended as the best way to ensure that chaplains in the military get respect while also being able to perform an independent role. Rank, it is argued, is necessary in order to effectively perform any function in a military setting. The lack of command means, among other things, that chaplains believe they can promise confidentiality to those they serve, officers as well as enlisted personnel.[46] There has been debate about all of these rules. Officer rank may be particularly important in the US context because of the diversity of religion. A position of leadership in a particular religious community is less legible and does not carry the authority it might in a more religiously homogenous society.

The chaplaincies of the various branches of the American armed services share much with each other and with other forms of chaplaincy today, but there are interestingly subtle differences among them, partly because of their very different living conditions and histories, as Hansen explains: "The Army's has generally been the quickest to adapt to increases in diversity, both racial and religious. The Air Force chaplaincy most resembles civilian ministry because chaplains 'don't go on airplanes' and are thus more likely to work out of a familiar chapel setting on a base. The Navy's chaplaincy is perhaps the most formal, given its maritime traditions and history of high church dominance."[47] So—to translate—the army is the largest and most inclusive, religiously speaking, welcoming Wiccans on their bases, for example. Army chaplains are deployed to the battlefield. The air force is the most evangelical, partly perhaps because it is located in Colorado Springs. And the navy is the most liberal—and global—in a theological sense, preferring a message of universal salvation.

The first army chief of chaplains was appointed in 1920, and the first official chaplain manual was published in 1926, *The Chaplain, His Place and Duties*.[48] There have been twelve more since, reflecting various changes in the demographic makeup of the army and in the religious views of the clergy. A historian of the manuals quotes the author of the World War II

45. Rivers, *The Law of Organized Religions*, 211. A reserve naval chaplain described his work thus to sociologist James Beckford (personal communication to author): "Unlike padres in the RAF and Army, chaplains in the Royal Navy don't carry a rank. We share the rank or rate of whoever we are talking to, whether that's an admiral or an able rate. Being alongside people on exactly the same level is for me exactly what the diaconate is all about—it's also a great model of chaplaincy and Christian service."

46. Hansen, *Military Chaplains and Religious Diversity*, 20.

47. Ibid., 7.

48. Nay, "The Operational, Social, and Religious Influences upon the *Army Chaplain Field Manual*, 1926–1952," 3.

edition to illustrate the crucial role of the chaplain in cultivating "spiritual forces and moral character":

> Centuries of experience show the necessity of the deliberate and systematic cultivation of spiritual forces and moral character in the Army. . . . [Chaplains] are necessary if cordial relations between the civil and military communities are to be maintained. Equally important is their contribution to military efficiency. The man of disciplined character and conscious rectitude, associated with comrades and led by officers who command his respect, can be trusted to endure privation and perform his duties in camp or on the battlefield.[49]

By the end of World War II, there were more than eight thousand Protestant, Catholic, and Jewish chaplains serving in the army. Stories of interfaith cooperation among and self-sacrifice by priests, ministers, and rabbis are common, particularly in stories of World War II and the Korean War.

Army chaplains became newly visible when they were drawn into the post–World War II military buildup against communism.[50] They were called upon by the Truman administration to design and deliver moral education to a force popularly believed to be suffering from venereal disease and overconsumption of alcohol. As the army professionalized, the chaplaincy did as well. After the war, in 1951, General George Marshall, former chief of staff of the armed services, now secretary of defense, mandated "Character Guidance" throughout the armed forces. As historian Anne Loveland explains, its purpose was "to assist the commander in promoting healthy moral, social, mental, and spiritual attitudes in the personnel under his command" and "to insure the continuance of the wholesome influences of home, family, and community." Character Guidance was a command responsibility, but chaplains were assigned the task of providing instruction in the program.[51] Implementation of the program was enthusiastically embraced by American evangelicals and others eager to serve as chaplains and change what was perceived to be the poor religious culture of the US Military.[52] There are different accounts of the expanded role of evangelicals in the military in the post–World War II period. Certainly evangelicals themselves deliberately organized such an effort, and a devotion to evangelization continues to be central for many conservative Christians and to be an issue in the military,

49. Ibid., 55.
50. Stahl, "God, War, and Politics."
51. Anne C. Loveland, *American Evangelicals and the U.S. Military 1942–1993* (Baton Rouge: Louisiana State University Press, 1996).
52. Ibid., 111–15.

but there is both exaggeration and an overly polemical coloring to many of the stories of proselytization in the military.

The Vietnam War was a challenging time for the army chaplaincy. While chaplains continued to win admiration for their shared sacrifice,[53] there is also documentation of soldiers deeply disillusioned by the reflexive patriotism of military chaplains. On the one hand, "accompanying the men on combat missions, living in the dust and the mud with them, eating the same rations, sharing the same trauma and losses of battle—that kind of intimate association, apart from their performance of the usual priestly and pastoral duties—earned chaplains the gratitude of many enlisted men and officers"; on the other, "the fact that army chaplains overwhelmingly supported the war, even to the point of endorsing it 'in the name of religion,' alienated many soldiers." As historian Anne Loveland explains, "After the war, in veterans' counseling programs and investigative hearings, Vietnam veterans offered examples of what they called 'chaplains bullshit': 'chaplains blessing the troops, their mission, their guns, their killing.'"[54] Vietnam also changed the perception of chaplaincy within US Protestant seminaries, particularly liberal ones. The constitutionality of the chaplaincy was challenged in a case that critically changed the chaplaincy's self-understanding, as will be discussed in chapter 4. The shift to an all-volunteer force brought new changes in the understanding of the role of the chaplaincy.

Changes in First Amendment jurisprudence coinciding with prosecution of the war in the Balkans, and then the impact of 9/11 and of the Iraq and Afghanistan wars on rethinking the relationship of religion and politics, have given rise to a more explicit embrace of new foreign policy–oriented roles for military chaplaincies, principally as advisors to commanders and in outreach to local clergy and local populations abroad.[55] In a recent publication by the Joint Chiefs of Staff, the new role—and a new public the-

53. For an admiring story of a chaplain in Vietnam, see Daniel L. Mode, *The Grunt Padre: Father Vincent Robert Capodanno, Vietnam, 1966–1967* (Oak Lawn, IL: CMJ Marian Publishers, 2000).

54. Anne C. Loveland, "From Morale Builders to Moral Advocates: U.S. Army Chaplains in the Second Half of the Twentieth Century," in *The Sword of the Lord: Military Chaplains from the First to the Twenty-First Century,* ed. Doris L. Bergen (Notre Dame, IN: Notre Dame University Press, 2008), 236.

55. Kenneth E. Lawson, *Faith and Hope in a War-Torn Land: The US Army Chaplaincy in the Balkans, 1995–2005* (Fort Leavenworth, KS: Combat Studies Institute Press, 2006). See also the 2010 report of the Chicago Council on Global Affairs on religion and foreign policy, particularly with respect to extraterritorial application of the Constitution. The Chicago Council on Global Affairs, "Engaging Religious Communities Abroad: A New Imperative for U.S. Foreign Policy" (R. Scott Appleby and Richard Cizik, cochairs; Thomas Wright, project director), 2010; see also Hurd, *The Politics of Secularism in International Relations.*

ology—is laid out. Now termed "religious support," the chaplaincy serves both the soldiers and a larger public—and religion figures as a significant and "dynamic" geopolitical force. As always foregrounding the key constitutional legitimation for the chaplaincy—that is, enabling the religious free exercise rights of soldiers—the Joint Chiefs explain that the chaplains are also responsible for advising commanders on religion in the operational arena: "Religious support in joint operations is dedicated to meeting the personal free exercise of religion needs of military and other authorized members and providing commanders with professional advice regarding the dynamic influence of religion and religious belief in the operational arena." The Joint Chiefs follow with a theory of the importance of religion for war:

> While it may not be the primary catalyst for war, religion can be a contributing factor. Some examples include religious overtones being invoked to develop an exclusivist vision and program for national and international action; governments or groups using religion as a motivating factor for socializing conflict; ideologies being linked with theological concepts that have mass appeal to achieve the ideal; conflicts "theologized" to justify existence, establish legitimacy, gain popularity, and enact policies, laws, and courses of action for internal and external activities; and, achievement of an end being gained by using theological concepts as a means.[56]

Although cast in the universalizing and legitimating language of social science research, it is, for the most part, the Global War on Terror and the perceived role of Islam in that war that has extended the task of the chaplain today. No longer focused just on the personal free exercise needs of the American "Judeo-Christian" solider, or even of a more general need to maintain discipline and morale within the military, religion, at least the religion of others, is now seen as "dynamic," "pivotal," even a catalyst or justification for war. The military chaplain is being asked to be the facilitator of religious freedom for the serviceman and also for the world; he is being asked to become expert on all religions and broker between good and bad religion writ large.[57]

56. US Joint Chiefs of Staff, "Religious Support in Joint Operations." Joint Publication 1-05, (2004); McLaughlin, "The Chaplain's Evolving Role in Peace and Humanitarian Relief Operations."

57. In taking on this task, the chaplain is arguably far in advance of the research in this area. Evidence for the mobilizing ability of religion *qua* religion is scanty. See Sullivan et al., *After Religious Freedom.*

Chaplain-to-chaplain meetings between the US Army and other armies are now routine. In March 2012, for example, the army announced such a meeting between US Army chaplains and chaplains of the Congolese Army chaplaincy: "U.S. Army Africa Chaplain (Col.) John McGraw, along with Africa Command Chaplain (Col.) Jerry Lewis, traveled to Kinshasa recently to provide resiliency training to [Democratic Republic of Congo's] Armed Forces chaplains . . . McGraw said. 'DRC is a vast nation and they have a large number of chaplains spread throughout the country.'" The report went on to explain how American chaplains could help the Congolese chaplains improve their pastoral care and contribute to the peace and stability of the DRC:

> "The Congolese are very spiritual people. There has been civil war and conflict in this region for nearly two decades," McGraw said. " . . . Our Chaplain Corps is now aligned to assist the Congolese chaplaincy with many of their issues and concerns," Lewis said. "The roles of chaplains can have big connections to peace and stability of this nation, and there are great contributions that our chaplains can make here in the future," he emphasized.[58]

In Afghanistan, American chaplains have been training chaplains for the Afghan army, training them in the ministry of presence.[59] At every stage in every theater of operation, underwritten with a faith in the natural spirituality of all people and the special expertise of the US army, the military chaplaincies have striven to argue for their value and importance, extending themselves, perhaps, in ways they are not prepared for and setting up expectations that cannot possibly be met, whether it is improving the moral character of the American soldier or achieving world peace.[60]

In 2005, complaints of coercive proselytizing were brought against the Air Force Academy. The official report concluded that "the HQ USAF team found a religious climate that does not involve overt religious discrimination, but a failure to fully accommodate all members' needs and a lack of

58. Rich Bartell, "USARAF Chaplains Teach Resiliency in Africa," US Army Africa Public Affairs Office, Kinshasa, Democratic Republic of the Congo, February 29, 2012. http://www .usaraf.army.mil/NEWS/NEWS_120229_CHAPS_DRC.html.

59. George Adams, "Chaplains as Liaisons with Religious Leaders: Lessons from Iraq and Afghanistan," *Peaceworks* 56 (2006): 20.

60. Comprehensively discussing the present threats to the legality, practicality, and moral legitimacy of the chaplaincy, see Robert J. Phillips "The Military Chaplaincy of the 21st Century: *Cui Bono?*" (paper presented at the International Society for Military Ethics Conference on Religion and the Military and the Military and Codes of Ethics, Springfield, VA, January 25–26, 2009). This paper and others presented at the conference are available at http://isme.tamu .edu/ISME07/isme07.html (accessed June 26, 2013).

awareness over where the line is drawn between permissible and impermissible expression of beliefs." The report recommended that commanders "be given a set of guidelines upon which to base decisions regarding how they recognize and build on the *inherently spiritual nature* of their people and create the conditions that demonstrate the value of and respect for the great diversity of belief systems within our Air Force."[61] Criticism brings a move toward universalism.

In 2009, the separate training schools of the air force, army, and navy chaplaincies were, somewhat to the dismay of each, merged to create the Armed Forces Chaplaincy Center in Fort Jackson, South Carolina. The center is dedicated to training new chaplains in each other's religion, as well as in how the military operates. An Associated Press article on the opening described the new center: "Setting the tone in the center's front lobby is a large stained glass portrayal of Gen. George Washington, kneeling in prayer with his Anglican chaplain and his soldiers in the snow at Valley Forge."[62] The article went on to describe "worship training labs" outfitted with items brought from the various military schools: "Golden icons line the walls in a small Greek Orthodox chapel; a Muslim prayer room is outfitted with prayer rugs and copies of the Quran; and a handwritten Jewish Torah is kept inside a wooden ark, alongside Sabbath candles and Seder plates to show how Passover is celebrated." Said Keith, a Baptist minister, "The school means we get to explore each other's traditions, history, culture. We think we are all going to be better off for it."

As religion comes to be named as *the* cause of difference and dissensions, on the one hand, and *the* hope for peace, on the other, the military chaplain's list of duties has become dauntingly long. Chaplains

attend chaplains' school in order to learn both how to be a military officer and how to serve as an effective chaplain in the U.S. military; serve as part of a command, and are responsible to a chain of command as officers; are paid according to rank and years of service as are other officers; comply with all official military regulations (e.g., regarding appropriate dress, behavior, etc.); wear the officer's uniform of their service, and have religious insignia on their uniform; serve in "camp" (barracks) domestically or are deployed outside the United States at the service's discretion; lead voluntary religious

61. See US Air Force, "Report of the Headquarters Review Group concerning Religious Climate at the U.S. Air Force Academy" (2005), 46.

62. Susanne M. Schaffer, "School for Chaplains Dedicated at Fort Jackson," Associated Press, May 6, 2010.

services, and facilitate leadership of such services by other clergy, as directed by the commanding officer; provide special services at weddings, memorial services, and on holidays; provide pastoral counseling; provide and facilitate post-traumatic stress disorder counseling; visit servicemen wherever they are, including combat, the brig, or in school; visit the families of servicemen where practicable; provide and monitor religious literature; provide death rites and funeral services; serve in hospitals and tend to the wounded; provide leadership in humanitarian projects; provide education and/or expertise on ethics; are enjoined from intelligence collection or target selection but are expected to participate in operational planning and advise the command and staff on matters related to religion; provide assistance in liaison with local religious leaders in a given area of operation; are part of, and generally the commanding officer for, a "Unit Ministry Team" (UMT), which includes non-commissioned officers as support for Religious Affairs; are prohibited from carrying weapons.[63]

As with chaplains in other secular institutions, the military chaplain, in addition to his pastoral duties, is being asked to pick up the slack by assuming responsibility for a range of duties that no one else wants—or perhaps knows how—to do.

Given the powerful need that any state has to persuade young people, against their inclination in most cases, to kill and to die, the role of the chaplaincy in fostering the smooth functioning of the military has always inevitably presented a profound challenge to its integrity, but the role of advisor to the command on the religions of the world today expands and challenges the responsibility of military chaplains in ways still being worked out. Chaplains are also now being assigned to those units charged with drone strikes.[64]

Prison Chaplains

The history of the prison is intimately tied to the history of religion in modern Europe and North America, particularly in the Anglo-American countries. The story has been told many times.[65] Eighteenth- and nineteenth-century

63. Pauletta Otis, "An Overview of the U.S. Military Chaplaincy: A Ministry of Presence and Practice," *Review of Faith & International Affairs* 7 (2009): 3–15.

64. Elisabeth Bumiller, "A Day Job Waiting for a Kill Shot a World Away," *New York Times*, July 29, 2012, A1.

65. A brief account of this history can be found in Sullivan, *Prison Religion*. Important sources include Norval Morris and David Rothman, eds., *The Oxford History of the Prison* (Ox-

Christian reformers in England and the United States sought to replace corporal punishment of various kinds with penitence and moral reform. The nature of today's prisons is greatly indebted to those early nineteenth-century reformers, their mistakes as well as their vision. In the United States, however, because prisons are instituted and regulated primarily at the state level, generalizing about prisons is hazardous. There are more than fifty-one separate corrections departments, at least one for each state, one for the District of Columbia, and one for the federal government, not to mention thousands of jails and detention centers at the municipal and county level. Religion figures in these institutions in different ways, varying because of differences in regional religious history and politics as well as the demography of prison populations.[66] Most have chaplaincies of some kind.

Courts and legislatures are generally very deferential to prison administrators, as they are to the military, with respect to the definition and scope of security needs, even when those security needs limit the ability of soldiers and prisoners to perform religious obligations.[67] Until the 1970s, prisoners were not understood to have rights at all, of any kind, including rights to religious freedom. They were legally, and quite literally, slaves of the state. Since the US Supreme Court's decision in *Cruz v. Beto*,[68] however, all US prisons are obligated to make provision for prisoners to exercise their rights under the First Amendment, albeit with the significant restrictions that govern all prisoner activity.[69]

---

ford: Oxford University Press, 1995); David Garland, *The Culture of Control: Crime and Social Order in Contemporary Society* (Chicago: University of Chicago Press, 2001); David Garland, *Mass Imprisonment: Social Causes and Consequences* (London: Sage, 2001); Michael Ignatieff, *A Just Measure of Pain: The Penitentiary in the Industrial Revolution, 1750–1850* (London: Penguin Books, 1970); John Lardas Modern, "Ghosts of Sing Sing or the Metaphysics of Secularism," *Journal of the American Academy of Religion* 75 (2007): 615–50; and James Q. Whitman, *Harsh Justice: Criminal Punishment and the Widening Divide between America and Europe* (Oxford: Oxford University Press, 2003).

66. The notorious Angola prison camp in Louisiana, for example, now houses a Baptist Bible college within the prison. Erik Eckholm, "Bible College Helps Some at Louisiana Prison Find Peace," *New York Times*, October 6, 2013, A15. But see also Andrew Cohen, "At Louisiana's Most Notorious Prison, a Clash of Testament," *Atlantic*, October 11, 2013. http://www.the atlantic.com/national/archive/2013/10/at-louisianas-most-notorious-prison-a-clash-of -testament/280414/ (accessed October 27, 2013).

67. The Supreme Court held in *Chappell v. Wallace*, 462 U.S. 296 (1983), a suit alleging racial discrimination, that soldiers could not sue superior officers for constitutional violations, because Congress had created two systems of justice, one for the military and one for civilians.

68. Cruz v. Beto, 405 U.S. 319, 322 (1972).

69. See Sarah Barringer Gordon, *The Spirit of the Law*, for an account of the role that Nation of Islam prisoners played in the effort to secure religious freedom rights for prisoners.

Some prisons have chaplaincy staffs who directly provide religious services. Others act primarily as coordinators or facilitators of religious services provided by outside volunteers. Many combine these models. In some prisons, these efforts are impressively inclusive. In the last couple of decades, with the privatization of social services across the governments of the United States, faith-based social service providers have also contracted to provide programs in prisons and have offered reentry programs in both government-run and private prisons.[70] But prison chaplains, like chaplains in the military, are constitutionally understood today to be there because prisoners cannot otherwise avail themselves of the free market in religion, which is the political and constitutional ideal in the United States. Prison chaplains are not legally understood to be there in order to effect conversion, that is, to engage in overt proselytization. Still, it is the government that is the "provider of religious experience" in prisons, a task administered largely through the chaplaincies, and the personal transformation sought by prisons can be understood to be religious in a more general sense. Self-improvement is both continuous in the United States with Christian theologies of the self and partakes of perennialist understandings of self and world.[71]

In the United States, a new era in the regulation of religion in prisons opened in 2000 with passage of the Religious Land Use and Institutionalized Persons Act.[72] RLUIPA, as it is known, was one of the legislative responses to the Supreme Court's declaration in 1990 in *Employment Division v. Smith* (the peyote case) that the free exercise clause of the First Amendment provides no right of religious accommodation by the government as long as any law that prevents a person from exercising her religion is neutral and of general application.[73] Congress's first effort to reverse the effects of *Smith,* the Religious Freedom Restoration Act (RFRA), was found unconstitutional as applied to the states in 1997 in *Boerne v. Flores.*[74] RLUIPA was an effort to restore a right to religious accommodation in prisons (and to a religious exemption from zoning restrictions) that Congress understood the Supreme Court to have eliminated in the *Smith* case.

70. For an account of a legal challenge to such a faith-based programs, see Sullivan, *Prison Religion.*

71. Sullivan, *Prison Religion;* for a look at prison chaplaincies in Guatemala, see Kevin O'Neill, "The Reckless Will: Prison Chaplaincy and the Problem of Mara Salvatrucha," *Public Culture* 22, no. 1 (2010): 67–88.

72. Religious Land Use and Institutionalized Persons Act, 42 U.S.C. § 2000cc-1, et seq. (2010).

73. Employment Division v. Smith, 494 U.S. 872, 890 (1990).

74. Boerne v. Flores, 521 U.S. 507 (1997).

RLUIPA provides that "no government shall impose a substantial burden on the religious exercise of a person residing in or confined to an institution . . . even if the burden results from a rule of general applicability, unless the government demonstrates that imposition of the burden on that person—(1) is in furtherance of a compelling governmental interest; and (2) is the least restrictive means of furthering that compelling governmental interest."[75] Justice Ginsburg, writing for the US Supreme Court, affirmed the constitutionality of RLUIPA in *Cutter v. Wilkinson*.[76] "RLUIPA," she wrote, "protects institutionalized persons who are unable freely to attend to their religious needs and are therefore dependent on the government's permission and accommodation for exercise of their religion."[77] Ginsburg explicitly recognized this accommodation as being a practical extension of the Constitution's—and the Court's—acknowledgment of the religiousness of Americans. "The Free Exercise Clause," she wrote, "requires government respect for, and noninterference with, the religious beliefs and practices of our Nation's people."[78] Prison chaplains are, on this theory, legally understood to be necessary to the constitutional task of recognizing the significant social fact that is American religion. But the role they perform in those institutions is far more complex. As with chaplains in other state institutions, chaplains work to serve both client (the inmate) and the secular employer (the prison authorities), while also striving to remain true to their religious commitments, both formal and organizational, as well as existential.

Prison chaplaincies, like military chaplaincies, are not without their critics. Leading First Amendment scholars Ira Lupu and Robert Tuttle, in a long article considering the constitutionality of prison chaplaincies, are far more skeptical than Justice Ginsburg about the capacity of government to "acknowledge" and "respect" religion in prisons. They argue that the government is constitutionally incompetent to determine what counts as religion and that decisions about accommodation for prisoners' requests for religious accommodation should therefore be made on entirely secular grounds. They would dispense with RLUIPA rights in favor of an entirely locally negotiated solution to conflicts between prisoner needs, whether secular or religious, and prison rules. Lupu and Tuttle describe RLUIPA's

75. Ibid., Section 2000cc-1.

76. Cutter v. Wilkinson, 544 U.S. 709 (2005).

77. Ibid. For a discussion of what RLUIPA does, see Ira C. Lupu and Robert Tuttle, "The Forms and Limits of Religious Accommodation: The Case of RLUIPA," *Cardozo Law Review* 32 (2011): 1907–36; see also, Taylor G. Stout, "The Costs of Religious Accommodation in Prisons," *Virginia Law Review* 96 (2010): 1201–39.

78. *Cutter*, 544 U.S. at 719.

prescription as "permitting prisoners the space to self-declare the substantiality of the burden they are experiencing on their religious exercise, and simultaneously giving prison officials wide authority to assert concerns of safety, security, and limited resources as reasons to refuse to make the requested accommodation."[79] Focusing on the incompetency of the prison fairly to provide free exercise opportunities for prisoners, Lupu and Tuttle regard the risk of "impermissible religious judgments" on the part of government and of discriminatory impact on those who do not share the prisoners' religious commitments, as reason enough to exclude special accommodations for the religious needs of prisoners. The value and effect of RLUIPA is still being debated,[80] but Lupu and Tuttle's view is a minority one. Prison officials in the United States today understand prisoners to be naturally spiritual and themselves to be generally expected to provide religious services for all prisoners on an equal basis subject only to defensible correctional needs. (Doing so for Muslim prisoners continues to be driven in large part by post-9/11 politics.[81])

The Correctional Chaplains Association explains what the new accommodation under RLUIPA means for the prison chaplain, beginning with a general description of the prison chaplain's role in providing professional pastoral care to both prisoners and staff, rehearsing the now well-worn explanation that prisoners, like others who are away from home, have a constitutional right to pastoral care. But they also make larger claims to the expertise claimed by chaplains. "Correctional chaplains," they insist, "are professionals, with specialized training in the unique dynamics of the corrections world."[82] The myriad tasks given to the prison chaplain are then listed. As with the military chaplain, it is a daunting grab bag of duties, combining traditional religious functions with those of other prison officers, suggesting obligations running sometimes to prisoners, sometimes to the prison authorities, insisting on the obligation to insure "that all prisoners are afforded the opportunities to practice the faiths of their choice . . . notifi-

79. Lupu and Tuttle, "The Forms and Limits of Religious Accommodation," 1935.

80. See also Derek L. Gaubatz, "RLUIPA at Four: Evaluating the Success and Constitutionality of RLUIPA's Prisoner Provisions," *Harvard Journal of Law and Public Policy* 28 (2005): 501–608.

81. The Office of the Inspector General of the Department of Justice commissioned a report in 2004 concerning the availability of Muslim chaplains. *A Review of the Bureau of Prisons' Selection of Muslim Religious Services Providers;* see also Hansen, *Military Chaplains and Religious Diversity,* on Muslim chaplains in the military, and Joshua Dubler, *Down in the Chapel: Religious Life in an American Prison* (New York: Farrar, Straus and Giroux 2013), on Muslim chaplains in prisons.

82. They may also be certified through the American Correctional Chaplains Association, http://www.correctionalchaplains.org/ (accessed January 8, 2012).

cation of death or other tragedy and Grief Counseling in such situations. . . . Marriage Counseling . . . clarifying issues involving various faith practices, religious articles, religious diets and other religious standards . . . insuring that volunteer activities are conducted in a diverse, yet secure manner . . . providing positive reinforcement and diffusing frustration, anger and stress amongst prisoners and staff, thereby lessening threats, assaults and other negative behaviors," and "averting harm to individuals and damage to facilities and the lawsuits that may result from such occurrences and issues of religious rights."[83]

The association's description of the chaplain's duties concludes with an endorsement of the importance of chaplains by the director of the Washington State prisons: "Chaplains are important in a correctional setting because they help offenders develop a healthy attitude toward themselves and staff . . . Chaplains help offenders develop a positive spiritual reality regardless of religious preference and they help promote spiritual growth."[84] A recent article on prison chaplaincies in Guatemala that emphasizes the focus on developing self-esteem through control of the will echoes the goals of US chaplains: "prison chaplains, men and women of faith who range from apocalyptic neo-Pentecostals to mainline charismatic Christians, have become such a valued resource for Guatemalan security officials. With no one watching, these pastors believe that active gang members, through the saving grace of Jesus Christ, can watch themselves—can internalize the panopticon."[85]

Like the military and health-care chaplain, the correctional chaplain has acquired a greatly enhanced role, one that arguably once again expansively integrates him into the prison project while embracing the prisoner as religious well beyond the specific constitutionally protected religious needs of the prisoner. Offenders are understood to need to acquire "a positive spiritual reality" through "spiritual growth," not just to have a constitutionally protected right to the "free exercise of religion." Correctional chaplains are expected to be experts on all religions and in religion in general, as well as to have expertise in behavioral psychology and "correctional issues," all while "positively impact[ing] the Finances of correctional facilities."

Sociologist Allison Hicks observes, based on her ethnographic research in prisons, that prison chaplains, often initially motivated by a sympathetic

---

83. http://www.correctionalchaplains.org/what_is_the_acca.htm (accessed January 8, 2012).

84. Tom Rolfs, director, Division of Prisons, Washington State Department of Corrections, http://www.correctionalchaplains.org/ (accessed January 8, 2012).

85. O'Neill, "The Reckless Will," 74.

desire to minister to the very particular needs of the incarcerated, learn over time to combine their ministry to the prisoners with implementation of the prison's behavior modification goals. Hicks describes the seduction of this shift: "Chaplains diminished the strain they experienced between the religious and correctional dimensions of their role through adapting and redefining their work . . . Through this adjustment chaplains were able to weave custodial concerns into their religious objectives, enacting their religious identity through practical behavior."[86]

Chaplains, integrated into the prison administrative hierarchy, not unlike hospital and military chaplains, frequently come to see prison officers, as well as prisoners, as being in need of spiritual care, as Hicks also observed:

> Not only were chaplains and officers now on the same team, assisting each other in managing and controlling the incarcerated population, chaplains also expanded their clientele to include officers. Originally expecting to humanize a cold institution in the service of the inmates, chaplains expanded this function to include addressing the emotional, psychological, and spiritual needs of the officers as well . . . As [one chaplain] said, "Corrections is a really, really difficult place to work . . . We see casualties in staff who don't die physically, but they die emotionally and spiritually and mentally." As a result, part of her ministry included "help[ing] staff find balance in their lives and come out of corrections on the other end as a whole person."[87]

The horror of the prison takes its spiritual toll on everyone.

Trained to serve virtually any people they come into contact with, and to be deeply universal, egalitarian, and perhaps naively optimistic and nonjudgmental in their theology, prison chaplains come to see themselves as ministers not to a specific denominationally defined group within the prison population, but as ministers to the whole situation, thereby in danger of becoming captured by institutional self-justifications.[88] Hicks recounts that,

86. Allison Hicks, "Role Fusion: The Occupational Socialization of Prison Chaplains," *Symbolic Interaction* 31 (2008): 400–421, 411; see also Jody L. Sundt and Francis T. Cullen, "The Correctional Ideology of Prison Chaplains: A National Survey," *Journal of Criminal Justice* 30 (2002): 365–85, showing that prison chaplains regard the incapacitation of prisoners as the primary objective of incarceration.

87. Hicks, "Role Fusion," 414.

88. Justice Brandeis, in his confirmation hearings, famously defended an alleged conflict of interest in his private legal practice in which he represented more than one party to a transaction by asserting that he was "counsel to the situation." (Professional legal ethics today prohibit representation of more than one party in a conflict.) *The Supreme Court of the United States: Hear-*

"as Daniel, the Catholic chaplain who had worked for ten years in a medium-security-level prison, phrased it, 'I think that for most of us, we are out for justice for all the people that we're serving, whether they're staff or offenders.'"[89] Another chaplain described her role this way to Hicks:

> Success from my chaplain point of view is that each person, each inmate, has the opportunity on a regular basis to pursue their religious convictions in a way that does not create conflict with safety and security and allows them to become deeper in their religious faith. But I'm also a correctional chaplain, so my objective from a correctional point of view, which I think aligns with those others, too, is that you [the inmate] are here in prison to address and correct the behaviors and the attitudes that cause you to be here. And part of that is "are you doing the right things? Are you getting into trouble, pushing at the rules, violating the rules, even the little ones?"[90]

Joshua Dubler, in his book describing a week in a Philadelphia prison chapel, comments on the tensions inherent to the work of the prison chaplain:

> Because they are trained in a caring profession, they are predisposed to distinguish themselves from the administration's custody-based approach, in which prisoners alternatively appear as dangerous criminals or tedious babies, requiring, in either case, the identical regimen of callous discipline. While the chaplain's aspiration to treat the prisoners as men is generally quite practicable, a conspiracy of factors nonetheless reinforces the prison's dehumanizing operating logic . . . periodically burned, and, before long, burned out, the chaplains come to deflect, to indulge in gallows humor, and to adopt as a default condition, a posture of sardonic remove, which in a roundabout way brings them into proper alignment with . . . "the World of No!" in which the prisoners live.[91]

While the constitutional excuse for their presence continues to be the free exercise needs of the prisoner, and there are prison chaplains who have heroically protected prisoners,[92] the prison chaplain, like the military chaplain,

---

ings and Reports on Successful and Unsuccessful Nominations of Supreme Court Justices by the Senate Judiciary Committee, 1916– (Roy M. Mersky and J. Myron Jacobstein compiled, 1975–).

89. Hicks, "Role Fusion," 414.

90. Ibid., 415.

91. Dubler, Down in the Chapel, 61.

92. Damian Echols of the West Memphis Three (all of whom were falsely accused of murder)

working out of a theology that has moved beyond the Constitution, is drawn into an enforcement role that attempts to effect an impossible task: "justice for all the people we're serving."

Hospital Chaplains

Hospital chaplaincy in the United States has changed shape in recent decades as health-care delivery has changed and as the religious lives of patients have come to reflect the greater diversity of the population. The training of hospital chaplains has become more specialized, and the center of professional self-understanding has moved from the sending denomination to the health-care setting where much of their training takes place. More, perhaps, than many other chaplaincy settings, hospitals challenge the religious practitioner in a very direct way to articulate and justify their work in a place of highly scientistic and market-based assumptions. US hospital chaplains today describe their understanding of illness as a crisis of meaning for the patient, not solely as a biological event; the chaplain is seen as expert in approaches to and translation of problems of meaning.[93]

In her new book on religion and spirituality in American hospitals, Wendy Cadge emphasizes the complex terrain that is hospital chaplaincy today, ranging from hospitals with no professional chaplaincy where spiritual care is delivered by local clergy to hospitals with a part-time differentially trained chaplain staff to hospitals with full-time professional chaplains. Those who work in these various contexts also have a range of understandings of their purpose. Some primarily visit patients from their own faith traditions. Some see themselves as able to switch-hit among traditions. Many understand themselves to be professionally expert in ministering to all comers, religious people of any faith tradition as well as those who are not religious; often, like chaplains in other settings, they see themselves as legally obligated to do so, whether or not that is formally the case.

The role of spirituality in health care is a topic of vigorous and contentious debate today, within the health-care community as well as outside of it, as the description of the *Nicholson* case in the last chapter showed. The

---

was freed after eighteen years on Death Row in Texas; he credited chaplains with saving his life in prison. http://www.texasmoratorium.org/archives/2131 (accessed January 20, 2013).

93. Nancy Cahners, "What Does a Hospital Chaplain Do Again? Trying to Explain the Meaning of Making Meaning in the World of Medical Ethics," in *Medical Ethics in Health Care Chaplaincy*, ed. Walter Moczynski, Hille Haker, and Katrin Bentele (Berlin: Lit Verlag 2009); Christopher Swift, "Speaking of the Same Things Differently," in *Spirituality in Health Care Contexts*, ed. Helen Orchard (London: Jessica Kingsley Publishers, 2001).

Joint Commission has required health-care providers to give attention to spiritual health since 1969, but the particular shape that attention should take in particular hospital settings has not been mandated or regularized. While there is much evidence that Americans, both patients and health-care providers, think spiritual health is important to overall health care, there is little agreement on exactly what care should look like. The importance of spiritual care to overall medical care manifests itself in the proliferation of traditional meditation and exercise regimens, as well as the integration of a variety of traditional healing methods and alternative therapies.

In the new holistic approach to health care, many doctors and nurses, as well as chaplains, see themselves as involved in spiritual care today. Cadge quotes a nurse describing her prayer at work in a public municipal hospital: "Different times in the middle of the night . . . when the chaplain had not gotten here yet and the baby is dying—we've [the nurses] been told that we are instruments of healing and we've actually taken water and blessed it and blessed the baby ourselves at 4 o'clock in the morning when a baby has passed away." Another nurse said, "One time in the middle of the night I remember a couple of the [Catholic] nurses, three of us, just started saying the 'Our Father, Hail Mary and the Glory Be' and we just prayed over the water and did the sign of the cross and just put it on the baby—you know heart, head, side, side." One gets the sense from Cadge's account, here and elsewhere in her book, that what she saw in her fieldwork at several secular urban hospitals was a remarkably diverse group of well-meaning people, doctors, nurses, chaplains, volunteers, trying to make their commitment to pluralism and spiritual care real—sometimes without strong models to determine how that should be done.

Hospitals originated as religious charities.[94] As Christopher Swift, Church of England chaplain and author of a book on hospital chaplaincy in England, explains, hospitals have always been profoundly part of the economy of salvation, here and hereafter. The fourth Lateran Council was already regulating hospitals in the twelfth century.[95] The council insisted on the relative importance of the state of the soul as being prior to the state of the body. Indeed, "hospital statutes from throughout medieval Europe always give priority to the spiritual over the secular well-being of sick inmates, to sacramental care over medical treatment."[96] In the early modern period,

94. Swift, *Hospital Chaplaincy*, 10.

95. James W. Brodman, "Religion and Discipline in the Hospitals of Thirteenth-Century France," in *The Medieval Hospital and Medical Practice*, ed. Barbara S. Bowers, (Burlington, VT: Ashgate, 2007)

96. Ibid., 123.

beginning in England with Henry VIII, with the suppression of religious houses, hospitals shifted toward a concern for bodies as well as souls, bodies arguably needed to serve the new states, bodies requiring moral *and* medical attention. Swift's book follows four hundred years of history of hospitals and their chaplaincies in a country with both an established church and, then increasingly, other churches and religious organizations, as well as a growing public commitment to universal health care.

A recent comprehensive history of the hospital by Guenther Risse summarizes their evolving and conflicting purposes, secular and religious, and the many interested parties that were involved in their growth, emphasizing the importance of hospitals in serving both political and economic, as well as spiritual, purposes: "From a religious point of view, hospitals have always been instruments of hope and pious benevolence . . . Social control and other rationales for welfare have also inspired hospital services over the ages, helping communities cope with the catastrophic displacements caused by famines, wars, and epidemics."[97] Risse goes on to explain that "new efforts to create 'patient centeredness' seek to modify current science and technology-centered management operations and hospital environments to ensure the delivery of a more humane care."[98] Like the prison and the army, the hospital is a place of arbitration as to the meaning of human life and death, the relationship of the individual and her community to the state, and a struggle for definition and control by a range of persons, governments, businesses, and churches.

In the United States, churches and other religious associations were involved in the founding of the first hospitals in the nineteenth century, first Protestants, then, with increased immigration, Catholic and Jewish organizations as well. These hospitals were initially mainly for the poor, as they had been for centuries in Europe; middle-class people were treated at home. In the twentieth century, however, the development of modern hospitals and scientific medicine led to the growth of a new kind of hospital and the greater use of hospitals by the middle and upper classes. Although priests, ministers, and rabbis have visited the sick throughout US history, the story of hospital chaplains as a distinctive religious vocation in the United States is primarily a twentieth-century story.

As Brooks Holifield explains in his history of clergy in the United States, only a handful of hospitals employed full-time chaplains in the 1940s, but

97. Guenter B. Risse, *Mending Bodies, Saving Souls: A History of Hospitals* (Oxford: Oxford University Press, 1999), 26–27.
98. Ibid.

by the 1950s hundreds of chaplains had become employed in general hospitals, mental hospitals, and VA hospitals. Hospital chaplaincy associations had also been formed. Holifield quotes Protestant observers who, already by the 1960s, were reporting "an accelerating movement of clergy toward preference for work in 'experimental' and 'specialized' ministries rather than the parish church."[99] Cadge describes US hospital chaplaincy over this time as moving from the work of the particularized ministry of separate religious communities to the work of professionals trained and dedicated to a more generalized spiritual support:

> the meaning of spiritual shifted from describing aspects of people's experiences within specific religious traditions to describing the ways people find meaning in any part of their lives. Chaplains today see themselves providing spiritual support not only when they pray with patients, as they would have in the past, but as they speak with them about pets, family members, favorite places, and anything else that provides meaning and purpose.[100]

Cadge sees these transitions as being pushed by demographic changes, by the decline of mainstream Protestantism, by the advocacy of doctors and nurses, and by the growing number of religious "seekers."[101]

One interesting way in which the ambiguous professional identity of the hospital chaplain today manifests itself is in the debate over whether chaplains should "chart" their visits. A desire for professional recognition and for greater integration into the health-care staff and their practices would suggest the appropriateness of chaplains recording their visits and

99. Holifield, *God's Ambassadors*, 252.

100. Cadge, *Paging God*, 21–22.

101. "Especially since the 1960s, increasing numbers of people have become seekers who combine aspects of multiple religious traditions with nature, exercise, and practices like meditation and yoga in their sense of what is personally meaningful. Such demographic changes coupled with the cultural decline of mainline Protestantism and increasing religious and ethnic diversity created by post-1965 immigration brought wider ranges of people with broader meaning making systems into hospitals. There they encountered Protestant and later Catholic and Jewish chaplains who were grappling with their own senses of professional identity as they struggled to stake consistent professional claims and collaborate with other healthcare professionals. Some of these struggles reflected chaplains' internal struggles to professionalize—which included efforts to medicalize—as they valued their identities as Protestant, Catholic and Jewish over a shared identity as professional chaplains. They also reflect Protestant chaplains' increasing efforts to make their work relevant in light of the numeric and cultural decline of mainline Protestantism, especially since the 1950s. Growing attention to spirituality in nursing and medicine over time resulted from similar demographic factors as well as from the advocacy of groups of physicians, nurses, and centers like the George Washington Institute for Spirituality . . . beginning in the 1990s." Cadge, *Paging God*, 21.

their observations, but both privacy concerns and a resistance to reducing and conforming the chaplain's role to a secularist model suggest otherwise. Christopher Swift describes the temptations inherent in this tension, referring to the hospital chaplain as a "technologist of the soul," referencing Foucault, but also citing the strictures of the Lateran Council insisting on the primacy to be given to the soul over the body.[102]

Medical anthropologist Frances Norwood, in her ethnographic study of hospital chaplains, sees the chaplain as addressing a different body from the medical community. It is through the concept of the "holy body," she says, that chaplains both differentiate and universalize their task.[103] Rev. Kate Braestrup, too, of the Maine Warden Service (see the preface), explains her role as a chaplain with reference to the sacredness of the bodies she encounters: "My uniformed presence signifies a human and humane understanding on the part of the wardens and the wider community that the body in the woods or in the water is not just a practical problem, but a matter of tremendous spiritual significance for those intimately involved. As a reverend, I can express our reverence."[104] And yet Cadge's and Swift's work would suggest that the holy body preoccupies the medical as well as the explicitly religious staff in the hospital, particularly, perhaps, when death threatens, complicating the separation imported from popular constitutionalism.

Jewish hospital chaplaincy in the United States shares in this longer history of the professionalization of hospital chaplaincy, but it also has a particular relationship to the development of other specialized ministries within the American Jewish community and their professionalization. Robert Tabak, in his history of Jewish hospital chaplaincy, explains that it finds its origins in ancient practices:

> Jewish chaplaincy builds on older traditions of *bikur holim*, visiting the sick, which continue today as a volunteer activity. This tradition is traced back in rabbinic literature to God, who visited Abraham: "The Holy One, blessed be he, visited the sick as it is written, 'The Lord appeared to him by the terebinths of Mamre (Gen. 18:1)'—and so you must visit the sick." It was viewed as part of deeds of loving-kindness—*gemilut hasadim*. This is an obligation, or mitzvah, for Jews.[105]

---

102. Swift, *Hospital Chaplaincy*, 45.

103. Frances Norwood, "The Ambivalent Chaplain: Negotiating Structural and Ideological Difference on the Margins of Modern-Day Hospital Medicine," *Medical Anthropology* 25, no. 1 (January–March 2006): 1–29.

104. Braestrup, *Here If You Need Me*, 103–4.

105. Robert Tabak, "The Emergence of Jewish Health-Care Chaplaincy: The Professionaliza-

The first Jewish hospital chaplaincies designated as such were in Philadelphia and New York City: "The Jewish Hospital in Philadelphia had a rabbi from the 1890s to the 1950s who led services for the elderly residents of the adjacent Home for the Jewish Aged. One Jewish geriatric facility in New York (on the Lower East Side, and after 1910 on the Grand Concourse in the Bronx) had a rabbi and *rav hamachshir* (kashrut supervisor) as early as 1902."[106] The work was sacramental, in the VA sense discussed in chapter 1, rather than clinical. Starting with the development of Hillel Houses at colleges and universities and then with the development of specifically Jewish health-care chaplaincies staffed by laypersons as well as by rabbis, Jewish chaplains, like their Christian counterparts, came to serve all comers, and increasingly to hold degrees and certifications in social work, pastoral care, and ministry.[107] In the mid-1980s, as will be discussed in chapter 4, several federal appellate courts established the conditions for the constitutionality of the administration of chaplaincies in government hospitals. As with the army and the prisons, one can see there reflected an increasingly universalist approach to religion.[108]

Not everyone is happy with the clinical partnership between religion and medicine. A 2004 public debate between theologian Stanley Hauerwas and physician Harold Koenig, both of Duke University, illustrates the persistent tension and ambiguity. Koenig argues for deep correlations between religion, spirituality, and medicine, and advocates for professional universalized spiritual care in hospitals.[109] Hauerwas resists what he sees as the dehumanizing scientism and secularization of spiritual care, arguing for scripturally based work by Christian ministers who understand the problem of suffering as fundamental to the human condition, a condition that cannot be "overcome."[110]

After their initial statement of positions, Koenig and Hauerwas each responded to a question about the appropriate response to the parent of a

---

tion of Spiritual Care," *American Jewish Archives Journal* 62, no. 2 (2010): 90. See "Our Mission." National Association of Jewish Chaplains, http://www.najc.org/about/mission (accessed January 31, 2013).

106. Tabak, "The Emergence of Jewish Health-Care Chaplaincy," 92.

107. Ibid., 100.

108. Wendy Cadge and Emily Sigalow, "Negotiating Religious Differences: The Strategies of Interfaith Chaplains in Healthcare," *Journal for the Scientific Study of Religion* 52, no. 1 (2013): 146–58.

109. Harold G. Koenig, "Religion, Spirituality, and Medicine: Research Findings and Implications for Clinical Practice," *Southern Medical Journal* 97, no. 12 (December 2004): 1194–1200.

110. Stanley Hauerwas, *God, Medicine and Suffering* (Grand Rapids, MI: Eerdmans, 1994).

dying child asked by the moderator: "How do you answer a parent who says, 'Why did my child become ill'? Must we turn to God or religion to overcome hopelessness?" Hauerwas answered, "Human agony is real. The worst thing you can do about the death of a child is give an explanation. The best thing you can do is be a presence. Encourage them to curse God— God can take it. The Psalms are filled with agonizing cries." Koenig responded, "A physician needs to take them to a quiet place and find out from cues what kind of information they want. If they want medical information, they should provide it. If the question is 'why?' then many times they are not looking for an answer. We are trained to give answers, but sometimes you have to just listen."[111] Pressed by Hauerwas to acknowledge that medicine does not have all of the answers and indeed that death is not avoidable, Koenig, too, turns to advocating the need for a listening presence.

The two were also asked about the effect of spirituality on health outcomes. In other words, does religion work? Koenig responded that "there is no doubt that frequency of religious attendance is a powerful correlate to health outcomes. This doesn't mean the deeply religious don't get sick. Often they aren't spiritual until they get sick." Hauerwas said, "For people with serious religious convictions, the outcomes may be as much negative as positive. Not all religious people have a positive worldview. Read Luther—we are an apocalyptic people."

Chapels

Chaplains, historically, were attached to a chapel, or *cappella* in Latin. Chapels denominated many different worship spaces in the medieval and early modern eras, but usually they were specialized worship spaces other than parish churches. Victorian hospitals and prisons, for example, had actual separate chapel buildings in their courtyards. Many still do. Today, while some lack dedicated spaces altogether, many of the institutions in which chaplains work have chapels—or, rather, spaces that have evolved over the centuries from highly particularized articulations of specific religious traditions to multipurpose rooms, some with revolving altars—places designed for a generalized spirituality.

Swift describes the newer chapels of English hospitals: "The space allocated for spiritual expression has been transformed from the task of promoting a particular religious story to a new role in permitting and embracing

---

111. Harold G. Koenig, "Does God Wear a White Coat?," *Inside Duke University Medical Center Employee Newsletter* 13, no. 20 (October 11, 2004).

an assortment of spiritual and religious expressions. Whereas the former provided cues and platforms for the place of the chaplain the latter offers no such privileges. . . . While truth was once both beyond and mediated by the presence of the chaplain it has now become immanent, personal and direct."[112] Today, increasingly, "The design does not tell a story except, perhaps, that it has become impossible to tell a single public religious story in the twenty-first century."[113]

Two architects at the University of Manchester, Ralph Brand and Andrew Crompton, have completed a comprehensive survey of multifaith spaces in the United Kingdom. Among the conclusions posted on the website displaying their photos is the following claim: "We would suggest that [multifaith spaces] exist on the boundary between religious requirement and secular accommodation, and because of this tension they should be viewed as *agents* in the active (re)configuration of public space, in addition to *symptoms* of wider social change."[114] Like chaplains, the religion these spaces enable both changes and is being changed by them.

The Cadet Chapel at the Air Force Academy in Colorado Springs, completed in 1963, illustrates both the range and limits of current possibilities as well as the transition of which Brand and Crompton speak, reflecting a mid-century pluralist sensibility giving way to that of an emerging universality:

> The Cadet Chapel was designed specifically to house three distinct worship areas under a single roof. The Protestant nave is located on the upper level, while the Catholic and Jewish chapels and a Buddhist room are located beneath it. Beneath this level is a larger room used for Islamic services and two meeting rooms. Each chapel has its own entrance, and services may be held simultaneously without interfering with one another. The All-Faiths Rooms are worship areas for smaller religious groups. They are purposely devoid of religious symbolism so that they may be used by a variety of faiths. Distinguishing faith-specific accoutrements are available for each group to use during their worship services.[115]

112. Swift, *Hospital Chaplaincy*, 4.

113. Ibid., 165; see also Cadge, *Paging God*, 51ff., and Sophie Gilliat-Ray, "The Use of 'Sacred' Space in Public Institutions: A Case Study of Worship Facilities at the Millennium Dome," *Culture and Religion* 6 (2005): 281–302.

114. An overview of Brand and Crompton's project and their findings, as well as hundreds of photos of multifaith spaces can be found at http://www.sed.manchester.ac.uk/architecture/research/mfs/ (accessed January 31, 2013).

115. US Air Force Academy website, http://www.usafa.af.mil/information/visitors/cadet chapel.asp (accessed January 31, 2013). Interestingly, this multipurpose space resembles those

Like the chaplain herself, the space of the chapel today in public and quasi-public institutions is increasingly unmarked by particularized religious identity. It is designed for everyone.

Chaplains Today

Chaplains have become today in the United States a remarkably versatile and flexible profession, eager to attend to the spiritual needs of all persons wherever they may find themselves. There is a specialized chaplaincy that serves the oil and gas industry, supplying chaplains for oil rigs.[116] The National Park Service has a chaplaincy.[117]

In 2009, the state of Indiana appointed a chaplain, Michael L. Latham, to its Department of Family and Social Services, partly in response to the privatization of social services. A joint interview with the Indiana chaplain and a spokesperson for the state published on the Pew Foundation website displays the continuities with other, more traditional chaplaincies while at the same time showing the newer context for this work. Reverend Latham, who also served on the Faith-Based Advisory Committee for the state of Indiana, explained enthusiastically what he saw his job as chaplain to be: "I thought it would be exciting to do ministry with the state. . . . The focus on *faith,* to me, is very important, because everybody in the state is not Christian. They have different faiths." "Faith" is for him and for many others a universalizing category enabling a universal ministry:

> We try to help our employees by bringing in other faith leaders to explain to
> employees the history of that faith. We had an Indian chief come in, we had
> a Muslim come in. We try really hard to get people to understand that just
> because I'm a Baptist minister, it does not mean that if you're a Muslim or if
> you're a Jewish person, that I can't assist you.[118]

---

of early modern Europe, as described by Benjamin Kaplan. He describes the many ways in which Protestants and Catholics shared spaces to serve a religiously diverse population. Benjamin J. Kaplan, *Divided by Faith: Religious Conflict and the Practice of Toleration in Early Modern Europe* (Cambridge, MA: Harvard University Press, 2007).

116. The UK Oil and Gas Chaplaincy, http://www.ukoilandgaschaplaincy.com/ (accessed January 31, 2013).

117. Charles Hillinger, "Ministry Reaches the Great Outdoors: Chaplains: Student Ministers Preach at National Parks in Spare Time, Offering Religious Services for Tourists," *Los Angeles Times,* February 1, 1992, http://articles.latimes.com/1992-02-01/entertainment/ca-1114_1_national-park-service (accessed January 31, 2013).

118. Pew Roundtable. Indiana has been particularly active as a state in promoting the new

Latham saw it to be his job to minister to employees distraught by the privatizing of social services: "Most of them that we talk to—and it's been probably in every office that we've been to—those kinds of conversations would
come up, because the state was going to do some privatizing. Employees
were so upset." The state had caused trauma to people because of privatization. Reverend Latham saw it as his job to assist everybody, Baptists, Muslims, Jews, and Indian chiefs.

The state spokesperson explained that what the state had in mind when
it hired Reverend Latham was "acknowledging that there was a dimension
of [employees'] personality in many cases that drove them to the positions
in social services. . . . So, just as our employee assistance program would
serve in sort of a secular sense some of the emotional and psychological
dimensions of people, so likewise the chaplain's program could serve that
spiritual dimension." State social service administration, like soldiering, being imprisoned, being sick, being a park ranger, has a spiritual dimension.
People have a spiritual dimension. The implication was that the state of
Indiana has an obligation to acknowledge that. FFRF filed a lawsuit challenging Reverend Latham's appointment, a case that became moot when
the Indiana social services chaplaincy program was subsequently ended, but
the state and other commentators insisted in their response to the suit that
such programs are not necessarily unconstitutional under current law.[119]

Chaplains are struggling to meet the demands of a complex religious
terrain.[120] Some are trying to professionalize by defining their tasks more
clearly, setting standards for certification, developing explicit ethical codes,
and developing research-based metrics as to what quality professional work
entails.[121] Others would resist the trend toward biomedical and behavioral
models of human flourishing that are implied by this kind of routinization
in favor of a more loosely defined spiritual field. While perhaps the tension is most acute in the military, ambiguous moral tensions exist for all
chaplains, as well as a tension caused by the strain perhaps of their newly
ambiguous religious identity.

accommodation of faith. In 2003 governor Mitch Daniels created FaithWorks (now called the
Office of Faith-Based and Community Initiatives) to implement the new faith-based initiative
authorized by Charitable Choice. http://www.in.gov/ofbci/ (accessed January 31, 2013).

119. Neela Banerjee, "Indiana, Faced with Suit, Takes Chaplain Off Payroll," *New York
Times*, September 28, 2007.

120. Swift, *Hospital Chaplaincy*, 63.

121. A set of essays considering these questions is published in "Can We Measure Good
Chaplaincy? A New Professional Identity Is Tied to Quality Improvement," *Hastings Center Report* 38 no. 6 (2008).

One chaplain who served in Iraq commented that "the ability to listen includes the willingness to accept people where they are in their own understanding of life and faith, not where the chaplain would like them to be. As a chaplain, I must realize that no matter how firm I feel about my own approach to God, I cannot have the last word for anyone else. This concept of pluralism is perhaps the most significant change in the chaplaincy from earlier times."[122] He described the demographic shifts that had led to this new approach: "In the Second World War, chaplains in the United States military included Roman Catholic priests, a very few rabbis, and ministers from six major Protestant denominations. By 1994, my last year in the navy, there were more than 150 faith groups providing chaplains to the military. Ten years later there are even more." As with other chaplaincies, "One of the major concerns for the chaplaincy in the US military is that individual interpretations of spirituality and conscience have become a substitute for creedal confession and denominational guidance."

Away from the safer, doctrinally defined spaces of their particular religious identities, chaplains must often improvise—inventing liturgies and pushing the boundaries of their theologies to accommodate the remarkably diverse clientele before them. Hospital chaplains are asked to baptize dead babies of unclear religious identity.[123] Military chaplains are asked to anoint the bodies of dead soldiers whose religious affiliation is unknown. Chaplains are both heroes and villains. They seem to be almost single-handedly trying to hold together the divine and the mortal, the sacred and the secular . . . and sometimes the apocalyptic. In a grim reflection on the moral challenges of military chaplaincy, some have quipped that the really successful military chaplains are all dead. They sacrificed themselves for God and country.[124] The living chaplains, this view implies, are the ones who sold out to defend the war—or whatever secular cause they serve. Wendy Cadge reports that hospital chaplains are often asked

---

122. Joseph F. O'Donnell, "Clergy in the Military, Vietnam and After: One Chaplain's Reflections," in *The Sword of the Lord: Military Chaplains from the First to the Twenty-First Century*, ed. Doris L. Bergen (Notre Dame, IN: Notre Dame University Press, 2008). The first Jewish rabbi in the Marine Corps, Rabbi Gittleson, delivered the eulogy at Iwo Jima. His well-known and often-quoted sermon, widely available on the web, reflects a midcentury irenicism about religious difference among Americans and the religion of the American way of life described in Will Herberg, *Protestant, Catholic, Jew: An Essay in American Religious Sociology* (Garden City, NY: Doubleday, 1955). On pluralist thinking in the United States, see also Courtney Bender, "The Power of Pluralist Thinking."

123. Cadge, *Paging God*, 176.; also Swift, *Hospital Chaplaincy*, 111–13.

124. Four hundred seventy-eight chaplains died in World War II (Hansen, *Military Chaplains and Religious Diversity*, 16).

to deal with death, what is termed the "dirty work" of hospitals, where the miracle cures of modern medicine have failed: "Hospital staff . . . often described dealing with death—with dead bodies, literal blood and odors, and the grief of families—as 'dirty' or low status work . . . [chaplain staff] described doctors quickly delegating families to nurses and chaplains after they tell them about a loved one's impending death, leaving it to them to handle families' emotions and any other 'dirty' work."[125]

Chaplains have a very specific history in the churches of the Latin West (the Roman Catholic Church and the protestant churches and their successors that emerged from the Reformations of the sixteenth and seventeenth centuries), one that has been adapted to serve the US context. In the last few decades, however, the pressure to accommodate all religions and all individual perspectives on all religions in a range of secular settings has stretched that historical legacy in many ways. Chaplaincy today is both recognizably connected to the older history and totally transformed by recent legal and religious changes.[126] Today, perhaps always, the attraction of chaplain jobs is partly a steady income, benefits, and a ready-made congregation, away from church politics and the humdrum dailyness of parish ministry, but it is also the exhilarating challenge of rising to the occasion of the complexity of the spiritual field today.[127] The secular institutions and their inhabitants seem to recognize that you are needed even if your traditional congregants do not. You also do not have to be an entrepreneur, and you do not have to commit to a lifetime of relationships.

Just as the chaplain is the indispensable person, spirituality is the indispensable faculty. There has been much helpful recent writing about the invention of spirituality as a mode of American religiosity as well as a more precise articulation of the relationship of an emergent American interest in spirituality in the nineteenth century with capitalism, but most of these accounts fail to consider how much church-state work this new spirituality

---

125. Cadge, *Paging God*, 256.

126. A recent edited volume canvassing the military chaplaincy from the first to twenty-first century displays both the continuities and the discontinuities. Doris L. Bergen, ed., *The Sword of the Lord: Military Chaplains from the First to the Twenty-First Century* (Notre Dame, IN: Notre Dame University Press, 2008).

127. Over the course of the twentieth century there was a well-documented decline in the United States in the status of clergy as well as increased competition from other professions. Holifield, *God's Ambassadors*, 267, 346–47. Swift discusses opportunities for employment in nineteenth-century England. Swift, *Hospital Chaplaincy*, 36. According to Swift, in the United Kingdom, chaplains in the military, in prisons, and in hospitals make up more than 10 percent of the employed clergy today. See also, Rivers, *The Law of Organized Religions*, 207n1.

has done and continues to do.[128] John Lardas Modern, for example, describes the invention of a particular style of American spirituality as "true religion" in the first half of the nineteenth century:

> This making of spirituality occurred within ostensibly religious venues such as Unitarianism as well as ostensibly secular ones like penny presses and etiquette books . . . spirituality was simultaneously a mode of haunting and a means of disenchantment . . . the concept of spirituality was integral to the imagination and maintenance of a subject who was wholly rational, truly religious, who felt at home in an uncanny world.[129]

Modern concludes that "as numerous studies and surveys now attest, spirituality has become the dominant tradition within recent American religious history, a way for individuals to signal their authentic mode of piety within, against, or alongside religious institutions."[130]

Modern insists that spirituality in this American mode is a fundamentally secular invention—by which he seems to mean that it finds its motivation in secular preoccupations. He even points to the moment of invention, the day that spirituality was introduced into the phrenological map to supplement "veneration" as the cranial location for religion:

> Before the embrace of mesmeric technics, Fowlers and Wells had most closely aligned "true religion" with Veneration. But as animal magnetism was establishing "the spiritual, immaterial existence of mind in a state separate from matter," the publications of Fowlers and Wells introduced the organ of Spirituality—the active and engaged faculty of religion that infused the element of agentive consent into Veneration's apparent *habitus* of submission.[131]

One might think of the chaplain today as the religious specialist detailed to spirituality and spirituality as true religion in this sense.

As with the phrenological map, spirituality also solves a problem for US law, supplying a necessary missing piece in the logical puzzle of the First Amendment. Importantly, American law comes into its own during the very

---

128. See, e.g., Schmidt, *Restless Souls*, and Modern, *Secularism in Antebellum America*.
129. Modern, *Secularism in Antebellum America*, 123.
130. Ibid.
131. Ibid., 165.

same period of which Modern writes.[132] Spirituality and American law, from the time of their emergence in the nineteenth century, both arguably finesse the line between submission and freedom, in their service to the enabling of American commercial interests. By defining what they do as "spiritual" care, rather than as religion, chaplains also finesse the separation versus establishment problem. If spirituality is universal, then it is not divisive the way religious affiliation and association is and so it's sponsorship and regulation arguably do not raise the same problems for public order as does the favoring of a particular religious community by the state.

A recent advertisement for chaplaincy positions outlines the job: "Chaplains and Chaplain Assistants must be multi-skilled, spiritually fit, agile, adaptive, innovative, self-aware, and mission-focused Spiritual Leaders. The Chaplaincy is focused on resetting the spiritual dimension of the Soldier, ensuring their present and future spiritual fitness and resilience."[133] How qualified professionals are prepared for this complex job of ministering to a universal human need, providing the religious services of particular religious communities, upholding the needs of the nation, and persuading people to conform to in an ambiguously designated secular and sacred world is the subject of the next chapter.

132. Melville, the central figure of Modern's book, was intensely interested in the kind of capitalism that was emerging in America and the law that enabled it. Alfred S. Konefsky, "The Accidental Legal Historian: Herman Melville and the History of American Law."

133. US Army Chaplain Corps, "The Army Chaplaincy Strategic Plan 2009–2014," http://www.apd.army.mil/jw2/xmldemo/r165_1/main.asp (accessed July 10, 2013).

THREE

Credentialing Chaplains

The chaplain in his first appearance in Europe was a figure of imperial Christianity and then, later, of the national churches. Pre-Constantinian Christian communities did not need chaplains. It was in the wars of the eighth and ninth centuries that military chaplains, posted away from their home churches and, therefore, necessarily holding multiple offices, began to be regulated by canon law to ensure both that they performed their duties—to church and to state—and to ensure that those to whom they ministered were properly served. Employment for chaplains increased as the cooperation and rivalry between church and state increased in medieval and early modern Europe. The established and highly regulated history of chaplains in England, and their institutionalization in a national church, as well as parallel forms in other European churches, might suggest their anomalous presence today in the United States and Europe. Yet chaplains continue to be indispensable to the modern state, even one as low church in ecclesiology as the United States. Indeed, the legal regulation of chaplains in the United States continues to reflect both their indispensable role as well as some of the same public concerns about their multiple obligations and lines of authority as concerned earlier regulators and reformers.

Martin Luther as well as Catholic reformers were critical of the abuses of what was called clerical simony and pluralism, the practice of clergy holding multiple offices in addition to their parochial duties, practices that were said to result in absenteeism, corruption, and neglect of duties; yet chaplains continued to be necessary even after the breakup of the Roman monopoly. More stringent regulation of church offices was instituted. Each of the post-Reformation churches and state establishments developed its own rules and practices with respect to the role of clergy, both parochial clergy and those who served specific purposes. In 1530, Henry VIII, for example, made specific legal provision for the granting of dispensations for the holding of multiple benefices for those who served as domestic chaplains in aristocratic households. Further English legislation to define and regulate church offices came after war, restoration, and revolution.[1]

With the establishment of the Church of England in the sixteenth and seventeenth centuries, chaplains developed a newly specialized position in and for the English church in particular. As Christopher Swift explains in his history of hospital chaplaincy in England, the Tudor reorganization of the royal hospitals shifted the purpose of the hospital from a medieval focus on salvation in the next life through a priority given to soul over body to a new focus on care of the destitute as workers for the state: "The preoccupation of the new hospitals is with government. It is a word that is constantly reproduced in the statutes, prayers and information books about the re-founded institutions. Emerging so strongly in the sixteenth century, it models the hospitals on the central principle of governing people and behavior according to the united sovereignty of God and King."[2] The role of the chaplain—and of the patient—changed in this period: "The patient [now] receives the chaplain as part of the new religion of the state, in which sovereignty unites temporal and spiritual power. The chaplain is charged with making the patient compliant to authority, a willing worker who contributes to the commonwealth. The surgeons are also expected to share in the task of ensuring the patient's moral improvement."[3] Swift traces the public role of the hospital chaplain through to the workhouses of Victorian England and the postwar establishment of National Health Care and its reform by New Labour.

Although more dispersed through the various legal and religious jurisdictions in the United States, one can see traces of this emerging focus on moral governance in the regulation of chaplains in the United States, most explicitly in the histories of military and prison chaplaincies, but also with their migration into other secular institutions. The formal interface between church and state in the United States today with respect to the hiring and regulation of government chaplains is provided by the endorsing organi-

---

1. Until recently, though, Church of England chaplains were still understood to be office-holders rather than employees, holding their positions as forms of private property. Church of England clergy held their offices as freeholds until 2005. Rivers, *The Law of Organized Religions*, 110; Swift, *Hospital Chaplaincy*, 2. Household chaplains declined in England in the eighteenth century as public common religious worship in parish churches was normalized for everyone. Gibson, *A Social History of the Domestic Chaplain*, 16–23.

2. Swift, *Hospital Chaplaincy*, 25.

3. Ibid., 27.

zations. Each endorsing body, that is, those religious organizations that warrant a chaplain's religious or doctrinal orthodoxy to the government, is the product of distinct institutional histories, many of them imported from elsewhere and transformed in the United States; each, that is, has its own legal culture. But other institutions, educational institutions as well as private and public regulatory bodies, also serve to define and regularize professionalism and orthodoxy in the provision of services. Secular employers of chaplains in the United States, private and public, select chaplains based on a combination of secular and religious criteria vetted by various proxies and subject to US employment law, state and federal. Those criteria are becoming increasingly uniform.

Although in many ways assimilated to the Protestant model of relying on endorsing church bodies, a somewhat different model of church administration of chaplaincy continues to be reflected in the distinctive regulation of Roman Catholic military chaplains in the United States (at least those who are priests), echoing an earlier ecclesiology, and to the US government's historic accommodation of that difference. (Although the difference is becoming more attenuated as the Catholic Church is Americanized, laicized, and protestantized.) This arrangement provides a glimpse of an earlier model of chaplaincy.

The special purpose Roman Catholic Archdiocese for the Military Services provides the Roman Catholic Church's pastoral and spiritual services to those serving in the US armed forces or other federal services overseas. This military ordinariate is a special diocese that was canonically erected in 1939 by Pope Pius XII. Each of its priests remains incardinated in his home diocese or religious order. The special purpose archdiocese has no territorial boundaries or "seat." Rather, the archdiocese has jurisdiction wherever American men and women in uniform serve, including all US government property in the United States and abroad, US military installations, embassies, consulates, and other diplomatic missions.[4] As for Catholic chaplains in other US institutions, such as hospitals and prisons, priest chaplains are usually subject to the authority of the local bishop, while male members of religious orders, as well as nuns and other lay Catholic chaplains, have historically had a more tangential relationship to the local Catholic hierarchy. Both in the military and in other US institutions, the ecclesiological difference between Protestants and Catholics has often been recognized and honored by government, notwithstanding the constitutional, social,

---

4. Archdiocese for the Military Services, USA, http://www.milarch.org (accessed January 8, 2012).

and cultural anomaly of American government officials deferring to Roman Catholic internal church orthodoxy and discipline.

Hiring a Chaplain

Although the religion that is practiced by government chaplains in the United States has been shaped by two centuries of both official and unofficial understandings of the Constitution and other social and cultural forces, it is principally today through credentialing that the religious dimensions of government and nongovernment chaplaincies are directly regulated across the various agencies and institutions in which they serve. The three credentials most often required for employment as a chaplain today are the MDiv degree (or, sometimes, its "equivalent"), CPE credits, and an ecclesiastical endorsement.

Excerpts from a recent online announcement of an opening for VA chaplains listed on the federal jobs website illustrates the extent of government regulation of these positions and their integration into a government project.[5] The announcement for the position of VA chaplain proclaims that the purpose of the chaplain is "to fulfill President Lincoln's promise—'To care for him who shall have borne the battle, and for his widow, and his orphan'—by serving and honoring the men and women who are America's Veterans," and asks, "How would you like to become a part of a team providing compassionate care to Veterans?" Formal qualifications for the position are proficiency in English, successful vetting by way of a background check, CPE credits, an ecclesiastical endorsement, and an MDiv degree from an accredited institution. Applicants are asked to note that "education must be accredited by an accrediting institution recognized by the U.S. Department of Education in order for it to be credited towards qualifications."

If hired, the duties will be many and challenging, what the VA calls "a complete religious ministry," illustrating once again a distinctive public understanding about what counts as religion in the United States in the twenty-first century and the mixed and sometimes conflicting expectations for those who do this work, insisting at once on the patient's right to choose while being attuned to the needs of the hospital:

> The chaplain has full responsibility for providing a complete religious ministry to veteran patients. Such ministry will encompass individual pastoral ministry. The chaplain will address religious, spiritual, moral and ethical

5. http://www.usajobs.gov/GetJob/ViewDetails/2388140 (accessed February 9, 2013).

problems of patients, and will provide appropriate ministration to the newly-admitted, pre and post-operative patients, the critically ill and the families concerned. The Chaplain also provides counsel and pastoral support to relatives of patients in difficult and trying situations to alleviate their anxieties, to win effective cooperation of these relatives with the treatment regimen of the medical center, and to help them deal with grief. The chaplain provides patients and personnel with guidance in the selection of religious literature and other resources to illumine and interpret the problems of person in difficulty. The chaplain responds to emergencies or crisis when pastoral care is appropriate. As appropriate within a therapeutic milieu, each VA chaplain is responsible for assuring that the right of each and every patient's free exercise of religion is upheld; and that patients are protected from proselytizing by staff, other patients, or visitors, regardless of faith group.

The chaplain must communicate effectively with persons of diverse races, cultures, religions, nationalities, ages, and persons having varying types and degrees of disability, in order to understand and address their specific needs.

Work Schedule: Intermittent. Scheduled as needed including weekend, evening, holiday and on-call.[6]

It is a daunting assignment. The chaplain "address[es] religious, spiritual, moral and ethical problems of patients . . . provides counsel and pastoral support to relatives of patients in difficult and trying situations to alleviate their anxieties, to win effective cooperation of these relatives with the treatment regimen of the medical center, and to help them deal with grief . . . provides patients and personnel with guidance in the selection of religious literature and other resources to illumine and interpret the problems of person in difficulty . . . and responds to emergencies." The announcement also reflects the extensive regulatory framework within which government chaplains now work, emphasizing the constitutional limitations on the work flowing from a legal anthropology that imagines religion to be freely chosen by the individual: "each VA chaplain is responsible for assuring that the right of each and every patient's free exercise of religion is upheld; and that patients are protected from proselytizing by staff, other patients, or visitors, regardless of faith group." Each credential provides an opportunity for the standardization of what qualifies as legitimate religious work.[7]

6. Ibid.

7. The published federal Bureau of Prisons' policy with respect to hiring is somewhat different from the army arrangement, as the following announcement makes clear: "The BOP does not advertise for chaplaincy positions by specific faith groups. Instead, BOP chaplain vacancies are announced continuously on the BOP website, the U.S. Office of Personnel Management

The job advertisement also extols the perks associated with being a VA chaplain:

> Every job at the VA impacts the Veterans that we serve. You can be part of that team, helping to make sure that our Veterans receive the top-quality care they deserve. VA professionals feel good about their careers and their ability to balance work and home life. VA offers generous paid time off and a variety of predictable and flexible scheduling opportunities.[8]

Historically, the professional identity of a chaplain in the United States was linked to his religious community. His training and supervision, as well as his authority to represent the community, was granted by the religious organization. Furthermore, the overwhelming majority of chaplains were supplied by Protestant and Catholic churches or by Jewish seminaries. Over the last half of the twentieth century, however, chaplaincy in the United States became more and more distinct as a professional identity, one that has developed its own professional skills and commitments, skills and commitments that are becoming abstracted from particular religious communities. If you are a young person in the United States today who is contemplating a career as a chaplain, it is increasingly likely that you will consider the path to such work to be through the acquisition of appropriate degrees and internships, parallel to those in other careers or fields you are considering, degrees and internships that may be independent of ordination and of your own religious community's tradition of religious specialization and leadership. Other religious or quasi-religious professions, such as alternative medical professionals, are also seeing a greater focus on credentialing and licensing, partly because of pressure from insurers.

All three of the typical credentials required for employment as a chaplain have their origins in Protestant institutions and have historically in the United States been controlled by mainstream Protestant churches. The content and style of the training that they represent also imply theological positions and practices that are deeply mainstream Protestant in structure and orientation. But all three have broadened considerably. They have been embraced by evangelical and Pentecostal Protestants across the spectrum

---

(OPM) website, and websites such as http://www.usajobs.com. The BOP also advertises chaplaincy vacancies with religious organizations and recruits at job fairs, theology speaking engagements, and conferences. Some chaplain candidates have applied to work for the BOP after serving as contractors in the institutions." "A Review of the Bureau of Prisons' Selection of Muslim Religious Services Providers."

8. http://www.usajobs.gov/GetJob/ViewDetails/2388140 (accessed February 9, 2013).

and by non-Protestants; the degrees in turn have adapted themselves to the religious diversity of the United States, the populist and egalitarian ethos of credentialing generally, and to the new "naturalization" of religion. All three are being shaped by cooperation between government agents (including law enforcement and the security services) as well as by private religious bodies—cooperation aimed at the standardization and professionalization of the services provided.[9] This chapter will consider government regulation of the work that chaplains do through the monitoring of the content and quality of these three credentials.

Chaplaincies today are staffed by full-time, part-time, and volunteer chaplains from a range of religious backgrounds. Chaplains from many different "faith" traditions are being trained to deliver pastoral care to all comers working with the assumption that such care is universally needed and can be delivered in a manner that does not depend on shared religious commitments among chaplains in a particular chaplaincy or between chaplain and client. The work is understood to serve a universal human need and right, the secular goals of the particular institutions in which they work, as well as a larger national mission, secular goals that are not understood to be at odds with particular religious goals. As the VA advertisement implies, if you do this work, you will be "fulfilling Abraham Lincoln's promise."

Updating and regulating these credentials provides occasions for the definition and shaping of religious phenomena. Recurrent phrases and traces of Christian theology and church history, constitutional litigation, popular spirituality, the languages of popular sociology and behavioral psychology, and the political language of equality and rights can all be found in the language of these regulatory bureaucracies, both legal and religious, and their texts. Many regulators emphasize an embracing inclusiveness, expressed as "faith," "spirituality," "holistic health," "wellness," "care," "pluralistic," and "multicultural," "nonsectarian," "nondenominational," or "nondiscriminatory." Yet, at the same time, the people and programs that implement this care are expected to be educated, licensed, certified, and ordained for such service, often by at least formally denominated sectarian bodies. And they are expected to serve the mission of their employers by facilitating their work, whether it is medical treatment, waging war, law enforcement, higher

9. Government interest in regulating chaplaincies increased after 9/11. See, e.g., *Hearing before the Subcommittee on Terrorism, Technology and Homeland Security of the Committee on the Judiciary*, 108th Cong. 43–49 (2003) (statement of Hon. Charles S. Abell, Principal Deputy Under Secretary for Personnel and Readiness, Department of Defense, Washington, DC).

education, punishment and rehabilitation, or making widgets. The state's interests in both control and protection of its citizens, as well as the advancement of government policy, are evident throughout. But one can also see the attraction for the person called to ministry. He or she has an opportunity to work at a place of intersection—or exception—riffing on and responding to the multiple themes of contemporary life in the context of the acute spiritual care of suffering individuals from all walks of life. She has an opportunity to argue for and celebrate the significance and importance of spirituality and religious community in the life of every individual.

Employment Law

All workers in the United States, including chaplains, are subject to a myriad of individual and collective labor and employment laws, including those regulating minimum wage, child labor, fair bargaining, antidiscrimination, safety, tax, and so on, laws promulgated at every level of government. Private, often discriminatory, standard setting as well as customary practices in various businesses and professions, also regulate who can work where, when, and for how much. It is very difficult, although not impossible, to work entirely off the public-private regulatory grid in the United States.

Certain occupations in the United States require a formal state license and specific credentials before it is legal to practice them at all—barbers and hairdressers, debt collectors, health-care workers, lawyers, embalmers, engineers, architects, pest-control technicians, and so on. The state is understood in these areas to have a particular interest in protecting the public from incompetent and unscrupulous workers. And that interest often coincides with the interest of workers in limiting access to their guilds. State licensing boards made up in large part of members of these professions oversee the setting of standards and the granting and withdrawing of licenses. Free market advocates criticize these regulatory efforts as being unduly restrictive of property rights, occupational freedom, consumer choice, and innovation; they argue that reliance on the free market in information about the quality of services and of workplaces is fairer to workers and a more efficient way of producing better services.[10] Furthermore, studies show that licensing regimes frequently result in increased discrimination against minority workers, ex-felons, and persons with various disabilities.

10. S. David Young, *The Rule of Experts: Occupational Licensing in America* (Washington, DC: Cato Institute, 1987). Milton Friedman, *Capitalism and Freedom* (Chicago: University of Chicago Press, 1962).

Religious professionals in the United States are not formally licensed by the state as they were historically in many countries and, in many countries, still are, for the same reasons as those asserted with respect to other regulated professions. American ministers and other religious specialists are not. They are licensed to preach by their religious communities, or they are self-appointed. But there are vestiges of the alternative model in the licensing of ministers to perform weddings and in the special tax privileges and exemptions from employment law that clergy and religious bodies enjoy—as well as in the regulation of government chaplains. Ministers must be licensed to perform weddings in most US states—licensed by their religious body and by the state—and marriages are legally (and often sacramentally) effective through the occasion of a joint church-state performative utterance. The minister at the wedding announces prior to the declaration of marriage that he speaks "by the authority vested in me by the state of x." (In most states now, weddings can also be performed by others, such as judges and other government officials; sometimes, as in Massachusetts, by specially deputized civilians.) And ministers hired by the government must meet minimum government-set qualifications for employment.

The Supreme Court, as well as various legislative bodies and agencies, federal, state, and local, have carved out exceptions for religious organizations in the regulation of employment, as, for example, from collective bargaining and the antidiscrimination provisions of the civil rights laws with respect to the hiring and firing of ministers. These vestiges of ecclesiastical immunity in employment and tax laws are arguably constitutionally suspect, granting religious organizations the power to violate standards mandated for all other employers, but they have rarely been successfully challenged.[11] In January 2012, the US Supreme Court denied a constitutional challenge to the judicially created ministerial exception by a schoolteacher who was terminated by a Lutheran day school.[12] The teacher alleged, and the Equal Employment Opportunity Commission (EEOC) found, that her dismissal was retaliatory and illegal under the Americans with Disabilities Act. The church answered that the court lacked jurisdiction under the ministerial exception, and further that the teacher had failed to seek recourse through the church's legal system and was therefore subject to dismissal under church discipline. The Court held that a ministerial exception to the ADA was constitutionally

11. See, e.g., NLRB v. Catholic Bishop of Chicago, 440 U.S. 490 (1979), granting an exemption from National Labor Relations Board regulation concerning collective bargaining for Catholic schools.

12. Hosanna Tabor Evangelical Lutheran Church and School v. EEOC, 132 S. Ct. 694 (2012).

mandated, although not jurisdictional, through a joint application of the two religion clauses and a reading of the prehistory of those clauses. The Court held that the church is entirely free to choose its own ministers and to define who is a minister, independent of state law. Whether the ministerial exception applies to discrimination in the hiring and firing of government chaplains in the United States has not been litigated. The courts do, however, retain the jurisdiction to administer the exception, examining the good faith and applicability of the exception in particular cases.[13]

A more indirect form of government regulation of religious work, perhaps, than state licensing boards and judicial exemptions, the state also regulates credentialing bodies. Many US jobs require the attainment of levels of educational achievement or other certificates of training and bona fides. For a variety of reasons, including studies purporting to show the better preparation of college graduates for employment and commitments to equal opportunity, but also to protect students and workers from fraud by diploma mills, formal credentials, credentials approved by government regulatory bodies, are increasingly demanded as a condition of employment throughout the American economy. Salary raises, particularly for public employees, are increasingly pegged to the acquisition of formal credentials. Malpractice and liability insurance policies also require certain kinds of credentials for covered employees for the protection of consumers.

Increased demand for licensed spiritual specialists is leading to increased supply. In addition to an increase in the availability of specialized chaplaincy degrees at established seminaries and universities, dubious quickie degrees and certification programs are proliferating across the labor market.[14] Credentialism, as it is sometimes called, is arguably resulting in discrimination against workers who are qualified but who lack the resources or opportunity to acquire such credentials, which may or may not actually be required to ensure appropriate job performance. The proliferation of degrees is also standardizing, and perhaps cheapening, the product. Legislative hearings investigating online degrees and degree mills have been held at the state and federal levels.

---

13. Justice Thomas, in dissent in *Hosanna-Tabor*, argued that the ministerial exception did deprive the courts of jurisdiction over such internal church matters. 132 S. Ct. at 710–11.

14. Creola Johnson, "Credentialism and the Proliferation of Fake Degrees: The Employer Pretends to Need a Degree; The Employee Pretends to Have One," *Hofstra Labor and Employment Law Journal* 23 (2006): 269–343; and "Degrees of Deception: Are Consumers and Employers Being Duped by Online Universities and Diploma Mills?," *Journal of College & University Law* 32 (2006): 411–90.

Let us consider each of the three credentials required for chaplaincy employment in turn.

The Master of Divinity Degree

The MDiv degree is the most common academic degree required for employment for ministers and other religious leaders today in the United States. A three-year postbaccalaureate professional degree, it corresponds to other terminal degrees that qualify students for professional, rather than academic work, such as the MBA, MFA, JD, MPP, and various degrees in the health fields. But the ascendancy of the MDiv as the defining degree for ministers is fairly recent. Authority to perform religious work in a religious community may be recognized in various ways by guardians and adherents of those traditions, but professional certification through an academic degree program does not seem a natural fit with the many communities which understand the qualities and training for religious leadership to be best recognized and nurtured according to their own standards of discernment and formation. For many, academic book learning is not necessarily required—or even desirable—beyond the basic literacy necessary for reading the Bible. Indeed, it is far from clear, except for the academically inclined and secularly oriented liberal Protestants who created the degree in the mid-twentieth century as a replacement for the previous bachelor of divinity, why other religious communities would themselves adopt such a credential apart from the requirements for government and secular employment and what might be called cultural mimesis.[15]

The MDiv degree, like other postsecondary academic and professional degrees in the United States, is regulated by state and federal governments in several ways.[16] Formal legal authority to grant postsecondary academic and professional degrees resides exclusively in state and federal governments and in Indian tribes; 98 percent of degree-granting institutions are licensed by state governments.[17] Legal authority to grant degrees is not the

15. Many churches and other religious bodies require would-be ministers to meet other requirements in addition before being ordained or licensed to preach, requirements beyond the academic demands of the program, including psychosexual evaluations.

16. Primary and secondary education in the United States is largely regulated at the state and local level, and local control of schooling is important to most Americans, although the state and federal governments are also increasingly involved in setting standards and defining curricula for elementary, middle, and high schools.

17. Most legal scholars agree that legal authority to grant degrees lies with the government, that is, that the granting of degrees is an inherently state function because the degree publicly certifies the holder as competent. Educational institutions must thus have formal power

same as accreditation of educational institutions. Degree-granting institutions, in order legally to award postsecondary degrees, must, under state law, be accredited in addition to having state authority to grant degrees. Accreditation attests to the meeting of educational and professional peer-reviewed quality standards. Individual states delegate accrediting power to private accrediting bodies, which are, in turn, legally "recognized" by the US Department of Education for federal loan purposes.[18]

Academic accrediting organizations are listed on the website of the US Department of Education, thereby providing an occasion for government endorsement of the orthodoxy and competence of the standards enforced by those organizations in their accrediting processes. The department website announces that "here you will find lists of regional and national accrediting agencies recognized by the U.S. Secretary of Education as reliable authorities concerning the quality of education or training offered by the institutions of higher education or higher education programs they accredit." The Association of Theological Schools, the leading accreditor of theological degrees, along with other religious accreditors including the Association for Biblical Higher Education, the Association for Clinical Pastoral Education, and the Association of Advanced Rabbinical and Talmudic Schools are listed as

granted to them by the state in order to award academic degrees. The leading national authority on the regulation of academic degrees is Alan L. Contreras. He summarizes the law in "The Legal Basis for Degree-Granting Authority in the United States" (2009) (unpublished manuscript, on file with State Higher Education Executive Officers), available at http://www.sheeo.org /resources/publications/legal-basis-degree-granting-authority-united-states (accessed February 4, 2013). Contreras concludes in this article that "the authorization of degree-granting entities is inherently a governmental function in the U.S., as it is in almost all nations. Although a state may decide not to authorize any degree-granting colleges, if it wants to allow any to exist, it has to make an affirmative written act to do that." See also George Gollin, Emily Lawrence, and Alan Contreras, "Complexities in Legislative Suppression of Diploma Mills," *Stanford Law & Policy Review* 21 (2010): 1–32.

18. The Database of Accredited Postsecondary Institutions and Programs of the Department of Education can be found on the department website, http://ope.ed.gov/accreditation/ (accessed July 6, 2013). Free market advocates challenge this tight regulation of higher education as well as the resulting limitation on consumer choice and academic freedom. See Judith Areen, "Accreditation Reconsidered," *Iowa Law Review* 96 (2011): 1471–94. Political concerns about government oversight of higher education have led to recent reorganization, as Areen notes: "Congress in 2008 prohibited the Department of Education from regulating the manner in which accrediting agencies assess student achievement. It also reorganized the body that recommends which accreditors the Department should recognize—the National Advisory Committee on Institutional Quality and Integrity [("NACIQI") http://ed.gov/about/bdscomm/list/naciqi .html (accessed July 6, 2013)]. Formerly, the Secretary of Education appointed all members of NACIQI. In a rather startling recognition of the politics of higher education today, one-third of its eighteen members are appointed by Congressional Democrats, one-third by Congressional Republicans, and only one-third by the Secretary." Ibid., 1484.

recognized accreditors under the overall professional educational category "Community and Social Services." These associations accredit schools that offer the MDiv degree, as well as other theological degrees. Theological education is thus the object of a form of public-private regulation that sets and polices the educational standards for professional ministry.

The MDiv is today increasingly offered in evangelical and Bible colleges, Catholic and Jewish seminaries, and in university divinity schools, as well as by the Protestant seminaries that originated the degree; in some programs, the MDiv degree may be pursued without a requirement that the candidate have a formal affiliation with any religious community. Buddhist seminaries are also offering the equivalent of the MDiv. The current Buddhist programs are at the Institute of Buddhist Studies (trying for accreditation and full inclusion in the Graduate Theological Union), Naropa (accredited in 1986), the University of the West (accredited in 2008), and Harvard Divinity School, where one can focus the MDiv in any of the nineteen areas of study offered (although there is still a required sequence on the history and traditions of Christianity for all students). Furthermore, persons from religious communities without a history of professional ministry at all, such as Mormons, are seeking an MDiv degree in order to qualify themselves for chaplaincy positions.

Naropa University, a "Buddhist-inspired" university in Boulder, Colorado, which describes itself as offering mission-based contemplative education, "informed by ancient Eastern educational philosophies," offers an MDiv with either a Tibetan Buddhist or a history of religions emphasis: "The Master of Divinity degree prepares students for professional work in the fields of pastoral care, chaplaincy, community development, and dharma teaching. This three-year program is firmly grounded in Buddhist philosophy and meditation practice while emphasizing an interreligious approach to individual and community care."[19] The MDiv degree has, in effect, become a professional degree oriented to secular employment without specific religious content or justification.

Locating the training of ministers in universities is relatively new for many religious communities in the United States. Even American Protestant Christians have long been divided as to the necessity of having an educated clergy.[20] In the United States, there has always been a substantial number, maybe at most times a majority, of American Christians who believe that

19. http://coursecatalog.naropa.edu/master-divinity (accessed February 9, 2013).

20. See E. Brooks Holifield, *God's Ambassadors: A History of the Christian Clergy in America* (Grand Rapids, MI: Eerdmans, 2007), 31–35.

pastoral leadership should be founded in a personal call from God and that the skills involved are not academic and professional but charismatic, oratorical, and pastoral, even shamanic. Belief in a priesthood of all believers leads many Protestants of all stripes to resist an overprofessionalization of the clergy and of pastoral care.[21] For many American Protestants, resistance to formal seminary education was founded in a profound reaction against Protestant denominations that seemed elitist and learned rather than being close to God and the people of God.[22] For Catholics, while both an undergraduate degree and a seminary education are usually required for priestly ordination today, the legal capacity for sacramental ministry depends fundamentally on consecration by a bishop, not on education or the acquisition of academic qualifications.

The oldest European universities were founded in the twelfth and thirteenth centuries with the study of Christian theology as their primary purpose, although most clergy then did not have university training. Formal university-based professional clerical education was first established in the sixteenth century. Indeed many colleges, seminaries, and universities in early modern Europe were founded for this very purpose—designed, it is said, to train clergy whose moral teaching and example would control an unruly populace in the emerging modern state.[23] Always, though, many Christians have also argued that all Christians are capable of reading the Bible in the vernacular without specialized training—and that the best preaching comes from the heart, with the guidance of the Spirit, whether clerical or lay, trained or untrained.

The development of the university in the United States in the second half of the nineteenth century, and its transformations in the twentieth century, is a complex story. How higher education in the United States became detached both formally and less formally from the Protestant Christian values and presuppositions of earlier times is also not simple or linear, as recent histories of the American universities have made clear, tied as these changes are to the rise of academic specialization and federal funding of research, among other factors.[24] A focus on education for citizenship of an increas-

21. Richard L. Hester, "Toward Professionalism or Voluntarism in Pastoral Care," *Pastoral Psychology* 24 (Summer 1976): 305–16.

22. Holifield, *God's Ambassadors*, 327–32.

23. Tomoko Masuzawa, "The University and the Advent of the Academic Secular: The State's Management of Public Instruction," in *After Secular Law*, ed. Winnifred Fallers Sullivan, Robert A. Yelle, and Mateo Taussig-Rubbo (Stanford, CA: Stanford University Press, 2011): 119–39.

24. See, e.g., John H. Roberts and James Turner, *The Sacred and Secular University* (Princeton, NJ: Princeton University Press, 2000).

ingly diverse public also played a role.[25] The twentieth century saw the creation of a hugely varied landscape of higher education in the United States, public and private, secular and sectarian, offering an astonishing range of models of higher education. It also saw a further specialization and instrumentalization of higher education. The landscape of ministerial education, if considered across the full spectrum of American religion, has also become more complex, occurring as it does today in a range of institutions: religiously affiliated colleges and universities, university divinity schools, free-standing denominational seminaries, and multireligious consortiums for the training of religious leaders, as well as smaller licensing and certificate programs. Religious studies programs have also influenced the development of a particular US public rhetoric about religion and its value.[26]

In the British colonies of North America before the American Revolution, the largest Protestant denominations were Presbyterians and Congregationalists, those who had founded the first American colleges in the seventeenth century, Harvard, Yale, and Princeton, and who continued such foundations through the eighteenth century. After the Revolution, Baptists and Methodists came to be the dominant Protestant denominations in the United States, emphasizing, as they did, the virtues of a part-time untutored ministry. These were the ministers initially responsible for evangelizing the west. Although many nineteenth-century colleges were founded by Protestant denominations and by Catholic religious orders, and periodic efforts were made to set higher standards for clerical education, Holifield estimates that the majority of American congregations have been and are still led by pastors without formal postsecondary seminary training.[27]

Periodic efforts have been made to reform and update the qualifications of US clergy, efforts increasingly under the shadow of the changing standards and expectations of higher education more generally and of a felt need across all religious communities to understand other religions and the modern secular landscape in which they all move. In 1936, the American Association of Theological Schools, as mentioned a recognized accreditor of theological degrees by the US Department of Education, was founded to

25. See Masuzawa, "The University and the Advent of the Secular," and Roberts and Turner, *The Sacred and Secular University.*

26. See on the effects of the decision in Abingdon v. Schempp, 374 U.S. 203 (1963), on the teaching of religion in the United States, Sarah Imhoff, "The Creation Story, or How We Learned to Stop Worrying and Love *Schempp*" (unpublished ms.).

27. Holifield, *God's Ambassadors*, 230. According to Holifield, only one-quarter of Protestant clergy had more than a high school education in 1926. Today he estimates that the number would be closer to 50 percent.

promote higher standards in Protestant seminary education, partially through the accreditation of seminaries. Begun by theologically liberal mainstream Protestant theological educators, today some two hundred and fifty schools from across the Christian theological spectrum are accredited through ATS. Buddhist and Muslim schools are affiliate members.[28]

The current ATS educational standards for the MDiv degree announce four curricular goals: understanding the religious heritage of the tradition of the community of faith in question; understanding the social and cultural context in which the community resides and addressing the global and multifaith nature of North America; personal and spiritual formation; and developing a capacity for ecclesial and public leadership.[29] There is strong emphasis in the ATS standards on the historicizing and contextualization of religious leadership—on responsiveness to the needs of congregants—and a deliberate abstraction and distancing from the nonnegotiable specificity of doctrinal matters. Proposed revisions to the standards are responding today to the growth in popularity of distance learning, an effort to maintain minimum residency requirements, and a broader cultural obsession with assessment of the efficacy of educational programs.

The MDiv curricular framework is designed to support programs across the full range of American religions that are willing to conform to it in order to participate in the professionalization and credentialism of today's job market. In 2010–11, there were roughly two hundred schools accredited by

28. Association of Theological Schools, Commission on Accrediting, www.ats.edu (accessed January 8, 2012); see also "Choosing a Seminary," Insights into Religion, http://religioninsights .org/theological-education/choosing-seminary (accessed January 8, 2012). The ATS developed from the Conference of Theological Schools, which met biennially beginning in 1918 to consider issues of "common interest and concern" to the Protestant theological schools in the United States and Canada. In 1936, the CTS became the ATS, with the announced aim of accrediting theological schools, which it began to do in 1938. In the 1960s, the ATS undertook a curriculum assessment and redesign in response to changes in ministry. See *Theological Education in the 1970s: A Report of the Resources Planning Commission*, issued by the ATS in 1968. In 1966, around the time that the ATS had begun to discuss, but not yet implement, sweeping curricular changes, five Catholic seminaries were admitted as ATS members. In *The Seminary: Protestant and Catholic* (New York: Sheed and Ward, 1966), Walter D. Wagoner (a Protestant examining the Catholic seminary system) advised Catholic participation and membership in ATS, calling it "an opportunity not to be missed" (87). He cited the "definite, really quite extraordinary correlation between the strength of the Protestant seminaries and the increasingly beneficial influence of the A.A.T.S." By 1968, fifteen Catholic seminaries had joined ATS; by the 1970s, "virtually all" the Catholic seminaries had sought and obtained ATS accreditation, according to Joseph M. White in *The Diocesan Seminary in the United States: A History from the 1870s to the Present* (Notre Dame, IN: University of Notre Dame Press, 1989). (Thanks to Kristen Tobey for this research.)

29. Current standards and proposed revisions may be found at "Basic Programs Oriented Toward Ministerial Leadership," Association of Theological Schools, Commission on Accrediting, http://www.ats.edu/memberschools/pages/degrees.aspx?pf=1 (accessed February 5, 2013).

ATS with 25,000–30,000 MDiv students enrolled in degree programs, depending on exactly how you count.[30] Another two hundred degree-granting
institutions are accredited by the Association for Biblical Higher Education,
also recognized by the US Department of Education as an accreditor of theological degrees. (The ABHE does not publicly list graduation statistics.) As
a comparison, in 2009–10, two hundred accredited American law schools
awarded forty-four thousand JDs.

Very consistently across Christian seminaries, the degree requirements
today include courses in basic Koine (New Testament) Greek and biblical
Hebrew, biblical exegesis, church history, doctrinal theology, ethics, and
practical theology, as well as courses in either cross-cultural contextualization or evangelism, depending on the orientation of the school. (The continuing importance of these classic courses are also reflected in required
credentials listed in job postings by the VA and other employers.) Cocurric-
ular requirements for the MDiv degree include field education, CPE credits,
and spiritual and character formation. Both conservative and liberal seminaries now offer courses in other religions, courses shaped by the development of religious studies as an academic discipline over the last half century
or so. Parallel curricula are being developed for non-Christian seminaries,
with core courses corresponding to the classic seminary trio, scripture, theology, and church history.

In the last seventy-five years then, many, perhaps most, American denominations, reflecting larger social trends, have come formally to favor
seminary training as the foundational credential for public ministry. And
seminaries increasingly offer degrees that are licensed by the state and accredited by national accrediting bodies recognized by the US Department
of Education. Catholic seminaries started offering the MDiv degree in the
1970s. Today laypersons as well as candidates for ordained ministry are
admitted to MDiv programs in Catholic seminaries in the United States.
Experimental programs in interreligious ministry are also arising. For example, Claremont School of Theology, a Methodist school in its origins,
announced in 2010 a new program for training in ministry with the following general requirements: courses in spiritual and vocational formation,
interreligious studies, Christian theological studies, and integrative studies,
with optional tracks for non-Christian students in Universalist Unitarian or

30. "2010–11 Annual Data Tables," Association of Theological Schools, Commission on
Accrediting, http://www.ats.edu/Resources/Pages/AnnualDataTablesFactBooks.aspx (accessed
February 5, 2013).

Muslim theology.[31] Harvard Divinity School requirements for admission to and completion of the MDiv degree program do not mention any specific religious tradition, offering rather preparation for ministry in any religious tradition. Harvard students are required to complete courses in theories and practices of scriptural interpretation; histories, theologies, and practices; and other religions and comparative courses; a relevant foreign language; and Meaning Making: Thinking Theologically about the Practice of Ministry. The University of Chicago MDiv program also admits non-Christian students. While these non-faith-specific programs are proliferating, for the most part they seem to model their curricula on an abstraction from the same triad of Bible, theology, and church history that has long been the foundation of Anglo-American Protestant Christian ministry studies, even though this very Protestant program of study does not necessarily correspond to the historic training of religious leaders in other religious cultures. All professional masters programs in ministry in the United States prepare students for a similar job, whatever the religious community, one that involves public worship, pastoral counseling, and cross-cultural mediation, as well as the management skills necessary to run a small organization.

In addition to the now ubiquitous MDiv degree, many seminaries and theological schools also offer degrees and certificate programs that concentrate in chaplaincy studies, in residential as well as in distance learning programs, degrees and programs that promise to prepare students for work as chaplains.[32] Liberty University, for example, in addition to a general masters degree in chaplaincy, also offers a masters degree in marketplace chaplaincy ministries, a specialized degree designed to prepare students for chaplaincies in businesses.[33] The Institute for Buddhist Studies in Berkeley, California, offers a general masters-level chaplaincy program, modeled on requirements set by the Association of Professional Chaplains, one of a number of professional chaplaincy organizations. Required courses include History of the Buddhist Tradition, Introduction to Shin Thought, Buddhist Practice, Buddhist Ethics, Buddhist Literature, Buddhist Psychology, Buddhist Services and Ceremonies, Buddhist Pastoral Care and Chaplaincy, as well as Clinical Pastoral Education, Buddhism in America/the West, and

---

31. http://www.cst.edu/degree-programs/mdiv/ (accessed January 21, 2013).

32. Kate Braestrup, chaplain to the Maine Warden Game Service, mentioned in the preface, went to Bangor Seminary where, as she explains, her teachers helped her to design her own independent study courses on law enforcement chaplaincy. *Here If You Need Me*, 60–61.

33. http://www.liberty.edu/online/masters/divinity/chaplaincy-72-hours/ (accessed January 21, 2013).

Spanish.[34] The Jewish Theological Seminary specifically trains Jewish seminary students for chaplaincy positions, the Jewish Welfare Board being the official endorser of rabbis from all of the major branches of US Judaism for service in military chaplaincy.[35] A concentration in chaplaincy studies is offered at Claremont, in cooperation with the US military.[36] Hartford Seminary offers training for Muslim students preparing for chaplaincy positions.[37]

It is through the acquisition of postsecondary degrees and certifications that training for chaplaincy is increasingly accomplished and where what one might call the legal secularization of ministry training and its assimilation to a larger credentialing culture is particularly evident. Indeed, Alan Contreras, the leading expert on US law with respect to academic degrees, argues that the granting of degrees is an inherently governmental, and therefore inherently secular, activity.[38] Authority to certify the credentials of ministers has passed from the churches to the government in the United States. The way in which challenges to that authority have been litigated illustrates the continuing public versus private tensions in the United States with respect to the regulation of property rights and the professions more generally, as well as the unfinished business of disestablishment. It is a story that both affirms state authority over professional degrees more generally and displays the ongoing contested effort to do so with respect to theological degrees in particular, raising the perennial issue in the regulation of religion as to whether religion is the same or different from other cultural and social formations.[39]

US case law regarding authority to grant academic degrees is sparse, but the struggle between church and state is evident as a boundary-setting concern in those cases. The leading case establishing the state's exclusive authority to authorize the granting of academic degrees to private educational institutions is *Townshend v. Gray*,[40] a Vermont decision from 1890. Mary J. Townshend, a graduate of Vermont Medical College, had sued demanding a

34. http://www.shin-ibs.edu/degrees/chaplain/ (accessed July 6, 2013).

35. "Military Chaplaincy 'The Basics,'" http://www.jtsa.edu/Documents/pagedocs/Rabbinical/military_chaplaincy_basic_information_sheet.pdf (accessed July 10, 2013).

36. http://www.cst.edu/financial-aid/military-benefits/chaplain-program/ (accessed July 6, 2013).

37. http://www.hartsem.edu/islamic-chaplaincy/program-details (accessed July 6, 2013).

38. See above note 18.

39. Winnifred Fallers Sullivan, "Neutralizing Religion, or What Is the Opposite of 'Faith-Based?,'" *History of Religions Journal* 41, no. 4 (2002). Reprinted in Hent deVries, ed., *Religion: Beyond a Concept* (New York: Fordham University Press, 2008).

40. Townshend v. Gray, 62 Vt. 373, 19 A. 635 (1890).

court order mandating the Vermont State Eclectic Medical Society grant her a certificate to practice medicine on the grounds of her having attained the requisite academic degree, the MD.[41] The Medical Society, explicitly authorized by the state of Vermont to grant such certificates, refused the certificate on the ground that the medical college she had attended did not possess the authority from the state of Vermont to award the MD.

The Vermont Medical College had been organized under a provision of the Vermont statutes permitting the formation of nonprofit corporations.[42] But, as the Supreme Court of Vermont explained, the fact that the college was legally formed according to the requirements of the Vermont law of corporations did not give it the power to grant degrees, for "the degree of M.D. is something more than a mere honorary title. It is a certificate attesting the fact that the person upon whom it has been conferred has successfully mastered the curriculum of study prescribed by the authorities of an institution created by law, *and by law authorized to issue such certificate.* It thus has a legal sanction and authority."[43] Furthermore, the court insisted, an academic degree does not simply signify the completion of a course of study: "In practical affairs, it introduces its possessor to the confidence and patronage of the general public. Its legal character gives it a moral and material credit in the estimation of the world, and makes it thereby a valuable property right of great pecuniary value."[44]

Mary Townshend might have met the academic requirements of her medical college, and her college might have had the proper corporate form to operate under Vermont law, but her college did not have the legal authority to grant a degree and thereby "introduce its possessor to the confidence and patronage of the general public" and "confer moral and material credit in the world." It did not have the authority to grant a valuable property right. Only authority granted by the state could do that. (I have been unable to learn more details about Dr. Townshend's predicament, that is, whether her being a woman was an issue or whether political issues within the medical establishment in Vermont were a factor. But the reported decision suggests

41. Eclectic medicine was a movement to establish herbal and homeopathic medicine in the United States, mostly suppressed by the efforts of scientific medicine in the late nineteenth and early twentieth century. Alex Berman and Michael A. Flannery, *America's Botanico-Medical Movements: Vox Populi* (Binghampton, NY: Haworth Press, 2001).

42. R.L. § 3664, subdiv. 10. The independence of private universities from state interference was famously established in Trustees of Dartmouth College v. Woodward, 17 U.S. (4 Wheat.) 518 (1819).

43. 19 A. 635, 636.

44. Ibid.

a connection with the long struggle between mainstream and alternative medicine and that struggle's connection with the history of US religion.[45])

The *Townshend* decision, notwithstanding its embeddedness in a very particular nineteenth-century Vermont history, remains the leading case in the United States on the state's exclusive authority to regulate academic degrees. More recently, the argument has been made that, while the degrees of secular institutions of higher education are indeed exclusively authorized by the state and the public moral authority of its law, religious institutions possess inherent authority under the First Amendment to issue degrees independent of state prerogative. In lengthy litigation in both the federal and state courts in New Jersey during the 1980s, Shelton College challenged the state's termination of its temporary license because it failed to comply with state standards concerning the awarding of baccalaureate degrees. On certification to the Supreme Court of New Jersey, the court held that the New Jersey statute intended to regulate both secular and religious colleges and that neither the free exercise clause nor the establishment clause of the First Amendment prohibited such regulation by the state, in spite of the burden on those religious practitioners who wish to attend and be granted degrees from unaccredited Bible colleges.[46] *Shelton College* is the current law in all states except Texas.[47]

Tyndale Theological Seminary and Biblical Institute was founded in Fort Worth, Texas, in the early 1990s, offering Bible courses in preparation for ministry. In 1998, in response to a letter to the school from the Texas Commissioner of Higher Education announcing the state's determination that Tyndale was in violation of state accrediting requirements, Tyndale sued the state challenging the state's authority to regulate degrees. The Texas Supreme Court, on appeal from lower court decisions largely upholding the state regulatory scheme, allowed an exemption for theological degrees.

The Texas court described the school at the time of the litigation: "Tyndale Theological Seminary and Bible Institute . . . consisted of a library, four or five classrooms, administrative offices, a small bookstore, and a computer department, and its enrollment was 300–350 students, with over three-fourths in correspondence courses." In 1999, at the time of the

45. See above note 41.

46. New Jersey State Bd. of Education v. Bd. of Directors of Shelton College, 90 N.J. 470 (1982).

47. The Supreme Court of Tennessee explicitly concurred with the Supreme Court of New Jersey in Tennessee *ex rel.* McLemore v. Clarksville School of Theology, 636 S.W.2d 706, 707–8, 711 (Tenn.1982). But see HEB Ministries, Inc. v. Texas Higher Educ. Coordinating Bd., 235 S.W.3d 627, 637 (2007).

Texas Supreme Court's decision, Tyndale offered diplomas described by the school as "equivalent" to bachelors, masters, and doctoral degrees. The Texas commissioner of education, vigilant in protecting the public from academic fraud, had fined Tyndale for violating the state's standards with respect to postsecondary education, asserting the public's interest in "assessing the competence of persons engaged in a wide range of activities necessary to the general welfare."[48] Tyndale, in response, argued that the Texas accrediting scheme, as applied to Tyndale, violated the religion clauses of the First Amendment and the Texas Constitution.[49] The Texas trial court found that the state was prohibited by state and federal constitutional guarantees from defining a seminary, but the court otherwise upheld the state's administration of degrees and the imposition of a penalty on Tyndale. The Texas Court of Appeals concurred. The Supreme Court of Texas, however, reversed, finding that Texas had violated Tyndale's state and federal constitutional rights.

In a lengthy opinion, the Texas Supreme Court described the ambiguous position of Bible colleges and seminaries in relation to state regulation, noting that Tyndale's own catalog expressed ambivalence with respect to accreditation—and to formal religious education more generally—reflecting a comprehensive distrust of elite academic expertise in matters of religion. The Texas court quoted from the 1997–98 Tyndale catalog: "Many seminaries are on shifting sands. They feel they must impress the world or the culture with their intellectualism . . . many schools seek *recognition* and *affirmation* from the state, from secular associations or professional groups that really have no business meddling in biblical matters." The catalog recalled an earlier more principled time: "In the 1960s, most Christian schools were not accredited, nor did the best want to be. . . . One of the largest Christian Universities in America has said, 'We will not become accredited!' That school today is highly respected and other schools want their graduates. Accreditation or lack of it has not had anything to do with the school's quality or mission."[50]

The Texas Supreme Court agreed with the authors of Tyndale's catalog that what it was doing was different from secular schools and that the dis-

48. Texas Education Code § 61.301. 235 S.W.3d at 669.
49. Article 1, section 6, of the Texas Constitution states that "All men have a natural and indefeasible right to worship Almighty God according to the dictates of their own consciences. No man shall be compelled to attend, erect or support any place of worship, or to maintain any ministry against his consent. No human authority ought, in any case whatever, to control or interfere with the rights of conscience in matters of religion."
50. 235 S.W.3d at 638–39.

tinction between secular and religious education was critical: "HEB Ministries does not challenge the State's authority to impose such standards on secular institutions and on religious institutions offering a secular education. Nor does HEB Ministries contend that the State cannot regulate use of the word 'degree.' It contends only that the State cannot deny the use of such higher education terminology to religious schools that do not meet its standards."[51] A plurality of the Texas court held that the Texas postsecondary regulatory scheme as applied to Tyndale violated both clauses of the First Amendment. Citing the US Supreme Court's decision in *Locke v. Davey* for the proposition that training for religious callings is fundamentally different from training for secular endeavors,[52] the court held that it was unconstitutional for Texas to require Bible colleges to meet secular standards of instruction in such matters as the educational attainment of its professors and, further, that the state process of accreditation involved the state in excessive entanglement in religious affairs. The New Jersey case was distinguished by the Texas court on the ground that Shelton College taught explicitly secular subjects as well as religious ones while Tyndale's curriculum was wholly religious.

Texas Justice Dale Wainwright, in dissent, underlining what he saw to be the critical distinction between the essentially private nature of religion and the essentially public secular nature of doctoral education, asserted that "typing the letters 'Ph.D.' on a parchment is an act that is not inherent to Tyndale's religious beliefs or engaged in for religious reasons, and should not be accorded constitutional protection under the religion clauses."[53] Both majority and dissenting opinions emphasized Texas's public interest in the prevention of, and strong record of response to, fraud by diploma mills.[54] Both majority and minority opinions also purported to know what distinguishes religion, seeing religious institutions as engaged in an essentially different project than secular ones. They differed only on whether granting degrees was a religious or secular event. (It is not clear that students in these

---

51. Ibid. at 641–42.

52. Locke v. Davey, 540 U.S. 712 (2004) held that it was not unconstitutional for Washington State to exclude students pursuing degrees in "devotional theology" from its Promise Fellowship, a state fellowship program for undergraduates.

53. 235 S.W.3d at 685.

54. The dissenters argued that the Texas statute was not an establishment of religion but was rather a neutral law of general application under *Employment Division v. Smith.* (see page 000 for a discussion of the *Smith* decision) and that regulation of religion was not of itself a violation of the free exercise clause, citing also *Bob Jones University v. United States,* 461 U.S. 574 (1983), holding that the IRS could withhold tax exempt status from Bob Jones on the grounds that its interracial dating policy violated federal racial policy.

schools make the same evaluations—seeing instead greater equivalency between secular and religious degrees, at least at the undergraduate level—in
part because of their recognition by the Department of Education.)

Tyndale's 2011 catalog gave economic and doctrinal reasons for its lack
of accreditation:

> *Tyndale Theological Seminary and Biblical Institute* is not accredited, and has
> no plans to pursue any type of accreditation for several particular reasons:
> (1) to keep our expenses low, enabling Tyndale to maintain its very low tui-
> tion rates—pursuit of accreditation would require a dramatic increase in costs
> passed on to the student; (2) to maintain doctrinal autonomy; and (3) to
> continue the utilization of Tyndale educated faculty to ensure theological and
> philosophical consistency with the doctrinal statement and mission of Tyn-
> dale—pursuit of accreditation would make this increasingly difficult.[55]

Today Tyndale offers masters programs in biblical studies, apologetics, counseling, church planting, Christian education, theological studies, messianic
studies, and biblical languages, as well as masters and doctoral programs
in divinity and theology, prophetic studies, and the philosophy of religion,
none of which are accredited. Its master of divinity course requirements
formally tracks that of other MDiv degrees, including required courses in
biblical exegesis, Greek and Hebrew, theology, church history, and cross-
cultural contexts. Adopted in 2009, the Texas Administrative Code now explicitly provides that "the Texas Higher Education Coordinating Board does
not regulate Religious Institutions of Higher Education which offer degrees
only in religious disciplines."[56] Texas is the only state that does not regard
academic degrees as inherently secular whatever the discipline.

Many chaplains serving today have been educated in Bible colleges such
as Tyndale, notwithstanding published standards requiring an accredited
degree. Administrators and judges have at times been receptive, for egalitarian and perhaps theological reasons, to the argument that religious legitimacy may derive from sources other than the acquisition of academic
degrees, although the standardizing effect of the MDiv degree remains
potent in a society that respects the equalizing effects in employment opportunity of formal, publicly announced credentials available to all who

55. Tyndale 2011 Catalog, 74.
56. Title 19, part I, ch. 7, subchapter A, rule § 7.9. Such schools may be subject to other
forms of regulation, however, including by the Internal Revenue Service. (See above note 54.)

are qualified for admission and can afford the tuition. And the curriculum prescribed for the degree has shaped even nonaccredited programs.

Clinical Pastoral Education

CPE certification is required for many government and private chaplaincy positions in the United States. While, broadly speaking, of course, pastoral care has always been a concern of Christian ministry, clinical pastoral education, in the contemporary sense, is an invention of the twentieth century, one product of a broader engagement first by liberal Protestants, then later by clergy of many denominations, with modern psychologies and medicine. Christians, laypersons as well as clergy, like many others, regard visiting the sick and those otherwise disadvantaged, to be a religious obligation. In the twentieth century, however, particularly within Anglo-American Protestantism, a new hybrid ministry developed, a clinical practice that was formally understood to be distinct from the work of both congregational ministers, on the one hand, and of doctors and nurses, on the other. This new practice would come to be the work of a new kind of health-care professional: the professional hospital chaplain trained in hospital settings. CPE has broadened since its first invention to encompass many other social service settings.

The story of the invention of clinical pastoral education as a distinct form of professional training bringing together emerging ideas about human psychology, medical ethics, professional education, and social work practice, as well as changes in Christian theology, is well known.[57] It has been told and retold many times among those within the health chaplaincy movement as well as by those seeking to understand the broader history of engagement between religion and medicine in the United States in the twentieth century. In 1925, Richard Cabot, a neurologist and cardiologist at Massachusetts General Hospital, issued a "Plea for a Clinical Year in the Course of Theological Study."[58] Cabot thought that Protestant ministers needed to encounter the real-life world of modern medicine in their training in order to prepare themselves for work in hospitals. The emergence of such professional clinical training for pastors paralleled similar educational

57. Summary accounts of this history may be found in Holifield, *God's Ambassadors*, 232ff., 242, 247; under "pastoral care" in the *Dictionary of Pastoral Care*; and Cadge, *Paging God*, at 25ff.. For longer treatments, see also Holifield, *A History of Pastoral Care in America* (Nashville: Abingdon Press, 1983), and Myers-Shirk, *Helping the Good Shepherd*.

58. Reprinted in Richard Cabot, *Adventures on the Borderlands of Ethics* (New York: Harper & Bros., 1926).

developments in law and medicine, professional educational programs that also newly focused at that time on what was known as the case method.[59] The need for such professional pastoral education has also resonated with more recent criticisms of American medicine from within the medical fields, particularly nursing.

Clinical pastoral education was first formally established by Anton Boisen, a chaplain at Worcester State Hospital in Massachusetts, working with Dr. Cabot. Boisen, himself a lifelong sufferer from mental illness, wrote extensively about the experience of illness as an opportunity for religious growth. Boisen was most interested in teaching pastors psychiatric and psychoanalytic skills while Cabot was more interested in the ethical formation of chaplains, but both emphasized a clinical year in which ministerial students would have the supervised real-life experience of interacting with patients, an experience that was later extended to other social service clients.[60] In the 1930s and 1940s, clinical pastoral education was institutionalized and given formal shape across the United States and Canada. New psychologies were combined with traditional clerical forms of ministry in formal CPE internships that taught ministers to convert their traditional forms of counseling into what might be called a form of religious psychotherapy or therapeutic religion specifically tailored for the modern hospital setting and the needs of the modern patient.

The primarily Protestant ministers who invented CPE, and other religio-psychological practices, have sometimes been dismissed as having reconceived Christian care of the soul from one focused on sin and salvation to one focused on self-realization, but that cheap narrative is belied by the seriousness of purpose and intellectual and practical work done by these reformers.[61] University of Toronto professor Pamela Klassen describes liberal Protestant theology's new engagement with psychology as resulting in the invention of a new "holistic trinity," a naturalistic concern to overcome the dualism of then current religious thinking in favor of an emphasis on the interconnectedness of body, mind, and soul, one that was impelled by a liberal Christian desire to make themselves into what she suggests might be called faith healers of a newly imagined Christian self.[62] She sees therapeutic

59. David A. Garvin, "Making the Case: Professional Education for the World of Practice," *Harvard Magazine*, July–August 2013.

60. See E. Brooks Holifield, *A History of Pastoral Education in America* (Nashville: Abingdon Press, 1983), 231–49.

61. The classic work is Philip Rieff, *The Triumph of the Therapeutic: Uses of Faith after Freud* (Chicago: University of Chicago Press, 1966).

62. Klassen, *Spirits of Protestantism*, 168.

religion as having a longer and broader genealogy, one that is related to and converges in various and complex ways with alternative spiritualities, both of the Eastern and of the more homegrown varieties, including Pentecostal and charismatic Christianities, all long a feature of the North American religious landscape. In the end, Klassen concludes that, notwithstanding the heroic efforts of these liberal Christian reformers, "the very demarcations of body, mind, and spirit in the holistic trinity . . . ended up not so much establishing the equilibrium of the healthy Christian self, as revealing the precariousness of its balance."[63] That precariousness is still evident in the practices of the ministry of presence by today's chaplains.

For those trained through CPE programs, spiritual health is understood to be a necessary, integral, and universal component of good health care. And human beings—all human beings—are understood to be spiritual as well as physical. While the story of the reception of various psychological and psychoanalytic ideas of the human into religious ideas and practices in the United States is complex, the existential encounter with the patient, an encounter that emphasizes a listening presence, remains at the heart of clinical pastoral education today. Hospital chaplains now describe their work as founded in understanding illness as creating a crisis of meaning for patients, one that demands specialized care, "meaning" being somehow a new catchall and universal vessel for the leftover business of naturalizing enlightenment philosophies and scientistic naturalism.

Today CPE certification in the United States is administered by the Association for Clinical Pastoral Education.[64] CPE has moved beyond hospitals to other institutional settings and beyond liberal Protestantism to other Christians and to non-Christians. Explicitly Jewish CPE programs, for example, have developed over the last half century; Jewish chaplains initially qualified themselves by obtaining social work degrees instead because CPE programs were initially seen by Jews as being Protestant. ACPE understands clinical pastoral education as a form of professional training independent of and open to all "faith traditions." The association now describes itself as "a multicultural, multifaith organization devoted to providing education and improving the quality of ministry and pastoral care offered by spiritual caregivers of all faiths through the clinical educational methods of Clinical Pastoral Education." It emphasizes the hands-on nature of its training with those termed "living human documents": "By 'living human documents,' we mean both the people who receive care as well as a study of ourselves,

63. Ibid.
64. http://www.acpe.edu/ (accessed February 7, 2013).

the givers of care. Through the practice of ministry and the reflection thereon with supervisor and peers, the experiential learning that is CPE takes place."[65]

Emphasizing the multicultural, multifaith character of CPE, and the universality of the need for spiritual care, as well as its government accreditation, CPE training today focuses on study of "the living human documents," using Boisen's words. Both the chaplain as caregiver and the patient are understood to be such documents. CPE is intended to develop and mature the pastor's ability to interact with persons in his care through his own development as a caregiver. Today CPE has no particular expressed religious identity, focusing rather on the praxis-oriented professional development of the minister of any tradition—or none.[66] CPE care is theorized using a fusion of the student's own theological tradition, behavioral and social scientific knowledge and methods, and a "multicultural" perspective of respect founded in popular constitutional ideas. The goal is to develop the pastor's own self-awareness as well as inculcating skills and knowledge of pastoral care. While most seminary students take units of CPE in the summer as a requirement for the MDiv, those contemplating a chaplaincy career may choose to apply for year-long paid residencies at major hospitals and other social service providers.[67]

CPE certification is one part of a larger effort to professionalize, and legally legitimate, the work of chaplains. Indeed, as historians and ethnographers of chaplaincies attest, CPE chaplains are constantly working to convince their employers of the value of their specialized training. As Wendy Cadge explains with respect to hospital chaplains: "CPE trained chaplains provided a new supply of workers for which they aimed to create a demand in hospitals. Professional CPE trained chaplains . . . argued that they, as professional chaplains, had new or unique skills, learned through Clinical Pastoral Education and evident in their commitment not to proselytize, that would help them support patients better than chaplains without such training and commitment."[68] As chaplaincy has self-consciously tried to develop itself as a true profession, it has worked to develop a corresponding profes-

65. Ibid.

66. There are religiously specific offshoots, or adaptations, of CPE that are explicitly theologically based. See, e.g., the College of Pastoral Supervision and Psychotherapy: http://www.pastoralreport.com/about.html (accessed February 9, 2013) and http://www.spirit-filled.org/endorsement.html (accessed February 7, 2013).

67. The Mayo Clinic, e.g., has such an internship: http://www.mayo.edu/mshs/cpe-res.html (accessed February 7, 2013).

68. Cadge, *Paging God*, 28–29.

sional education that is founded in research and academically respected evidence through specialized journals and professional organizations. Part of the cost of CPE training is now reimbursable to hospitals through Medicare, as an allied health-care education activity.[69] The federal government's discussion of this rule in the Federal Register reflects the success of CPE's campaign and its consequent acceptance of hospital chaplains as allied secular health professionals receiving professional education to qualify them for board certification just as do other health professionals.[70] Acceptance of this narrative by judges likewise legitimates the profession.[71]

Ecclesiastical Endorsement

Finally, a candidate for a chaplaincy position must usually provide evidence of an endorsement from his or her "faith community." According to the Veterans Health Administration, an ecclesiastical endorsement certifies "that an individual is in good standing with that religious faith group, and stat[es] that the individual is, in the opinion of the endorsing agent, qualified to conduct all offices, functions, sacraments, ordinances, ceremonies, rites, and/or observances required to meet the needs of patients of this particular group."[72] (Interestingly, this definition continues to reflect, in the use of the word "required," an understanding of the role of clergy as necessary mediators in the sacrificial economy, rather than, as Braestrup would say, glad companions for the journey.) Ecclesiastical endorsement is a guarantee of the orthodoxy and good character of the chaplain applicant by the sending religious community and signifies a commitment on the part of that community to monitor continuing compliance.

The endorsement also constitutes one more credentialing interface between the private regulatory regimes of the churches, on the one hand, and those of the government, and other secular employers, on the other. The chaplain must meet the requirements of the secular institution that employs him, the professional organizations that give him his training and certification, and, finally, the religious body that authorizes his ministry and vouches for his orthodoxy and ministerial competence on an ongoing basis. Together the law created by these private and public regulators legally defines acceptable religious work and identifies who can perform it.

69. "2003 Final Rule for Medicare Pass-through Funds for CPE," Association for Clinical Pastoral Education, Inc., http://www.acpe.edu/AdminMedicare.html (accessed January 8, 2012).

70. Ibid.

71. See discussion in chapter 4

72. VHA Handbook 1111.1.

It seems quite straightforward. If you present yourself as a candidate for a job as a chaplain, you need a statement from your church saying you are in good standing as a minister in that church. The ecclesiastical endorser certifies that you are a genuine Presbyterian minister, for example—or Lutheran pastor or Catholic priest or Buddhist monk. The endorsement is also an acknowledgment that the government or other secular employer is not competent to make that determination. On one reading of this arrangement, the employer is simply matching providers of services with clients. In theory, the employer is not interested in the applicant's particular doctrinal positions.

It is not so straightforward in practice—at least in the United States—for both practical and constitutional reasons. Most importantly, US religion is simply not organized enough, or institutionally "established" enough—or is organized in ways that are at cross-purposes to the preservation over time of orthodoxy—and so cannot consistently fulfill that role for the many who are otherwise qualified to do the work that chaplains do, work that is largely removed from the creeds and confessions that historically define orthodoxy. Continuing to require an ecclesiastical endorsement as a condition of employment for positions in chaplaincy also seems anachronistic—even perhaps unconstitutional—in the United States, where the work of chaplains is increasingly understood to be universalist and nonsectarian, and orthodoxy is often regarded not only as unnecessary but also as undesirable. Furthermore, of course, religious orthodoxy is understood not to be within government competence—or even interest. These American cultural and regulatory reflexes distance the chaplain employee from the endorsing body even while endorsement continues to be a qualification for employment.

The continued demand for an ecclesiastical endorsement provides a regulatory link that disregards a constitutional jurisprudence that insists that each person in the United States is free to interpret her own faith and tradition as she wishes.[73] Such an endorsement also contradicts the generalizing and equalizing impulse of credentialing professional chaplains broadly to

73. This doctrine is founded, in part, on the cases interpreting the conscientious objector provisions of selective service legislation, including U.S. v. Seeger, 380 U.S. 163 (1965), which extended conscientious objector status beyond those with membership in the historically pacifist churches to anyone with a genuine objection to all war, even if founded in a nonreligious personal philosophy. While not constitutionally based, these cases have had a large influence on both legal and lay understandings of the nature of religion for constitutional purposes. For advocacy by a health-care chaplain against endorsements on theological grounds, see Paul Brassey, "Eliminate Endorsement," *Plain Views* 6, no. 4 (March 18, 2009).

minister to all humans as naturally in need of spiritual care without regard to the particulars of any particular religious tradition. In these senses, ecclesiastical endorsements are an ongoing vestige of an older regulatory model, an establishment one, more similar to those in other parts of the world.

To be sure, the endorsement model continues to make practical sense even in a disestablished religious context. Part of some chaplains' jobs continue to involve ministering to members of that chaplain's own religious community in ways exclusive to that community, such as in the provision of sacraments. Ecclesiastical endorsements also preserve the notion that legally protecting the free exercise of religion has an organizational, as well as an individual, aspect to it—protecting the rights of churches as well as that of believers. Outsourcing religious orthodoxy and discipline to the endorsing bodies may further be understood to provide some constitutional cover for employers, including the government, who do not wish to be involved, or to be seen to be involved in, evaluating orthodoxy. But there is increasing strain on what has become a rather hodgepodge arrangement.

The most organized group of ecclesiastical endorsers is that which is recognized by the army. The Armed Forces Chaplains Board keeps a list of its more than two hundred currently approved ecclesiastical endorsing organizations on the web.[74] (This list is reproduced in the appendix.) It is a curious group, which includes Buddhists, Muslims, Jews, Native Americans, Quakers—lots of evangelicals and Pentecostals—and every possible kind of ecclesial and quasi-ecclesial body, including Buddhist Churches of America, Camelback Bible Church, First Church of Christ, Scientist, Greek Orthodox Archdiocese of Vasiloupolis, the Union of Messianic Jewish Congregations, and more than twenty-five different kinds of Baptists. Joining this list is usually a matter of applying, although there have been in the past difficulties with the creation and recognition of endorsing bodies for Mormons, Muslims, and Wiccans, among others—Mormons because they lack a professional ordained ministry,[75] Muslims because of suspicion directed

74. http://prhome.defense.gov/rfm/mpp/CHAPLAINS%20BOARD/endorsements.aspx (accessed December 27, 2012). This list is reproduced in the appendix.

75. According to a 1975 dissertation by Joseph F. Boone, "The Roles of the Church of Jesus Christ of Latter-Day Saints in Relation to the United States Military, 1900–1975" (Brigham Young University), "Mormons had periodic trouble getting appointments to the military chaplaincy because they lacked formal training. In 1941 a policy was introduced whereby Mormons (and only Mormons, it seems) could become chaplains by demonstrating equivalency in theological education through an exam, and could substitute for ordained ministry an appropriate 'secular occupation'—teaching is then given as the secular occupation 'considered the nearest approach to the occupation of a clergymen' (592). In 1944 it was suggested that the two years

against Muslim organizations since 9/11,[76] and Wiccans partly because of their small numbers but also because of their antiorganizational bent. Mormons and Muslims now both have endorsing bodies.[77]

The most bureaucratically formal churches in the United States have an office that produces printed forms on which the church officially warrants

of teaching and one year of a mission might be accepted in place of three years of teaching. As other religious groups began to threaten Protestant hegemony in the late 1950s, the army and navy returned to the former standards, insisting on formal ministerial training, so that no Mormon could qualify. (The air force kept more flexible standards at first but repealed them in 1960.) Mormon chaplaincy declined precipitously, and in 1965 the graduate education requirement was again waived for Mormons. In 1968 Brigham Young began to discuss the possibility of implementing a graduate chaplaincy training program, which was instituted in 1969. Credit hours would come from coursework, and from completing missions." (Thanks to Kristen Tobey for this research).

76. A report to the Department of Justice by the Office of the Inspector General with respect to chaplains for federal prisons describes the BOP effort to find a partner for Muslim endorsement: "Obtaining an endorsement from a national Islamic organization presents special challenges for Muslims because, unlike other religions, there is no national Islamic decision-making body to recognize official Islamic religious leaders or authorize them to minister to others. The BOP Muslim chaplains explained that in Muslim countries the government, not organizations, endorses religious leaders. They said that Muslims in the United States have created national organizations to unify and represent them, such as the Islamic Assembly of North America, the Islamic Circle of North America, and the ISNA. However, the chaplains noted that these organizations are not as large, organized, or established like other religions' organizations, such as the Catholic Church or the Southern Baptists, and several of the organizations have received scrutiny for allegedly advocating radical beliefs or supporting terrorism." http://www.justice.gov/oig/special/0404/index.htm (accessed January 21, 2013).

77. Today, the requirements for Mormon chaplains are listed on the church website:

Marriage. All LDS applicants must be married in the Temple and remain Temple worthy while serving as a chaplain.

Mission. It is desirable that all chaplain applicants serve a mission, but it is not absolutely required.

Church Leadership. The Department of Defense Directive 1304.19 requires that each applicant must have at least two years of practical ministerial experience following completion of the master's degree. Although we do not have a paid clergy, most of our applicants will meet this requirement by having sufficient practical Church leadership experience by the time they graduate, especially if a mission has been completed.

BYU Religion Class. BYU Religion 540 "Preparation for the Military Chaplaincy" (Section 1 and 2), six (6) semester hours. This may be completed via distance learning.

Age Requirements. Must complete all requirements for application and be selected by the Chaplain's Board by the following maximum age:

No prior service: less than age 40

With prior service: less than age 45 depending on length of service

Reserves and National Guard: less than age 48 depending upon length of service with the Reserves

http://www.lds.org/pa/display/0,17884,5062–1,00.html (accessed February 7, 2013).

to the employer that the minister in question is, for example, a good Lutheran, and that the Lutheran endorsing body undertakes to continue to be responsible for the chaplain's religious orthodoxy and good behavior. One solution for independent Pentecostal and holiness churches has been the creation of the Coalition of Spirit-Filled Churches, a group that was organized to serve as an endorser for such churches; chaplains pay a percentage of their income as a fee for receiving the endorsement.[78]

The military endorsers are gathered together in the National Conference on Ministry to the Armed Forces.[79] A simple graphic design combining an American flag and a shepherd's crook decorates their website, which explains their purpose:

> Our common goals are to recruit, endorse and provide oversight for clergy-persons who desire to serve as chaplains in any one of the branches of our armed forces. We want clergypersons to serve who are credible, committed to their faith, open to all persons, able to meet all military standards, and who represent the highest standards of their own faith communities.[80]

The National Conference also provides a code of ethics for military chaplains and their endorsing bodies, requiring them to follow the regulations of the army, to be faithful to their own theologies, and to be respectful of all others.

The lengthy Endorser's Code of Ethics reflects the mixed history and ambiguous status of chaplains, combining multiple and often conflicting obligations toward the sending community, chaplaincy as a profession, the Department of Defense, other endorsers, the families of armed forces personnel, the equal status of all religions, and a commitment not to engage in unfair discrimination on the basis of gender, race, religion, or national origin:

78. "The Coalition of Spirit-filled Churches (CSC) is an incorporated, non-profit 'religious endorsing body' ministry. We are a coalition of independent churches and groups of churches from Pentecostal, Renewal, and Charismatic traditions who have united for the exclusive purposes of the credentialing and promotion of Spirit-filled clergy and lay caregivers for pastoral care in specialized settings. These settings include, but are not limited to: the US Armed Forces; Veterans Affairs and civilian healthcare facilities; federal, state, and local correctional facilities; federal, state, and local law enforcement agencies; public and private schools; the workplace; and professional pastoral counseling practices." http://www.spirit-filled.org/ (accessed February 7, 2013).

79. http://ncmaf.org/ (accessed February 7, 2013)

80. Ibid.

Endorsers' Code of Ethics

I will hold in trust the traditions and practices of my religious body.

I will show personal love for God in my life and ministry as I strive together with my colleagues to preserve the dignity, maintain the discipline, uphold the ethical standards and promote the integrity of the profession to which we have been called.

I will adhere to whatever requirements are provided by the Department of Defense through the Armed Forces Chaplains Board for endorsing organizations.

I will respect, participate with and work collegially with other endorsers in the same ways expected of the chaplains I endorse.

If a chaplain I endorse desires to change endorsement to another NCMAF member endorsing body, or if a chaplain endorsed by another endorsing body seeks endorsement by my faith group, I will follow NCMAF and Service branch policies regarding change of endorsement.

I will not initiate or encourage any chaplain to change endorsement to my faith group.

I will support my endorsed chaplains with communication, guidance and prayer. When possible, I will make pastoral visits to chaplains I endorse and their family members at their duty locations.

During endorser visits to my chaplains, I will seek to provide care and ministry to other chaplains as requested by the chaplain.

I will respect the beliefs and traditions of my colleagues to include persons of religious traditions different than my own.

If and when I have an issue of misunderstanding or conflict with a colleague endorser, military chaplain or military official, I will seek to resolve any differences directly with that endorser, chaplain or official. If that approach is unsuccessful, I will seek resolution through the NCMAF Executive Director or the lowest level possible before elevating the said issue to a higher and/or legal venue.

I will honor the confidences of my colleague endorsers as well as those chaplains I endorse and will at all times perform my duties with the highest ethical standards.

I will support all of my endorser colleagues in ministry by building constructive relationships through all of my associations with the National Conference on Ministry to the Armed Forces.

I will adhere to all of NCMAF approved policies and guidelines.

I will defend my colleagues against unfair discrimination on the basis of gender, race, religion or national origin.

> Recognizing the special power inherent in my pastoral/endorser office, I will
> not abuse that power to violate the personhood of any human being, re-
> ligiously, emotionally, or sexually. I will use my pastoral/endorser office
> only for the good of those with whom I minister and relate to in my role
> as endorser.

The code reflects the often contradictory current US religious, military, and legal expectations with respect to any professional employment, as well as a universalistic and egalitarian theology which finds its roots in a broad Christian ecumenicism.

The employment contract for chaplains usually specifically anticipates and allows for the possibility that a chaplain may be terminated either by the employer or by the endorsing body, an arrangement that can present difficulties for chaplains moving from one faith tradition to another. Sociologist Hansen describes the Catch-22 situation of an army chaplain who decided to convert from being a Pentecostal to being a Wiccan chaplain. He hoped simply to be picked up by another endorsing agency:

> In 2006, a Christian Army chaplain . . . decided to convert to Wicca and con-
> tacted the Sacred Well Congregation, a Wiccan organization that was already
> trying to get the Department of Defense to recognize them as an endorsing
> agent for Wiccan chaplains. Having been told by the Army chaplaincy that
> they had met all requirements of an endorsing agency except putting forth a
> viable candidate, they thought Larsen would be ideal, given that he already
> was an Army chaplain. Unfortunately for Larsen, his original endorsing
> agency, the Chaplaincy of Full Gospel Churches, found out from the Army
> that he was planning to convert and . . . rescinded his ecclesiastical endorse-
> ment, which made it impossible for him to continue serving as a chaplain.[81]

Such situations raise both constitutional and other legal issues of discrimination in employment.

In most cases, in order to qualify to provide an ecclesiastical endorsement, a religious organization must have tax exempt status under section 501(c)(3) of the Internal Revenue Code.[82] While it is sometimes inaccurately said that it is the IRS that generally supplies the legal definition of religion in the United States through its regulation of tax exemption, the significant gatekeeping performed by the IRS through the tax laws

---

81. Hansen, *Military Chaplains and Religious Diversity*, 79.
82. I.R.C. § 501(C)(3)(2006).

unquestionably affects the phenomenology of US religion.[83] Lacking a government ministry whose job it is to vet and approve religious organizations for all legal purposes, as many countries have, in fact each government body in the United States is free to make its own decisions about what qualifies as religion, within the very vague and broad mandate of US Supreme Court jurisprudence. Some use the IRS as a proxy for this decision. But it is important to remember that the IRS definition is only available if an organization wishes to qualify for tax exemption, or for another government benefit that is conditioned on 501(c)(3) status. No law requires a religious organization to apply for such status simply in order to operate.

Enrollment as a section 501(c)(3) organization provides then a convenient crystallization and regularizing of an official ecclesiology for a specific range of purposes. For the purposes of chaplaincy, it is the orientation within the IRS definition toward the provision of pastoral care to a lay constituency that so clearly enacts into law a distinctively protestant Christian form of religious self-understanding, notwithstanding its explicitly inclusive stance toward other religious organizations. Section 501(c)(3) of the Internal Revenue Code exempts from taxation contributions made to "corporations . . . organized and operated exclusively for . . . religious purposes." A "church," which is a special subsection of a purely religious organization under the tax code, is not necessarily Christian, has special legal protections, and is currently assessed by the IRS according to a fifteen-point set of judicially defined criteria.

In order to qualify for these special legal protections, according to the IRS, a church must have some, not necessarily all, of the following:

> (a) a distinct legal existence, (b) a recognized creed and form of worship, (c) a definite and distinct ecclesiastical government, (d) a formal code of doctrine and discipline, (e) a distinct religious history, (f) a membership not associated with any other church or denomination, (g) an organization of ordained ministers, (h) ordained ministers selected after completing prescribed studies, (i) a literature of its own, (j) established places of worship, (k) regular congregations, (l) regular religious services, (m) Sunday schools for religious instruction of the young, (n) schools for the preparation of its ministers, and

---

83. For commentary, see Nathan M. Boyce, "From Rubik's Cube to Checkers: Determining Church Status Is Not as Hard as You Think," *Exempt Organization Tax Review* 68 (2011): 27; Nicholas A. Mirkay, "Losing Our Religion: Reevaluating the Section 501(C)(3) Exemption of Religious Organizations That Discriminate," *William & Mary Bill of Rights Journal* 17 (2009): 715–64.

(o) any other facts and circumstances that may bear upon the organization's claim for church status.[84]

In an article recommending that tax exemption be conditioned on nondiscrimination in the administration of its services, Nicholas Mirkay comments that "the criterion that courts most consistently rely on in determining the existence of a church is the presence or absence of an established and regular congregation." He explains that "because charitable organizations must primarily confer public benefit, the congregational or associational facet of a church comports with that requirement."[85] The IRS regards the congregation as the defining feature of a "church," whether Christian or not, and regards the congregation as being of obvious public benefit. That the IRS takes a broad view of its own criteria, as long as it does not believe that the application is merely a pretext for tax avoidance, can be seen by looking carefully at the list of endorsers.

In May 2011, the Veterans Health Administration released a new handbook governing ecclesiastical endorsements for chaplains in the VA system.[86] Its purpose is to "define the administrative procedures and requirements that religious faith groups must meet to provide ecclesiastical endorsements of individuals for Department of Veterans Affairs (VA) Chaplaincy." The handbook is basically a how-to book on the way to be a faith group that interacts with the government. The VHA requires an endorser to meet the following requirements:

(1) Be organized and function exclusively or substantially to provide religious ministries to a lay constituency.

(2) Possess authority to both grant and withdraw initial and subsequent ecclesiastical endorsement.

(3) Be recognized by the Internal Revenue Service (IRS) as a tax-exempt religious organization under section 501(c) (3) of the Internal Revenue Code.

---

84. American Guidance Foundation v. United States, 490 F. Supp. 304, 306 n.2 (D.D.C. 1980). Modified by Foundation of Human Understanding v. U.S., 614 F.3d 1383 (2010). See Matson Coxe, "Here Is the Church, Where Is the Steeple? *Foundation of Human Understanding v. U.S.,*" *North Carolina Law Review* 89 (2011): 1248–72. Instructing that the criteria "are not exclusive and are not to be mechanically applied," the IRS chief counsel recommended the addition of the fifteenth criterion, (o) any other facts and circumstances that may bear upon the organization's claim for church status.

85. Mirkay, "Losing Our Religion," 728.

86. VHA Handbook 1111.01.

(4) Agree to abide by all Federal, VA, and VHA laws, regulations, policies, and issuances on the qualification and endorsement of persons for service as VA chaplains, Federal employment, and Veterans health care.

(5) Agree to notify the VA National Chaplain Center of any withdrawal of an existing ecclesiastical endorsement.

(6) Provide to the VA National Chaplain Center the information and documents specified in paragraph 7 of this Handbook.

(7) Acknowledge that:

(a) Acceptance of an ecclesiastical endorsement by VA does not imply any approval by VA of the theology or practices of a religious organization, nor does it obligate VA to employ the endorsed individual or any other members of the organization;

(b) VA's mission to provide health care to Veterans is always paramount, and VA reserves the right to restrict or prohibit within its facilities any practices that it deems detrimental to the health or safety of patients;

(c) Individuals endorsed by the organization must function in a pluralistic environment and must support, directly and indirectly, the free exercise of religion by all Veteran patients, family members, and others authorized to receive VA health care.

Like the IRS, in order to be recognized as a religion for VA endorsing purposes, a religious body must minister to a lay constituency. This provision, perhaps a lingering legacy of anti-Catholicism, intentionally excludes contemplative religious orders, organized without a lay congregation, which are regarded as lacking a public charitable purpose.[87] But there are other embedded public policy goals as well. An endorsing body must agree to abide by all laws and regulations and be nondiscriminatory and pluralistic. It is a curious historical phenomenon to have the US government doing such theological work—regulating the shape of acceptable religious life—in quite so open a way.

Qualifying to Be a Chaplain

If you want to get a job as a chaplain delivering spiritual care to Americans, you will most likely need an MDiv degree in any religious tradition, or

87. It is hard to say whether that requirement would hold up today, given widespread public belief in scientific proof of the efficacy of prayer. British law of charitable exemptions excludes religious communities organized solely for prayer, the work of enclosed monastic communities being understood to have no public benefit. Rivers, *The Law of Organized Religions*, 163.

none; certification of completion of a clinical internship of generalized spiritual dimensions; and endorsement by a religious body that can qualify for tax exemption. You must be willing to work in a multifaith environment. You must accept at least publicly the idea that proper religion is something that is vital, voluntary and varied but tolerant, compliant and oriented to the ends of the secular institution in which you work.[88]

One new employment opportunity for chaplains, beyond the conventional settings of hospital, prison, and the military, is in one of the new municipal crisis ministries created after 9/11 and Hurricane Katrina. Legal scholar Mary Jean Dolan has described one such ministry, the Seattle Community Chaplaincy program, and the financial support it received from the federal government.[89] She explains that "they are expected to provide 'nonsectarian, nondiscriminatory support' to all and asked not to proselytize."[90] The Seattle Community Chaplaincy program was, according to Dolan, funded by the US Department of Justice's Office of Victims of Crime, which has also given grants to Community Chaplaincy, a self-described not-for-profit organization that assists local police departments in creating community chaplaincies.[91] Such chaplaincies, designed to minister to residents in the case of crime, natural disaster, or terrorist attack, are proliferating in the United States.

The regulation of chaplains as workers reflects a convergence among a credentialing boom, populist religion, and egalitarian approaches to employment. It is also profoundly driven by a national project of interfaith equity and moral education. As the Church of Jesus Christ of Latter-day Saints website explains, "Chaplains go where the troops go. They are in the barracks, in the offices, and in the training areas, as well as in combat zones ministering to men and women of all faiths, denominations, and persuasions. They must be able to work in a pluralistic religious environment, respecting and accommodating members of all faiths without compromising their own beliefs."[92]

The peculiar educational formation and credentialing of chaplains is not driven just by the force of law, the needs of government, and the social

---

88. For a discussion of a shift in the understanding of pluralism among sociologists of religion from a mid-twentieth-century focus on a shared civic faith to a market-based understanding, see Courtney Bender, "Pluralism and Secularism."

89. Mary Jean Dolan, "Government-Sponsored Chaplains and Crisis: Walking the Fine Line in Disaster Response and Daily Life," *Hastings Constitutional Law Quarterly* 35 (2008): 505–46.

90. Ibid.

91. http://fcsministries.org/collective/community-chaplaincy/ (accessed July 6, 2013).

92. https://www.lds.org/callings/military-relations/military chaplains (accessed July 11, 2013).

facts of religious diversity. That training is also enabled by the success of religious studies in naturalizing its own religious practices. The work done by the religious studies department in many colleges and universities in the United States reflects a broadly irenic and inclusive voice on behalf of *Homo religiosus* in all his guises. Needing both to differentiate its work from that of other departments and to justify itself in a secular academy, religious studies in the last fifty years or so, like chaplaincy, has attempted to separate itself from the particularity of Christian theology and to universalize its gaze, all the while insisting on the importance of understanding religion and its distinctiveness as a human activity. Religious studies has fostered the production of a strange and hybrid discourse that incorporates Christian universalism, anthropological histories, and the peculiar erasures of minority and nonconforming practices through world religions language. It has also been successfully popularized through the work of Huston Smith, Joseph Campbell, and Karen Armstrong, among many others.

This style of religious studies is not without its critics. Jonathan Z. Smith, Tomoko Masuzawa, Bruce Lincoln, Russell McCutcheon, and many others have argued that the representation of religion as diverse but sui generis and essentially valuable is both false and dangerous.[93] The predominance of such a religious studies discourse in both academic and media settings is, nevertheless, helping to make the work of the chaplain legible to, and legal for, Americans.

93. See, e.g., Christopher Lehrich, ed., *On Teaching Religion: Essays by Jonathan Z. Smith* (Oxford: Oxford University Press, 2012); Tomoko Masuzawa, *The Invention of World Religions, or How European Universalism Was Preserved in the Language of Pluralism* (Chicago: University of Chicago Press, 2005); Bruce Lincoln, *Gods and Demons, Priests and Scholars: Critical Explorations in the History of Religions* (Chicago: University of Chicago Press, 2012); and Russell McCutcheon, *Critics Not Caretakers: Redescribing the Public Study of Religion* (Albany: State University of New York Press, 2001).

FOUR

Chaplains and the Constitution

Religious freedom, American style, constitutionally speaking, begins, in some sense, with the important claim that the default position for most Americans is that the United States is rightly understood not as a secular state, but as a proudly religious country. Disestablishment does not mean secularism. Disestablishment prohibits government coercion in religious matters and government control of religious associations, as well as religious control of government; it does not mean that religion is entirely privatized or understood to be unimportant to the common good. Just as presidents must ask God to bless America, the Supreme Court must find a way to acknowledge, over and over again, as Justice Douglas did in 1952, that "we are a religious people."[1] There are important ways in which what that religiousness looks like has changed since 1952, but for now those obligations are secure and the Court seems content to find new ways to recognize that reality even while its approach to interpretation of the religion clauses is changing once again.

Abandoning the high separationism of the second half of the twentieth century, the Court has shifted in recent decades to a position that seeks to accept and enable the religiousness of Americans. This shift reflects, in part, wider changes in law and in constitutional jurisprudence over this time, including a growing disenchantment with national government, and with judicial capacity for social engineering, in favor of a neoliberal faith in free

---

1. Justice Douglas writing for the majority in Zorach v. Clauson, 343 U.S. 306 (1952). Plaintiffs in the *Zorach* case challenged a New York law permitting schools to grant "release time" for students to attend religious education classes. Those who did not have such permission were required to stay in school. The Court found the law not to violate the establishment clause of the First Amendment.

enterprise, the rights of corporations (including religious corporations), and a populist faith in local management.

Bringing to an end a fifty-year experiment with federally enforced church-state separation, the religion clause lawsuits that were litigated in the 1980s and 1990s transformed US First Amendment law. The Court withdrew from a strong commitment both to a hard-edged exclusion of religious institutions and symbols from the public square and from public funding as well as to selective free exercise accommodation. The new jurisprudence is still in a formative stage, but the regulation of chaplaincies is one place where one sees the law working out the terms on which religion will be sponsored by the state in this new dispensation. The work that chaplains do is shaped by these changes to law as well as changes in religion.

Religiously speaking, the mainstreaming of Catholicism, a decline in the authority of traditional religious institutions, particularly of their leadership, growing religious diversity, the absorption of psychology by theology, the practical and technological bent of American approaches to pastoral care, and transformations in the training and professionalization of clergy, as well as the politics of religious freedom and the restructuring of the churches away from denominationalism, have led to the further deinstitutionalization of American religion.[2] Legally speaking, the goal of much law about religion today in the United States is the celebration and fostering of a universalist and irenic spirituality that mirrors American politics and upholds the rule of law while containing or excluding forms of religion that are perceived to threaten stability, sexual mores, or national security. Chaplaincies have become an acceptable form of established religion because they are understood to be necessary to the enabling of this version of the free exercise of religion. Yet that has not entirely robbed them of their capacity to interrupt and surprise the established order.

The Supreme Court has only once addressed the constitutionality of government chaplaincies, in 1983, in *Marsh v. Chambers*,[3] a case challenging the practice of chaplains being attached to state legislatures. This chapter will consider that decision as well as other recent lower court decisions addressing the legality of government chaplaincies, but we will begin with *Katcoff v. Marsh*,[4] a challenge to the constitutionality of the army chaplaincy in the early 1980s, because the prosecution of *Katcoff* more completely il-

2. See Robert Wuthnow, *The Restructuring of American Religion: Society and Faith since World War II* (Princeton, NJ: Princeton University Press, 1988), for an early, prescient description of the changes to the sociology of American religion.

3. Marsh v. Chambers, 463 U.S. 783 (1983).

4. Katcoff v. Marsh, 582 F.Supp. 463 (1984) ; *aff'd* 755 F.2d 223 (2d Cir. 1985).

lustrates the constitutional challenges presented by government chaplaincies than does the case of legislative chaplaincies—and because it continues to be cited. We will then return to the appeal from the *Nicholson* decision, discussed in chapter 1, about the VA practice of spiritual assessment, and consider the regulation of religion in the United States today more generally given the current state of religion clause jurisprudence.

Suing the Secretary of Defense

The *Katcoff* case was initiated by a couple of Harvard law students while they were still in law school. Joel Katcoff and Allen Wieder met at Harvard Law School in the late 1970s. Moved by their newly gained legal knowledge, and having absorbed the First Amendment separationism of the 1970s, they sued John O. Marsh, then secretary of the army, as taxpayers, *pro se*, asserting that the army chaplaincy constituted an establishment of religion. They further claimed that the religious needs of soldiers could and should be provided by a volunteer civilian clergy rather than through a government-paid chaplaincy. A Harvard law professor was reported in the Harvard student newspaper to have said at the time that they would lose but that it would be good experience for them.[5]

At the beginning of its opinion in *Katcoff*, the district court observed dismissively that the "plaintiffs, who brought this action while they were still Harvard law students, have never served in the military," and that "there are some who might argue that this question is more the grist of a moot court competition than a case or controversy to occupy the energies of a federal court."[6] Nevertheless, two of the lawyer-chaplains who worked on the army defense, Israel Drazin and Cecil B. Currey, thought the case important enough that they wrote a memoir about their experience, *For God and Country*,[7] and, while, legally speaking, the *Katcoff* case is not usually regarded as a significant decision in the canon of First Amendment jurisprudence, the actual process of the litigation had a transformative effect on the army chaplaincy, and arguably on chaplaincy more generally. As John Wesley Brinsfield, author of a history of the chaplaincy from 1975 to 1995,

5. Stephen R. Latham, "Law Students File Suit against Army: Charge Funding of Chaplaincy Is Unconstitutional," *The Crimson*, November 30, 1979.

6. 582 F. Supp, at 464.

7. Israel Drazin and Cecil B. Currey, *For God and Country: The History of a Constitutional Challenge to the Army Chaplaincy* (Jersey City, NJ: KTAV Publishing, 1995); see also Richard D. Rosen, "*Katcoff v. Marsh* at Twenty-Two: The Military Chaplaincy and the Separation of Church and State," *University of Toledo Law Review* 38 (2007): 1137–78.

says, "In many fundamental ways the Army's spiritual care system would never again be the same."[8]

The work and legacy of the *Katcoff* litigation can be seen in retrospect to have consolidated over time in a new and enduring rationale on which to found the case for government provision of spiritual care. Notwithstanding the fact that this was a case cooked up, as the professor and the judge had observed, by a couple of smarty-pants law students, the army took the case very seriously, actually entertaining the possibility that the chaplaincy would be abolished by the court. Interrogatories filed in *Katcoff* resulted in a massive discovery effort by the army, detailing the entire then current administration of the chaplaincy; the litigation also led to a serious reexamination of the purposes and practices of the military chaplaincy in the United States at a time when the military was undergoing profound soul-searching after the Vietnam War and its transformation into an all-volunteer army.[9]

In addition to statistics on the number and denomination of the clergy employed as chaplains, Katcoff and Wiener sought information

> on chapels, retreats, religious libraries, worship services, construction costs, salaries and expenses, prayer breakfasts, religious education, devotional programs . . . the number of civilian employees involved in the Army's religious-support program, sacred items, denominational literature purchased with Army funds, contracts with civilian religious organizations, the availability of civilian houses of worship near each Army facility, and religious training and professional development programs.[10]

A special team of active-duty and reserve chaplains was assembled, led by Drazin, himself a retired army reserve chaplain and rabbi; the team was charged with defending the army and developing the factual record in the case.

The army's need to respond to this lawsuit was taken by the army chief of chaplains at the time, Kermit Johnson, as an opportunity to review all of the practices of the chaplaincy. The *Katcoff* litigation and the response it evoked from the army thus led to a fundamental rethinking of the chaplaincy's foundation in law and to the now ubiquitous assertion that the central raison d'être of the military chaplaincy is to protect and enable the

---

8. Brinsfield, *Encouraging Faith*, pt. 1, 120.

9. Ibid., 120–30. See also, Beth Bailey, *America's Army: Making the All-Volunteer Force* (Cambridge, MA: Harvard University Press, 2009).

10. Drazin and Currey, *For God and Country*, 74.

free exercise rights of those who serve in the various branches of the armed services.[11] Other government chaplaincies are also now justified in a similar way. Earlier rationales for the army chaplaincy had tended toward an open foregrounding and fostering of a civil religion theology, "For God and Country," as the army chaplaincy motto still expresses it. This shift illustrates the broader shift noted by Courtney Bender in the way religious pluralism is explained by sociologists in the United States. Bender suggests that while mid-twentieth-century sociologists such as Robert Bellah and Will Herberg saw religious pluralism as leading to the creation of a common civic creed, sociologists today see US religious pluralism on a free market model as fostering vitality and competition.[12]

The 1983 decision of the district court in *Katcoff*, on a motion for summary judgment, finding the chaplaincy program constitutional, came almost five years after the case was originally filed. In a 1985 opinion, the Second Circuit Court of Appeals affirmed,[13] emphasizing the voluntary nature of religious participation in the military and the deference due to Congress's authority under the War Powers Act, authority which is granted "for the purpose of 'preserving the peace and security, and providing for the defense, of the United States.'"[14] Congress, according to the act,

> has specifically authorized that as part of this establishment there be "Chaplains in the Army," who shall include the Chief of Chaplains, and commissioned and other officers of the Army appointed as chaplains . . . each chaplain is required, when practicable, to hold religious services for the command to which he is assigned and to perform burial services for soldiers who die while in that command. The statute also obligates the commanding officer to furnish facilities including transportation, to assist a chaplain in performing his duties.[15]

The court also noted that military chaplains are recognized by the Geneva convention as having noncombatant status.[16] Chaplains thus have a recognized place in international, as well as domestic, law.

11. Brinsfield, *Encouraging Faith*, pt. 1, 130.

12. Bender, "Pluralism and Secularism."

13. Katcoff v. Marsh, 755 F.2d 223 (2d Cir. 1985). The Second Circuit remanded for the limited purpose of determining whether different arrangements should be made for military personnel permanently stationed in the United States in large urban areas. 755 F.2d at 237–38.

14. U.S. Constitution, Art. I, § 8.

15. 10 U.S.C. § 3073 and § 3547.

16. 755 F.2d at 226.

"The primary function of the military chaplain," according to the Second Circuit Court of Appeals, "is to engage in activities designed to meet the religious needs of a pluralistic military community, including military personnel and their dependents."[17] Yet the congressional mandate clearly understands the chaplaincy's obligations also to extend to "the command," that is, to the commanding officer; chaplains are required to "hold religious services for the command to which he is assigned and to perform burial services for soldiers who die while in that command."[18] Chaplains are also now obligated to advise the command on religious issues that arise in the field. While the *Katcoff* suit was ultimately unsuccessful in the terms on which it had been filed, that is, it was unsuccessful in eliminating the chaplaincy, in the six years since the original filing, army chaplaincy procedures had been extensively reformed in line with a new legal theory, one that in some ways acknowledged the establishmentarian tendencies of the civil religion model. No petition for review from the Second Circuit decision was filed in the Supreme Court.[19]

Katcoff and Wiener had argued not just that a government-paid chaplaincy was an unconstitutional establishment of religion but that churches and synagogues would easily be able to pick up the slack, supplying volunteer clergy willing to serve as military chaplains. The evidence they offered for this confident prediction was the practice of one of the Lutheran churches in the United States that had developed a special program for supplying clergy to the military.[20] Both the district court and the court of appeals questioned the practicality of such an arrangement being extended across the entire army and across all religious communities. Both courts found that it was not a violation of the establishment clause for Congress to authorize a government chaplaincy as a means of addressing what both plaintiffs and defendants, reflecting a larger social consensus, even now including the FFRF, have agreed is the army's obligation to provide for the free exercise needs of soldiers, enabling them to avail themselves of the free market in religion seen as the constitutional gold standard for religious freedom.

---

17. Ibid. See Terry A. Dempsey, "Asymmetric Threats to the United States Army Chaplaincy in the 21st Century," USAWC Strategy Research Report, US Army War College, April 10, 2000.

18. 755 F.2d at 225.

19. Presumably because Katcoff and Wiener had lost interest.

20. First Amendment scholar Kent Greenawalt has also argued in favor of a voluntary chaplaincy. See chapter 12, "Chaplains in the Military and in Prisons," in Kent Greenawalt, *Religion and the Constitution*, vol. 2, *Establishment and Fairness* (Princeton, NJ: Princeton University Press, 2008), 218.

Beyond the sheer impracticality of managing a volunteer chaplaincy, the Second Circuit explained why volunteer local clergy cannot supply the same services. Referring to the situation in which soldiers are deployed outside the United States, the court concluded that "in most of these areas the Judeo-Christian faiths of most American soldiers are hardly represented at all by local clergy and the average soldier is separated from the local populace by a linguistic and cultural wall."[21] Even in the United States, though, there was an issue: "Within the United States . . . although the linguistic or cultural barrier may be absent, local civilian clergy in the rural areas where most military camps are centered are inadequate to satisfy the soldiers' religious needs because they are too few in number for the task and are usually of different religious denominations from those of most of the nearby troops."[22] American troops, the court asserted, are bound together overseas by their "Judeo-Christian" faith and linguistic and cultural difference from local populations while at home they are separated from local clergy by their denominational differences. Religious difference loomed large in envisioning a volunteer chaplaincy. The problem was one of fit—a need for fit between plural particularized religious identities and corresponding religious services. A specialized professional chaplaincy attuned to the particular needs of soldiers and of the country was clearly necessary to address this complex religious situation.

The court of appeals was also concerned with cultural and spiritual dislocation from what it calls the "natural habitats" of their "respective faiths" and with their "separation from their homes, loneliness when on duty in strange surroundings involving people whose language or customs they do not share, fear of facing combat or new assignments, financial hardships, personality conflicts, and drug, alcohol or family problems." When at home the court envisioned that these problems would be addressed because "the soldier . . . would usually be able to consult his spiritual adviser."[23] A professional military chaplaincy would address these needs as well.

Imagining soldiers whose pre-army life would have included ready consultation with a "spiritual advisor," the court sees the spiritual health of soldiers as both an individual and a community concern. Ultimately, however, the need for the chaplaincy was a matter of national defense: "Unless there were chaplains ready to move simultaneously with the troops and to tend to their spiritual needs as they face possible death, the soldiers would be left

21. 755 F.2d at 227.
22. Ibid. at 227 28.
23. Ibid. at 228.

in the lurch, religiously speaking . . . unless chaplains were made available in such circumstances the motivation, morale and willingness of soldiers to face combat would suffer immeasurable harm and *our national defense* would be weakened accordingly."[24] It was not just that soldiers would be "left in the lurch" as to their constitutional right to the free exercise of their religion. The country needed soldiers able and willing to face combat. While speaking the language of freedom, the court concerns itself with creating the conditions necessary for preparing soldiers for the fight.

The Second Circuit described in detail the comprehensive responsibilities of army chaplains in this effort to supply religious services, assist in the smooth running of the unit, and foster spiritual reflection and renewal. The court further explained how the extensive administrative structure of the army chaplaincy was necessary to do this well:

> The Chief of Chaplains, a major general of the Army, is in general supervision and management of the Army's chaplaincy. His office contains three divisions: (1) Administration and Management, which, among other things, maintains liaison with religious and secular organizations, (2) Plans, Programs and Policies, and (3) Personnel and Ecclesiastical Relations. These divisions work closely with the Department of Defense Armed Forces Chaplains Board. Over the years the Army has built or acquired more than 500 chapels which are used for the conduct of religious services of many different denominations. In addition it has built more than 100 Religious Educational Facilities, which are used for religious services and classes in religious education for soldiers and members of their families of all ages (including children). The Army has purchased and made available for voluntary use by various denominations numerous chaplain's kits, vocational kits, communion sets and vestments, and religious publications (including Holy Scriptures and Prayer Books for Jewish Personnel, the New Testament of our Lord and Savior Jesus Christ, and a Book of Worship), and has developed a Cooperative Curriculum for Religious Education of the Armed Forces.[25]

Providing chaplaincy services to soldiers, sailors, and airmen requires the government to provide ministers, chapels, educational facilities, and religious goods. Accommodating the religious needs of such a large and diverse population is a large and complex task, one the court understood as not easily replicated through the hit and miss of volunteer efforts.

24. Ibid.
25. Ibid. at 228–29.

It is not just worship and counseling, as the court noted. The army has also always been involved in procuring religious goods for members of the armed forces. Special Bibles have long been printed for army use. As the armed services have become more diverse, other religious paraphernalia have been added. A key aspect of the expansion beyond Christianity and Judaism has been the need to supply religious goods beyond Bibles, goods such as "solo seder kits," and the wafers and wine needed for celebration of the Eucharist. Through a special arrangement with the Church of Jesus Christ of Latter-day Saints, for example, desert-colored temple garments can be purchased by Mormon soldiers.[26]

The plaintiffs in the *Katcoff* case proposed substituting this vast effort with volunteer private religious services, restricting the army's role to one they called "a neutral provider of opportunity."[27] The court of appeals described this suggestion as "bordering on the frivolous."[28] Rejecting the then prevailing *Lemon* test for determining whether or not a particular action of government violated the establishment clause as inappropriate in the military context,[29] and placing *Katcoff* within the small group of cases in which long-standing practice confers constitutionality, the court of appeals further announced that the free exercise clause is the source of the authority for the chaplaincy: "the morale of our soldiers, their willingness to serve, and the efficiency of the Army as an instrument for our national defense rests in substantial part on the military chaplaincy, which is vital to our Army's functioning."[30] An affirmative commitment to fostering religious practice on a national scale is expressed in these opinions.

It is never quite spelled out in these decisions how the chaplaincy and its facilitating of an opportunity to exercise their rights to religious freedom underwrites the soldiers' willingness to serve and contributes to the national defense. One explanation may lie in the Cold War origins of America's

26. http://www.lds.org/pa/display/0,17884,4878-1,00.html (accessed February 8, 2013). Mormon men and women wear white temple garments under their clothes to signify purity. "Temple garments serve as a personal reminder of covenants made with God to lead good, honorable, Christlike lives. The wearing of temple garments is an outward expression of an inward commitment to follow the Savior" (from lds.org FAQ, accessed February 8, 2013). Viewing and purchasing temple garments on the LDS website is limited to Mormon Church members who must enter a Mormon ID number in order to access the information.

27. Plaintiffs' Brief of October 4, 1982, at 6, quoted by the district court: 582 F. Supp. at 475.

28. 755 F.2d at 236.

29. See footnote 57 in chapter 1 for a description of the *Lemon* test.

30. 755 F.2d at 237. See footnote 1 of the opinion for a chart of the distribution of denominations in the army chaplaincy in 1980 and 1981.

renewed commitment to religious freedom in the twentieth century.[31] The religiousness of Americans comes to be understood as tightly linked to the exceptional quality of freedom in the United States more generally, the freedom for which soldiers are asked to kill and die. The vital role attributed to the chaplaincy may also reflect a longer-standing Old Testament biblicism whose militant God sanctions a nation's cause, suggesting that the free exercise rationale acts as a constitutional pretext for a more problematic establishment.

It is doubtful that the Supreme Court would be interested now, several decades later, in comprehensively considering the constitutionality of the military chaplaincy—and law students now also have different preoccupations—but any appraisal of the overall constitutionality of the military chaplaincy today would require a new analysis under the Supreme Court's 1990 decision in *Employment Division v. Smith* (the peyote case),[32] a decision that substantially revised free exercise jurisprudence, as well as more recent establishment clause decisions that limit standing in such cases, and are largely accepting of government funding of religion in other contexts, such as in schools and the provision of social services. *Smith* rejected the argument that the First Amendment mandates affirmative protection for religious free exercise through exemptions from laws of neutral application. Commentators agree that under *Smith*, the *Katcoff* conclusion that the chaplaincy is mandated by the free exercise clause would likely not hold. The military chaplaincy would more probably be viewed today either as a permitted accommodation of religion under *Cutter v. Wilkinson*,[33] finding legislative protection for the exercise of religion in prisons constitutional, which cited *Katcoff* with approval, or as an anomaly of the *Marsh v. Chambers* variety, that is that legislative chaplaincies are constitutional solely because hallowed by time.[34] The constitutional difficulty in harmonizing the two clauses in the case of justifying government chaplaincy reveals an ongoing unresolved tension between them. When does the accommodation of religion become an establishment? And, conversely, when does the outlawing of an establishment hamper free exercise?

31. Samuel Moyn, *The Last Utopia* (Cambridge, MA: Harvard University Press, 2010), and "From Communist to Muslim: Religious Liberty in European Human Rights Law."
32. 494 U.S. 872 (1990); and, of course, taxpayer standing is no longer available for such cases, under Hein v. FFRF, 551 U.S. 587 (2007), as will be discussed later in the chapter.
33. Cutter v. Wilkinson, 544 U.S. 709 (2005).
34. For a strong critique of the constitutionality of the chaplaincy, see Steven K. Green "Reconciling the Irreconcilable: Military Chaplains and the First Amendment," *West Virginia Law Review* 110 (2007): 167.

That tension continues to haunt the effort to administer fairly the chaplaincy, as the navy cases discussed below suggest; how to accommodate the various needs of military personnel—and of the state—in a military that is far more diverse than that of the early 1980s and in which the currency of the rhetoric of free exercise rights has raised expectations beyond what can reasonably and coherently be achieved.[35] One response of the military has been to move beyond the free market pluralist model, one of catering to the particularist needs of the troops, to one that accommodates and integrates a naturalized universal spirituality as its motivating force and model of religion. This move might be seen as part of a larger cultural shift away from pluralism as a political project.[36]

Constitutionality of Government Chaplaincies in the United States Today

Recent shifts in interpretation of the religion clauses that suggest a greater tolerance on the part of the Supreme Court toward government funding of religious entities have been accompanied by the always present proviso that there are core activities that the establishment clause prohibits government from directly funding or sponsoring, that is, worship and proselytizing. Government chaplaincies would seem to fit squarely within this prohibited realm, as the court of appeals in *Katcoff*—and many commentators—have noted. Government chaplaincies hire religious specialists to conduct worship and preach the word. Government chaplains engage in religious education and lead retreats, all in a context of hierarchical discipline. And yet, notwithstanding these apparently obvious constitutional difficulties with having ministers hired by and working for the government, there is relatively little law about the constitutionality of government-run chaplaincies. The selection, payment, and supervision of chaplains, the licensing and accrediting of theological programs, as well as the ongoing relationship of government to ecclesiastical endorsing bodies, all might be thought to violate the establishment clause of the First Amendment to the US Constitution, at least on a strong separationist reading. There have been challenges

---

35. See, e.g., Charlotte E. Hunter, "The Ethics of Military Sponsored Prayer," Defense Equal Opportunity Management Institute, http://isme.tamu.edu/ISME07/Hunter07.html (accessed February 8, 2013).

36. See "Habits of Pluralism" by Pamela E. Klassen and Courtney Bender, introducing the history of the rhetoric of religious pluralism, in Courtney Bender and Pamela Klassen, eds., *After Pluralism: Reimagining Religious Engagement* (New York: Columbia University Press, 2010). Also Courtney Bender, "Pluralism and Secularism."

to these practices from time to time, before and after *Katcoff,* some of which will be discussed in this chapter, but the continued presence of chaplains in the military, in police and fire departments, in the park services, in prisons, in hospitals, in legislatures and city councils, in colleges and universities, and in countless other venues persists. Their presence in private but government-regulated entities such as schools and businesses also raises serious issues of employment discrimination and indirect establishment through the regulation of credentials and tax exemption.

US military, medical, and prison chaplaincies are now commonly justified as a necessary means of accommodating the free exercise needs of prisoners, of patients in public hospitals, and of servicemen and women who are away from home for reasons of the state. The rationale is that these folks are unable to avail themselves of the free market in religion understood to be the constitutionally prescribed ideal in the United States. The actual duties of such chaplains and the rationale for their continued existence arguably far exceeds, however, that necessary to provide such an accommodation. These chaplaincies and others clearly serve other purposes, purposes both of the government or the secular institution that employs them and of the chaplains that staff them, as well as larger social purposes.

The only Supreme Court decision with respect to the constitutionality of government-funded chaplaincies, *Marsh v. Chambers,* decided while *Katcoff* was still in discovery, ruled that legislative chaplaincies do not violate the establishment clause.[37] Ernie Chambers, Nebraska state senator, had sued Frank Marsh, treasurer of Nebraska, challenging the expenditure of state funds to support the cost of hiring a full-time chaplain whose duties included the opening of each senate session with a prayer. Legislative chaplaincies, the practice of having a chaplain attached to a legislative body and serving as an officer of that body, common throughout American history at the federal, state, and local levels, may have originated and may continue, in part, as a response to the need of legislators for pastoral care while away from home—similar to the rationale for soldiers and prisoners—but that motive is largely ignored today. Legislative chaplaincies, like other government chaplaincies, serve a more priestly role, celebrating and legitimating political authority and the civil religion of the nation in the prayers that are offered at the beginning of each session and performing such services as

---

37. Marsh v. Chambers, 463 U.S. 783 (1983). For a discussion of the constitutionality of legislative chaplaincies, see Jeremy G. Mallory, "'An Officer of the House Which Chooses Him, and Nothing More': How Should *Marsh v. Chambers* Apply to Rotating Chaplains?," *University of Chicago Law Review* 73, no. 4 (Autumn 2006): 1421–53.

burial of deceased members. These activities are tolerated as largely harmless even though, when focused on, it is difficult to imagine them as secular in a strong sense.[38]

In his opinion for the majority in *Marsh*, finding the Nebraska practice constitutional, Chief Justice Burger listed the constitutional challenges and rejected each of them, almost in the same breath: "Beyond the bare fact that a prayer is offered, three points have been made: first, that a clergyman of only one denomination—Presbyterian—has been selected for years; second, that the chaplain is paid at public expense; and third, that the prayers are in the Judeo-Christian tradition. Weighed against the historical background, these factors do not serve to invalidate Nebraska's practice."[39] In other words, for many years a Presbyterian minister had been paid to pray a Christian prayer to open the legislative day in Nebraska. The fact that such a practice was "historical" was sufficient to make it constitutionally permitted. Here, as elsewhere, history can have a distancing and secularizing effect for the Court. Once passions have cooled, and religion has become routine, then it becomes constitutional.[40] While *Katcoff* suggests that passions can be reheated, the courts who heard that case were also impressed with the weight of history—including the presence of a chaplain in George Washington's army.

Burger's telling of the history of legislative chaplains in *Marsh* began with the Continental Congress, that is, he begins before the drafting and passage of the Bill of Rights.[41] Noting that provision was made for a chaplains' prayer in the first Congress, Burger concluded that "the delegates did not consider opening prayers as a proselytizing activity or as symbolically

38. The current chaplain to the US Senate has served for ten years. Jeremy W. Peters, "Give Us This Day, Our Daily Senate Scolding: Senate Chaplain Shows His Disapproval during Morning Prayer," *New York Times*, October 6, 2013, A1. Before the Court in the October 2013 term is *Town of Greece v. Galloway*, a Second Circuit case challenging the practice of opening city council meetings with prayers.

39. 463 U.S. at 793.

40. The secularizing effect of history is evident in other establishment clause decisions including *Lynch v. Donnelly* (see below note 47) and the Ten Commandments display cases. Historicizing, has long been understood to have a secularizing effect on religion more generally, particularly in the United States. Historical-critical readings of scriptures split the American churches in the nineteenth century. The US government has made efforts to foster a historical reading of the Qur'an, for similar reasons. See Saba Mahmood, "Secularism, Hermeneutics, and Empire: The Politics of Islamic Reformation," *Public Culture* 18 (2006): 323–47.

41. The official history of the US congressional chaplaincies also begins there. Ida A. Brudnick, "House and Senate Chaplains: An Overview," *Congressional Research Service* (May 26, 2011).

placing the government's 'official' seal of approval on one religious view."[42] Rather, he said, the Founding Fathers looked at invocations as "conduct whose . . . effect . . . harmonize[d] with the tenets of some or all religions" and recognized that "to invoke Divine guidance on a public body entrusted with making the laws is not, in these circumstances, an 'establishment' of religion or a step toward establishment; it is simply a tolerable acknowledgment of beliefs widely held among the people of this country."[43] It is hard to say from the opinion how he knows what the Founding Fathers thought about opening prayers. What makes the invocation of "Divine guidance" secular, though, according to the chief justice, is that that it rests on widely held beliefs that "harmonize with the tenets of some or all religions." Burger here distinguishes between what everyone agrees on, which is what might be termed secular, or even civil, religion—that is, historically sanctioned, universalist, and widely held—and established religion, which is ahistorical, divisive, dogmatic, proselytizing, and not widely agreed upon. Actual widely held beliefs in the United States can be seen to figure on both sides of this distinction, as both established and disestablished at the same time, calling into question the very possibility of the distinction. It is in part the capacity of Christianity and the Judeo-Christian "tradition" to figure as universal and particular in turn that supports this jurisprudence.[44]

Justice Brennan's dissent in *Marsh* displayed a very different and vastly more complex reading of the nature of prayer and of the religious sensibilities of the American public. "Prayer," Brennan announced, "is serious business—serious theological business and it is not a mere 'acknowledgment of beliefs widely held among the people of this country' for the State to immerse itself in that business."[45] He went on to describe a wide spectrum of views about the nature of prayer:

> Some religious individuals or groups find it theologically problematic to engage in joint religious exercises predominantly influenced by faiths not their own. Some might object even to the attempt to fashion a "non-sectarian" prayer. Some would find it impossible to participate in any "prayer opportunity" marked by Trinitarian references. Some would find a prayer *not* invoking the name of Christ to represent a flawed view of the relationship between human beings and God. Some might find any petitionary prayer to be improper.

42. 463 U.S. at 792.
43. Ibid. at 791.
44. See Gil Anidjar, "Secularism." *Critical Inquiry* 33(2006): 52-77.
45. Ibid. at 819.

Some might find any prayer that lacked a petitionary element to be deficient. Some might be troubled by what they consider shallow public prayer, or non-spontaneous prayer, or prayer without adequate spiritual preparation or concentration. Some might, of course, have *theological* objections to any prayer sponsored by an organ of government. Some might object on theological grounds to the level of political neutrality generally expected of government sponsored invocational prayer. And some might object on theological grounds to the Court's requirement that prayer, even though religious, not be proselytizing.[46] (citations omitted)

Justice Brennan's familiarity with the history of religion and his passionate and intelligent sensitivity to religious difference underwrote his strongly separationist political position, a sensibility and position not now represented on the high court since Justice Souter's retirement. As with his dissent the following year from another majority opinion by the chief justice in an establishment clause case, *Lynch v. Donnelly* (the Pawtucket crèche case),[47] Brennan's attention to the specifics of religion subverted the happy, irenic establishmentarian assumptions underlying Burger's opinion.

At the time, *Marsh* and *Lynch* seemed anomalies—exceptions to the reigning separationism of the Court's decisions in the contemporaneous school cases. And while recent Court decisions validating the new faith-based politics, including those approving the constitutionality of school vouchers and rejecting a challenge to the White House Office on Faith-Based Initiatives, among others, may be understood to mark the undoing of that earlier separationist jurisprudence and also of a new tolerance, even blessing, of nondenominational Protestantism as a constitutionally permitted form of secular practice, the spiritual politics underwriting that affirmation arguably have a much longer history.[48] Beginning in the early republic, Protestant sensibilities and Protestant morality have been central to public life in the United

46. Ibid.

47. Lynch v. Donnelly, 465 U.S. 668 (1984). In *Lynch,* Brennan countered Burger's assertion for the majority that a crèche displayed as a part of a town Christmas display was secular because sanctioned by a holiday "long celebrated in the Western World," with a lengthy discussion of the history and theology of Christmas celebrations in the United States. For a discussion of legal models of religion in the *Lynch* case, see Winnifred Fallers Sullivan, *Paying the Words Extra: Religious Discourse in the Supreme Court of the United States* (Cambridge, MA: Harvard University Press, 1995).

48. In an important article, Richard Schragger argues that establishment clause jurisprudence is best understood as having been characterized throughout its history by deliberate underenforcement. Richard Schragger, "The Relative Irrelevance of the Establishment Clause," *Texas Law Review* 89 (2011): 583–649.

States in more and less formal ways.[49] De facto establishment today, though, after the rejection of separation, has moved beyond evangelical Protestantism to embrace a more universal and naturalized religious field, enabled, in part, by changes to the semantic reference of the word "religion."

The Supreme Court has not spoken since *Marsh* on the subject of government chaplaincies, but a line of lower court decisions, citing *Marsh* and following *Katcoff*, have found both military and public hospital chaplaincies to be constitutional in the face of establishment clause challenges. As with *Marsh* and *Katcoff*, these decisions understand chaplaincies to have a dual purpose, one pastoral and one priestly, the necessary provision of religious services for soldiers and patients who are away from home, on the one hand, and the furthering and blessing of the national endeavor, on the other. But the overwhelming sense in the language of these judges is that the chaplaincies also serve an important and appropriate public governmental role in serving what is newly understood to be a natural and universal spiritual need.

In its 1988 decision in *Carter v. Broadlawns Medical Center*,[50] the Court of Appeals for the Eighth Circuit considered whether a county psychiatric hospital violated the establishment clause by hiring a chaplain. The court began by introducing the chaplain, Maggie Rogers: "Rogers has a Masters of Divinity degree and is trained in grief counseling and Clinical Pastoral Education, or C.P.E. She is not an ordained minister, but is a deacon of the United Church of Christ."[51] Emphasizing CPE's noncoercive and patient-centered approach, the court quoted Deacon Rogers on the nature of her work: "You listen very carefully to their story, to their faith language, to the symbols that are important to them, and you help them find the resources of faith and the resources of their life whether that be family or their church or their faith or their own history. . . . To do anything else than that, according to the philosophy of CPE, is unconscionable."[52] The court further noted that "she testified that she was trained to counsel atheists as well as theists of all persuasions, since CPE teaches its adherents 'to facilitate just human expression whether that person be atheist or something else.' "[53] CPE-trained

49. See David Sehat, *The Myth of American Religious Freedom*.

50. Carter v. Broadlawns Medical Center, 857 F.2d 448 (1988).

51. Ibid. at 450. The United Church of Christ, a generally liberal Protestant church today, was created in 1957 as a successor to the Congregational churches founded by New England Puritans.

52. Ibid. at 451.

53. Ibid.

chaplains serve all. And, by not proselytizing, by serving atheists as well as theists, their practice is secularized and constitutionalized.

Supervising doctors who testified at the *Broadlawns* trial emphasized the importance and universality of the chaplain's role. Dr. Berry Engebretsen "testified that the hospital should use a 'wholistic' approach to medicine, and that this means that the patient's 'spiritual' as well as bodily, social and emotional states affect his health."[54] The court explained that "by using the word 'spiritual,' he did not mean to imply adherence to 'a particular denomination or world religion.' "[55] Broadlawns' approach was understood by the court to be spiritual, not religious. The other medical expert, Dr. Timothy Olsen, testified concerning the chaplain's special role in treating mental illness. He testified, echoing the justification for prison and military chaplaincies, that "psychiatric patients often need the support provided by a chaplain and stressed those patients' inability to leave the hospital at will and the isolation from ordinary sources of support frequently caused by their mental illness itself." Furthermore, "it was necessary to have an experienced chaplain who was able to work with the doctors in caring . . . particularly [for] those with religious delusions."[56] Presumably the chaplain would be able to identify and educate the psychiatrist about what counts as a "religious delusion," a special form of mental illness with which the doctor would be inexpert.

The *Broadlawns* court found that hiring Deacon Rogers to provide spiritual care to county mental health patients was not a violation of the establishment clause. Citing *Lynch* and *Katcoff*, the court held that "the finding that Broadlawns hired Rogers to enhance its wholistic treatment approach to patient care establishes a valid secular purpose under the *Lemon* test."[57] Universalist spiritual care is a constitutionally appropriate role of government. In a case of circular reasoning, it seems that all that is necessary to constitutionalize religion is to say that it serves a secular purpose.[58] Secularity for the court guarantees constitutionality. Indeed it is not too much to say that constitutionality implies secularity as well.

54. Ibid.
55. Ibid.
56. Ibid.
57. Ibid. at 455.
58. "The Court has invalidated a government act because it violated the 'secular purpose' requirement only five times since *Lemon*." Schragger, "The Relative Irrelevance," 593. *Lemon* has been widely criticized by academics. See, e.g. Steven G. Gey, "Religious Coercion and the Establishment Clause," *University of Illinois Law Review* 463 (1994): 467–72.

Excessive religious particularity can disqualify a chaplain under this reasoning. In 1988, the dismissal of a Pentecostal minister who was serving as a chaplain in a VA hospital in Illinois was upheld against a constitutional challenge on the ground that the minister was insufficiently ecumenical in his practice.[59] Franklin Baz, a Pentecostal minister who had been fired from his job as chaplain at a VA psychiatric hospital, had brought an employment discrimination and free exercise claim alleging that his dismissal was the result of bias based on his religious identity. Mr. Baz complained that he was discriminated against because his theology differed from that of the VA. The court, upholding the dismissal, contrasted the parties' differing understandings of the chaplain's role: "The plaintiff saw himself as an active, evangelistic, charismatic preacher while the chaplain service and the medical staff saw his purpose as a quiescent, passive listener and cautious counselor. This divergence in approach is illustrated by the plaintiff's listing 'twenty-nine decisions for Christ' in his quarterly report of activities of the Veterans Administration."[60] "Decisions for Christ" denominate conversions.

The Seventh Circuit Court of Appeals affirmed the trial court in *Baz*, holding with the lower court that Baz's dismissal was for secular reasons having to do with the job of a chaplain, a job that was fundamentally secular, and that there was therefore no violation of the Civil Rights Act or of the free exercise clause: "A VA chaplain . . . is not simply a preacher but a secular employee hired to perform duties for which he has, by dint of his religious calling and pastoral experience, a special aptitude." The activity of proselytization sacralizes the chaplain's role and makes it unfit for government employment, as the court explained: "Far from defining its own institutional theology, the medical and religious staffs at Danville are merely attempting to walk a fine constitutional line while safeguarding the health and well-being of the patients."[61] Performing duties according to detailed instructions for which he has a special aptitude "by dint of his religious calling and pastoral experience" is secular and constitutional. "Unleashing" a proselytizer on a captive audience is not. One wonders what Justice Brennan might have said about the distinction. And one wonders also whether the comparative effectiveness of such care can in fact be distinguished and measured. In any event, it is, for the most part, the more generic version of chaplaincy and spiritual care that is being blessed as secular by the courts today.

59. *Baz v. Walters*, 782 F.2d 701 (1986).
60. Ibid. at 704.
61. Ibid. at 705, 709.

Murphy v. Derwinski,[62] a 1993 Tenth Circuit case, suggests, however, that, although the universalist model predominates, the courts were still struggling to stay out of theological matters in the administration of chaplaincies. Mary Wilson Murphy applied for a job as a Catholic chaplain in a VA hospital in Denver. She was informed that her application could not be considered because she was not ordained. At that time, ordination was required for employment as a VA chaplain, whether Catholic or not. Murphy, who met all of the other formal requirements for a position as a chaplain, filed a sex discrimination claim against the VA with the EEOC under Title VII of the Civil Rights Act of 1964.[63] On appeal from the decision of the secretary finding no violation, the district court held that the VA's ordination requirement had a disparate impact on women in violation of Title VII because some churches restricted ordination to men. It further found that the VA's expressed interest in providing a full range of services for Catholic patients could, in any event, be met through the ecclesiastical endorsement requirement. In other words, the court acknowledged that providing "a full range of sacramental rites" is an appropriate goal, but it argued that the way to do that, constitutionally, was by leaving ordination requirements to individual endorsing agencies to regulate because they are free to discriminate on the basis of sex. That is one of the purposes, or at least one of the effects, of the ecclesiastical endorsement requirement; it privatizes discrimination.[64]

While the language describing the employment of government chaplains is usually couched in a universalist manner, Catholics have often been treated differently, both in terms of employment requirements and in terms of the relationship between the church and various government agencies. Catholics are also often used as the test case because Roman Catholic doctrine and sacramental law is assumed to be distinctively material, mediating, and nonnegotiable. Also it is assumed to be clear and well defined. Priests *must* be male, and only priests can perform sacraments. Catholics *must* receive last rites before they die. Administrators of government chaplaincies often cite these rules as constituting limit cases in the challenge

62. Murphy v. Derwinski, 990 F.2d 540 (1993).

63. The administrative law judge in *Murphy* found a violation of the act, but the secretary disagreed. Ibid. at 542.

64. A dramatic instance of the failure of such an effort at outsourcing religious discrimination is seen in the first judgment of the British Supreme Court, a case concerning admissions to the Jews' Free School, a government-funded "faith school" in London: *R v. The Governing Body of JFS*, 2009 UKSC 15. Whether or not applicants were Jewish was determined by the Office of the Chief Rabbi (an Orthodox institution), rather than by the school. The arrangement was found to be in violation of the Race Ralations Act. Whether such outsourcing can continue in the United States remains to be seen.

158 / Chapter Four

of a universalist ministry—although the shortage of priests is straining the Roman Church's capacity to provide services, and in some respects Catholics themselves are changing their understanding of such an exclusivist non-negotiability understanding of the administration of sacraments.

The *Murphy* court of appeals concurred with the district court's opinion, but it also showed some skepticism about the narrow definition of Catholic pastoral work and, citing the *Baz* decision, emphasized the secular nature of a chaplain's duties:

> The record shows that outside the VA hospital system, women may and do serve as Roman Catholic chaplains without disruption of service. . . . Most of a chaplain's duties would be unaffected by the removal of the ordination requirement. A VA hospital chaplain is "not simply a preacher but a secular employee hired to perform duties for which he has, by dint of his religious calling and pastoral experience, a special aptitude."[65]

The court then reviewed the duties of a chaplain, comparing hospital chaplains to prison chaplains:

> The VA Manual states that the Chaplain Service's primary objective is to "provide for the spiritual welfare" of patients by establishing relationships with individual patients. . . . Priests are not needed to administer these functions. The VA desires that its chaplains . . . follow an ecumenical practice that stresses blending "general or universal truths and traditions." In these respects, the VA program is similar to prison chaplain services in which each chaplain's particular religious affiliation is a matter of secondary importance.[66]

Religious particularity is "of secondary importance" to a job whose "primary objective is to 'provide for the spiritual welfare of patients'" by "blending 'general or universal truths.'" Chaplains are no longer there primarily to provide specialized rituals. They are there to minster to a universal need. The appellate court's opinion in *Murphy* reflects a growing universalism in how the role of the chaplain is understood, putting further pressure on the use of the ecclesiastical endorsement to insulate government from claims of discrimination.[67] The tension persists between the government's claim to

---

65. 990 F.2d at 545.
66. Ibid. at 545–46.
67. Jane Rutherford, "Equality as the Primary Constitutional Value," *Cornell Law Review* 81 (1996).

serve a universal need equally, on the one hand, and the chaplain's three-way obligations to his secular employer, his client, and his own religious community, on the other.

Whether the particular religious affiliation of a chaplain could be considered a BFOQ, or "bona fide occupational qualification" under employment discrimination laws, and therefore exempt from strictures against discrimination, was considered in 1988 in *Rasul v. District of Columbia*, which did not reach the constitutional issue.[68] The *Rasul* court held that the Washington, DC, Department of Corrections could not claim that being a Protestant minister was a BFOQ for a position as chaplain in the face of a challenge by an otherwise qualified imam. The court explained: "The nature of the chaplain's duties suggest that an applicant's religious affiliation is, at best, a matter of secondary importance. Lorton chaplains . . . are entrusted with the task of 'planning, directing, and maintaining a total Religion program' for all inmates in a particular section who request such services, whatever their respective denominations might be."[69] More than a decade before 9/11, the courts were seeing imams as interchangeable with Protestant ministers when it came to doing the work of chaplains. In other words, being Protestant was not a prerequisite for being universal.

In the most recent and most dramatic challenge to the labor practices of government chaplaincies, more than eight hundred Evangelical and Pentecostal navy chaplains have sued the navy in a series of ongoing lawsuits claiming that the navy's theology unconstitutionally privileges non-Evangelical Christian chaplains, particularly in hiring, but also in assignments, promotion, and retirement practices.[70] These cases demonstrate the administrative complexity of meeting denominational needs of military personnel in a diverse navy. The Evangelical and Pentecostal plaintiffs allege that "the Navy has created a culture and system which has allowed and allows certain senior chaplains to exercise their religious bias and destroy plaintiffs' and other Non-liturgical chaplains' careers with no accountability." They expressly challenge the Navy Chaplain Corps' "systematic

68. Rasul v. District of Columbia, 680 F. Supp. 436, 442 (D.D.C. 1988).

69. Ibid. at 440–41.

70. See *In re* Navy Chaplaincy, 850 F. Supp. 2d 86 (2012) for the most recent decision in the cases. Also, Ward Sanderson, "War in the Chaplain Corps," *Stars and Stripes*, November 23, 2003; Steven H. Aden, "The Navy's Perfect Storm: Has a Military Chaplaincy Forfeited Its Constitutional Legitimacy by Establishing Denominational Preferences?," *Western State University Law Review* 31 (2004): 185; and Hansen, *Military Chaplains and Religious Diversity*, 177ff.

hostility and culture of prejudice," which "chill plaintiffs' free exercise and free speech rights."[71]

Kim Hansen, writing of the relationships among chaplains of different religious commitments in the navy, tells of a joke that expresses the problem the Evangelical chaplains perceive: "The running joke among evangelical chaplains was that for a baby-baptizer to get promoted, he only needed to be able to chew gum and walk at the same time. A non-baby-baptizer on the other hand would have to be able to chew gum and walk . . . on water."[72] Baby-baptizers include Catholics and what the navy calls liturgical Protestants. The accusation is that the navy favors Catholics and liturgical Protestants over Evangelical and Pentecostal Christians. Promotion is a serious issue in the navy chaplaincy because if you are passed over twice you will be removed from active duty. Hansen says that the chaplains he interviewed offered various explanations for the disparity of treatment, personal, institutional, and theological. Few agreed that there is in fact actionable discrimination occurring.[73]

The leading academic chroniclers of the legality of faith-based governmental activities, Ira C. Lupu and Robert W. Tuttle, advocate for something they call "minimal pluralism" in public prayer settings in the military and in the practical accommodation of the needs of service members.[74] Considering the various jurisprudential frameworks under which the constitutionality of government chaplaincies might be considered, Lupu and Tuttle conclude that they are best understood as a permissible (not required, as *Katcoff* suggests) accommodation of the needs of service personnel. Lupu and Tuttle argue that, since *Katcoff*, the following four criteria have been developed to consider the constitutionality of accommodations:

1   The Accommodation Must Relieve a Significant Government-Imposed Burden on the Private Exercise of Religious Freedom
2   The Accommodation Must Facilitate Private and Voluntary Religious Practices
3   The Accommodation Must Be Available on a Denominationally Neutral Basis

---

71. 850 F. Supp. 2d at 116.
72. Hansen, *Military Chaplains and Religious Diversity*, 177.
73. Ibid., 178.
74. Ira C. Lupu and Robert W. Tuttle, "Instruments of Accommodation: The Military Chaplaincy and the Constitution," *West Virginia Law Review* 110 (2007): 89–166. Lupu and Tuttle trace the origins of the idea of permissible accommodation to Justice Douglas's opinion in *Zorach*.

4   The Accommodation Must Not Impose Significant Burdens on Third
    Parties[75]

Lupu and Tuttle rely on the work of religion scholars Mircea Eliade, John
Hick, and George Lindbeck to define religion and religious pluralism. Announcing that funding worship is constitutionally suspect and "worship,
for most faiths, is the heart of religious experience . . . the center and source
from which other obligations and practices radiate," they express skepticism
about the capacity of government to provide constitutionally appropriate
religion through its chaplaincies.

Lupu and Tuttle also raise doubts about the constitutionality of the government's promotion of what they call "maximal pluralism" on the grounds
that pluralism itself makes a theological "truth claim": "In both its universalist or relativist modes, . . . maximal pluralism represents a substantive
and highly contested set of religious commitments. Officially compelled
proclamation of these religious commitments would raise serious problems
under both the Establishment and Free Exercise Clauses."[76] Having been
persuaded by religion scholars that maximal pluralism is in fact religious
because it makes a "truth claim," Lupu and Tuttle are wary of the government purveying such a position.[77] They are sympathetic to the claims of
Evangelical chaplains that they are being made to subscribe to a theology in
which they do not believe, the equal value of all religions, but they are also
clear in asserting that military chaplains, like other military personnel, do
not enjoy the same free speech protections as private citizens.[78]

The courts do not, on the whole, seem to agree with Lupu and Tuttle.
Increasingly, US courts are saying that the government can compel universalist religious commitments by chaplains because such commitments are
founded not in a sectarian religious or theological position raising constitutional red flags, but, rather, in a view of the human person that understands

75. Ibid., 113–16.
76. Ibid., 135.
77. Many political philosophers would resist the notion that pushing pluralism is necessarily a religious project. See, e.g., the work of Cécile Laborde, who is currently the primary
investigator for a five-year project funded by the European Research Council (ERC) entitled "Is
Religion Special? Reformulating Secularism and Religion in Legal and Political Theory."
78. Lupu and Tuttle, "Instruments of Accommodation," 137. Their position would be consistent with recent trends in free speech jurisprudence limiting the free speech rights of government employees more generally. See, e.g., Garcetti v. Ceballos, 547 U.S. 410 (2006). Some
military chaplains have asserted a First Amendment right to promote exclusivist religious positions. See, e.g., David E. Fitzkee and Linell A. Letendre, "Religion in the Military: Navigating the
Channel between the Religion Clauses," *Air Force Law Review* 59 (2007): 1–71.

him to be naturally spiritual, a view that should not be understood to be suspect under the establishment clause.

Appealing the *Nicholson* Decision

Returning to *Nicholson*, the VA case discussed in chapter 1, where do the US courts stand today on the constitutionality of the VA actively assessing and offering treatment for spiritual needs through its relocated chaplaincy? In 2008, having lost the *Nicholson* case on a motion for summary judgment in the district court, the Freedom from Religion Foundation appealed to the Court of Appeals for the Seventh Circuit, arguing that "the VA's policy choice to promote a faith infused model of medical treatment is not something the government can constitutionally do under the Establishment Clause. The government cannot camouflage its policy preference for religion over non-religion as merely an accommodation of Free Exercise rights."[79] While trends in the courts toward the voluntary accommodation of religion and spirituality might suggest that the Seventh Circuit would have likely affirmed the lower court opinion in *Nicholson*, what in fact happened was that before the appeal could be argued an intervening decision of the US Supreme Court in another FFRF case, *Hein v. FFRF*,[80] appeared to trump the questions presented in *Nicholson* and to complicate discussion of the issues at oral argument.

Hein is arguably one of the most important establishment clause cases decided by the Supreme Court in the last half century.[81] The *Hein* case had also been brought by the FFRF to challenge what it understood to be government preference for religion over nonreligion. As with *Katcoff* and *Nicholson*, and many other challenges to government activity under the establishment clause, *Hein* was a taxpayer case, that is, the court's jurisdiction in the case depended on the plaintiffs' standing as taxpayers. In *Hein*, FFRF represented taxpayers who were challenging the government's use of federal tax funds,

79. Brief of Appellants and Appendix, Freedom from Religion Foundation, Inc. v. Nicholson, 536 F.3d 730, 737 (7th Cir. 2008).

80. Hein v. FFRF, 551 U.S. 587 (2007).

81. For legal commentary on the decision, see Douglas Kmiec, "Standing Still—Did the Roberts Court Narrow, but Not Overrule, *Flast* to Allow Time to Re-think Establishment Clause Jurisprudence," *Pepperdine Law Review* 35 (March 2008): 509–22; Mark C. Rahdert, "Forks Taken and Roads Not Taken: Standing to Challenge Faith-Based Spending," *Cardozo Law Review* 32 (January 2011): 1009–97; Steven K. Green, "The Slow, Tragic Demise of Standing in Establishment Clause Challenges," issue brief published by the American Constitution Society (September 2011). Schragger argues that *Hein* only reinforces what was already the Court's tendency to underenforcement of the establishment clause. Schragger, "The Relative Irrelevance," 599.

arguing that White House promotion of faith-based initiatives through White House conferences designed to increase awareness and participation of faith-based providers in bidding for government contracts for social services violated the establishment clause.[82] A majority of the Supreme Court found in *Hein* that federal courts lacked power to hear FFRF's challenge to the faith-based initiative under Article III of the US Constitution.

Article III of the Constitution, which establishes and delimits the judicial power of the federal government, provides that federal jurisdiction will be limited to "cases" and "controversies."[83] These words have been interpreted to mean that both the Supreme Court and the lower federal courts established by Congress under Article III may rule only in what are known as "justiciable" controversies. These courts cannot decide what are understood to be essentially political questions, or rule on issues that are hypothetical or moot. To do those things is understood to invade the provinces of the other two branches of government and thus to violate the US constitutional doctrine of separation of powers. It is a bedrock principle of the US constitutional order that legal questions are better decided when presented in an actual case or controversy because the facts of a live controversy sharpen the issues before the court.[84] The relevance of this jurisdictional doctrine to taxpayer suits was first articulated in 1923 in *Frothingham v. Mellon.*[85]

In its decision in *Frothingham,* the Supreme Court held that lawsuits initiated by federal taxpayers, simply in their capacity as taxpayers, in order to challenge the constitutionality of congressional statutes, are not constitutionally justiciable because individual taxpayers, solely on the basis of their individual tax burden, lack an "injury in fact," or, what Justice Scalia calls in his concurring opinion in *Hein* a "pocketbook" injury, rather than a "psychic" injury, that is, they lack a sufficient personal financial stake in such

82. The entire faith-based initiative, originating under President Clinton in the Welfare Reform Act, and continued under President George W. Bush, might be said to exemplify the new affirmation of the universality and naturalization of religion. Executive branch programs to facilitate faith-based social service programs continue under the Obama administration, although there is strong sociological evidence that many religious providers lack the interest and ability to avail themselves of these opportunities. See Mark Chaves and Bob Wineburg. "Did the Faith-Based Initiative Change Congregations?," *Nonprofit and Voluntary Sector Quarterly* 39 (2010): 343–55.

83. U.S. Constitution Art. III § 2.

84. The US Supreme Court differs in this respect from many other national constitutional courts that are explicitly authorized, sometimes designed exclusively, to give legal opinions as to the constitutionality of legislation whether or not there is a live controversy, sometimes before the legislation goes into effect. In some constitutional systems, such challenges may be brought only by certain designated persons, such as members of parliament.

85. Frothingham v. Mellon, 262 U.S. 447 (1923).

cases to qualify their challenges as real cases or controversies under Article III. Individual US taxpayers can sue the government over issues specific to their own tax bills, but they cannot sue the government as watchdogs on behalf of the public at large to challenge how the government spends the general funds it raises through taxes.

Only one exception has been made to this rule against taxpayer suits since the *Frothingham* decision. In 1968, in *Flast v. Cohen*,[86] the Court allowed such taxpayer actions specifically in order to challenge the constitutionality of congressional acts alleged to be in violation of the establishment clause of the First Amendment. Religion is special, the Court said in 1968, and its financing by the government is especially dangerous. The *Flast* taxpayer-plaintiffs had challenged a federal grant of assistance to local schools, including religious schools, to purchase textbooks and other instructional materials for disadvantaged students. In an eight-to-one decision, the Supreme Court held in *Flast* that the foundational and structural importance of the principle of church-state separation to the US government demanded that an exception be made to the rule in *Frothingham*. Citing James Madison, special emphasis was placed by the majority in *Flast* on the evil of using any government funds whatsoever, however small, to support religion.[87] In his concurring opinion in *Flast*, Justice William Douglas, in anti-Catholic language characteristic of him and of the time, described the "mounting federal aid to schools" as "notorious" and warned that any money given to parents of parochial school children would be given directly to "the priest."[88]

But that was 1968. In a prophetic dissent to the *Flast* decision, Justice John Marshall Harlan cautioned against an ahistorical reading of the religion clauses: "The historical purposes of the religious clauses of the First Amendment are significantly more obscure and complex than this Court has heretofore acknowledged. Careful students of the history of the Establishment Clause have found that 'it is impossible to give a dogmatic interpretation of the First Amendment, and to state with any accuracy the intention of the men who framed it.' "[89] Anticipating, one might say, both the decline of anti-Catholic sentiment and a return to social acceptance of overt

86. 392 U.S. 83 (1968). But see Nancy C. Staudt, "Taxpayers in Court: A Systematic Study of a (Misunderstood) Standing Doctrine," *Emory Law Journal* 52 (2003): 771–804.

87. Authority for this proposition was found in James Madison's *Memorial and Remonstrance*: "The same authority which can force a citizen to contribute three pence only of his property for the support of any one establishment, may force him to conform to any other establishment in all other cases whatsoever." 392 U.S. at 103.

88. 392 U.S. at 119 n.9.

89. Ibid. at 128.

government support of religion that was to occur some thirty or forty years later, Harlan insisted in his decision in *Flast* that "the difficulty with which the Court never comes to grips, is that taxpayers' suits under the Establishment Clause are not . . . meaningfully different from other public actions."[90] Religion is not different. Harlan's dissent in *Flast*, which reaffirms the rule against taxpayer standing in *Frothingham* and rejects the majority's conclusion that the establishment clause is in some sense more "structural" than other constitutional limitations on congressional spending, significantly foreshadows both the recent reworking of establishment clause jurisprudence in general, the Court's decision in *Hein* in particular, and the current legal phenomenology of religion. Extending Justice Harlan's reasoning, one might argue that religion today is increasingly regarded by the Court as not particularly threatening, not perhaps even essentially different from other sociocultural phenomena, at least when it comes to government funding.[91] Religion does not need to be separated.

The vote in *Hein* was five to four, and there were four different opinions filed in the case. The three opinions of the justices in the majority differed on precisely why FFRF lacked standing and as to whether they should formally overrule *Flast*, but what united them was their assertion that the danger of religious establishment no longer requires special constitutional vigilance. All three announced that such special treatment is the legacy of an earlier, now anachronistic, anti-Catholicism, and that it therefore ought to be abandoned. The president can promote the value of religion, they said, just as he can promote any other social policy, limited only by electoral politics. And taxpayers—simply in their role as taxpayers—have no standing to complain about it in federal court. The full reach of the *Hein* precedent is still unclear.[92] The decision limited *Flast* to taxpayer establishment clause challenges to certain kinds of specific funding allocations by Congress, distinguishing as exempt from such taxpayer challenges other kinds of

90. Ibid. at 128.

91. The Court's recent decision in *Hosanna-Tabor* might be said to complicate this claim. *Hosanna-Tabor* recognizes a ministerial exception to the civil rights laws, and implies that the ministerial exception is, in some sense, structurally mandated. The ministerial exception is apparently limited to the hiring of ministers by churches, however, not by the government. And the majority opinion in *Hosanna-Tabor* focuses almost exclusively on "the church," not on religion more generally. Putting *Hein* together with *Hosanna-Tabor*, the Court seems to regard the church as having a special constitutional identity but not one that requires special vigilance. See note 33 on p. 15 above.

92. *Hein* was extended in Arizona Christian School Tuition Organization v. Winn, 131 S. Ct. 1436 (2011) to taxpayer challenges to tax credits. For a critique of this decision, see William P. Marshall and Gene R. Nichol, "Not a *Winn*-Win: Misconstruing Standing and the Establishment Clause," *Supreme Court Review* (2011): 215–52.

congressional action and the activities of the White House Office on Faith-Based and Community Initiatives as a part of the executive branch.[93] But, as Justice Scalia wrote in his concurrence in *Hein, Flast's* days seem clearly to be numbered.[94]

Souter's opinion on behalf of the four dissenting justices in *Hein* is long and impassioned, but somewhat dated, relying as it does on a social understanding of the dangers of religious establishment more characteristic of the *Flast* era. Souter insists that individual conscience must be protected by a high wall of separation from the necessary discrimination resulting from a state-church alliance. "Favoritism for religion," says Souter, citing James Madison and invoking Justice O'Connor's test for the establishment clause introduced in *Lynch*, " 'sends the . . . message to . . . nonadherents' that they are outsiders, not full members of the political community."[95] The majority's opinions in *Hein* reflect a shift away from such separationist arguments—a shift away from understanding the establishment clause as a structural bulwark against the favoring of religion. As long as there is no coercive government proselytizing of an identifiable person, government can promote and fund religion as it chooses. In other words, government is free to favor religion in general because religion in general is presumed to be noncoercive in a sectarian sense, even beneficial.

In the oral argument in the *Nicholson* case in the US Court of Appeals for the Seventh Circuit, the lawyers and the judges discussed both the significance of *Hein* and the substance of FFRF's complaints about the VA chaplaincy program.[96] With respect to the merits of the case, that is, the constitutionality of the VA assessment program, the judges repeatedly asserted their concern that forbidding the spiritual assessment and care provided by the VA chaplaincy might amount to preventing the government from offering veterans the best treatment. The judges characterized as desirable those programs that "are the most medically effective regardless of religious orientation," with one worrying aloud that "if services that would promote a positive health outcome aren't allowed solely because they are religious in nature that promotes non-religion over religion in violation of the estab-

93. An earlier decision limiting the *Flast* doctrine, Valley Forge Christian College v. Americans United for the Separation of Church and State, 454 U.S. 464 (1982), found that the federal courts lacked jurisdiction in a taxpayer challenge to the transfer of government property without cost to a Christian college.

94. 551 U.S. at 637.

95. Ibid. at 643.

96. Oral argument in Freedom from Religion Foundation v. Nicholson, 536 F.3d 730 (7th Cir. 2008), 07-1292, available as an mp3 file at http://www.ca7.uscourts.gov/fdocs/docs .fwx?caseno=07-1292&submit=showdkt&yr=07&num=1292 (accessed February 8, 2013).

lishment clause, doesn't it?" and also that "the patient who is susceptible to making progress in a faith-based program really is put at a disadvantage." One judge asked the FFRF attorney: "Aren't you committing the Veterans Administration to giving sub-standard care in these areas simply because it is a government organization?" Standard care naturally now includes spiritual care.

The Seventh Circuit judges seemed prepared at oral argument to accept the notion that spiritual care might be the best care in some circumstances and that the government therefore has an obligation to provide it to veterans. Religion is good for you. Separation is not. But the case was not decided on those grounds. To conform with the new rule announced in *Hein*, the Seventh Circuit court in *Nicholson* vacated the decision of the district court and ordered that court to enter an order dismissing the complaint in its entirety: "Allowing taxpayer standing under these circumstances would subvert the delicate equilibrium and separation of powers that the Founders envisioned and that the Supreme Court has found to inform the standing inquiry."[97] Other taxpayer actions challenging government expenditures under the establishment clause have also been dismissed since the *Hein* decision. These dismissals reflect broader shifts in the Court's attitude toward the desirability of this sort of constitutional litigation, but they also reflect specific shifts away from reliance on the judiciary in managing the spiritual life of the nation.

FFRF did not challenge the constitutionality of the chaplaincy itself in *Nicholson*, but only the particular use to which it was being put in the spiritual assessment policy and in the VA's integration of chaplains into the clinical team. Questions about the constitutionality of government-sponsored chaplaincies linger, however, particularly as no appeal was taken from *Katcoff* and the Supreme Court has not subsequently directly addressed the issue. (Legislative chaplaincies, approved in *Marsh*, are often considered a special case in the literature because of their use in the Continental Congress and because legislators are viewed as a less captive and vulnerable a population.[98]) The administrative entanglements revealed in the ongoing litigation concerning the navy chaplaincy have raised a host of thorny issues. As Steven Green, a leading First Amendment scholar, puts it

97. 536 F.3d 730, 737 (7th Cir. 2008). The Seventh Circuit had already dismissed another appeal under *Hein*: Hinrichs v. Speaker of the House of Representatives of the Indiana General Assembly, 506 F.3d 584, 598 (7th Cir.2007), a case challenging the Indiana legislature's Minister of the Day program, the legislative prayer scheme of the Indiana state legislature.

98. But see *Town of Greece* (see note 38 above), concerning chaplain prayers in a town council meeting in New York State, argued in the US Supreme Court on November 7, 2013.

with respect to the military chaplaincies, "The military chaplaincy system is a constitutional train-wreck waiting to happen."[99]

Rethinking Legal Religion

A prominent public expression of the new salience of religion for law and politics is the enormous enthusiasm today for the active promotion and legal protection of religious freedom. Virtually every country in the world today guarantees religious freedom. Religious freedom is being incorporated into legal instruments across the globe at every level of government.[100] In pursuit of the spread of legally free religion, religion is being legally remodeled to suit it for globalization. Why and when freedom of *religion* became so salient politically is complex and incompletely understood. Even while religious freedom proliferates as a universal political and legal goal, religion remains subject everywhere to the laws of a remarkably diverse set of local, national, and transnational regimes born of complex historical and cultural interactions.

Among other products of this political effort, the global conversation about law and religion displays a fascinating array of possible religio-legal arrangements, provincializing the American story. For many in the United States, the legal administration of religion in this country has been understood to stand apart from the larger story, motivated by a unique and historic commitment to and achievement of religious freedom. The prevailing narrative in the United States has been that religious freedom originated in the decision of English Puritans to flee persecution and come to North America. Cut free from the political tyranny and religious authoritarianism of Europe, American religion then flourished as a voluntary and apolitical commitment of a free people to live virtuously. This story is less persuasive than it once was. The history that supports this claim of exceptionalism is being rewritten, and the history and legal phenomenology of US religion is being redescribed in light of a longer and broader story. Too long Americans have assumed that disestablishment and free exercise structure a distinctively free religion for Americans. We now know better. Religious freedom is not a single phenomenon. Further, advocacy for religious freedom has multiple motivations, figuring at times unambiguously as a cover for projects of domination and at others seeming to persist as an expression

99. Green, "Reconciling the Irreconcilable," 168.
100. See Politics of Religious Freedom Project, http://politics-of-religious-freedom.berkeley.edu/ (accessed July 21, 2013).

of more inchoate contemporary anxieties about the nature and future of what it means to be human.

Two dominant stories are now being told. One story is of conscience. This version depends on a particular stitching together of ancient Greek and Christian philosophies, often culminating in an Enlightenment liberation of the individual. Antigone is succeeded by Paul and then by John Stuart Mill. Another story tells of the freedom of religious communities to be self-governing. This version tells the story of religiously plural empires and states that have provided limited legal subjurisdictions to enable such self-government: Romans, Ottomans, the Moguls, followed by India, and others. The early Christian community is succeeded by the Jewish Diaspora, by the separatist churches of the radical reformation, and then by indigenous claims to self-rule and Muslim personal law jurisdictions, among others, the descendants of which continue to claim communal sovereignty. These two stories are in tension because in the first story multiple religious communities are replaced with a single civic community and in the second the freedom of the individual in the minority community is submerged in the push for the community's continued existence. The ongoing tension between these two models can conceal at times the fact that all individuals are formed by and participate in communities, civic and religious.

A less heroic account might see religious freedom today as naming the convergence of a series of political, economic, and religious changes that are enabling a rethinking and reshuffling, of religious and civic identities and commitments, parallel perhaps to that of the early modern period, one whose outcome is uncertain. On this account, religious freedom emerges discursively as an adjunct to the early modern emergence of the sovereign nation-state and the autonomy of the modern individual over against the community and as a product, later, of post–World War II politics; deep uneasiness remains about the precise articulation of individual and community as seen in the history of minority rights under this international law and politics. In the twentieth century, the articulation of the sovereignty of the nation-state as over against both individuals and minority populations supports both nationalist and internationalist forms of domination.[101]

Historian Evan Haefeli sets the United States, and its particular form of legal religion, in the context of the British imperial history of the seventeenth and eighteenth centuries.[102] Reviewing and rejecting various accounts

---

101. See Saba Mahmood, "Religious Freedom, the Minority Question, and Geopolitics in the Middle East," *Comparative Studies in Society and History* 54 (2012): 418–46.

102. Evan Haefeli, "Toleration and Empire: The Origins of American Religious Diversity,"

of American exceptionalism in this area, Haefeli concludes that "what made America exceptional was its English context," not a commitment to toleration. The English context to which he refers was the fluctuating religious politics in Britain over the period of American colonization and founding. Haefeli explains that "the Elizabethan legacy was not the founding of American colonies but the emergence of religious tensions within the national church that ultimately undermined England's ability to create a religiously homogenous empire." He concludes that "American pluralism was born in England's religious chaos."[103]

Samuel Moyn sees the twentieth century as further transforming what was essentially an explicitly Christian project from the beginning:

> Primarily a federation of Protestants agreeing to put aside their once bitterly divisive differences in the name of common geopolitical interests, the FCC [Federated Council of Churches] and its European allies were in the van of history in perfecting "freedom of religion" as the main principle with which to oppose communism, before the wartime alliance frayed or the Cold War even began. . . . One of the most important developments in Cold War historiography of late is to show, even as the US Supreme Court turned to impose a "wall of separation" between church and state, how the country's self-avowed Christian statesmen viewed their task as a holy crusade against secularism. It was at this point that Americans pledged allegiance to a nation united "under God" and therefore indivisible.[104] (citations omitted)

Moyn's account would coincide with others for whom modernity is a euphemism for Christian exceptionalism and imperialism, particularly in a context of the invention and protection of Christian minorities and of Christian missionaries and the overt or concealed demonization of Islam and other non-Christian religions.[105]

Paralleling these histories of religious freedom and of the legal regulation of religion is the history of the modern study of religion, another messy story, to be sure. But scholars of religion have cooperated in various ways in the effort to remodel religion for modern government.[106] One result has

---

Oxford History of the British Empire, suppl. vol. (Oxford: Oxford University Press 2013).

103. Ibid.

104. Moyn, "From Communist to Muslim."

105. Gil Anidjar, "Secularism."

106. On the role of expert witnesses, see Winnifred Fallers Sullivan, "The Religious Expert in American Courts," in "Expertise publique et religion," special issue, *Archives des Sciences Sociales des Religions* 155(2011): 41–60.

been that Christians have been able to be a "religion" when it suits them, when they feel the need of legal or political protection, and not a "religion" when that is advantageous, when they wish to be aligned with "secular" political and legal authorities against other religions; this capacity to engineer a win-win situation by darting back and forth across the secular divide has allowed Christians to be the arbiter of what counts as good religion and what counts as bad religion for law.[107] This book describes a new effort to escape the bobbing and weaving of religious politics. In the United States today, there is a sense that law's subject is increasingly a person naturally religious but also scientifically comprehensible, that is, a person in need of spiritual care. The provision of that care is understood to be the end of religious freedom.

---

107. For a tracing of this theme in US literary history, see Tracy Fessenden *Culture and Redemption*.

FIVE

A Ministry of Presence

While in the past chaplains were mostly religious specialists legally detailed from a particular church to a particular secular setting in order to provide necessary, even mandatory, religious services specific to a particular religious tradition (e.g., private masses and spiritual formation for nobility, last rites for soldiers, or baptism for dying babies) but also in order to provide pastoral counseling for church members who were away from their home religious communities (soldiers, prisoners, patients, and perhaps legislators) as well as to serve as an advocate for social justice, the role has been transformed in the last several decades in the United States and elsewhere. Secularizing processes of various kinds, including the effects of late capitalism and the apparent explanatory power of sciences such as medicine, evolutionary psychology, and neuroscience; greater mobility; a shift in religious authority from traditional leadership to various forms of lay authority; increased religious diversity and intermarriage; and, not least, the press of the politics of religious freedom, have all set the stage for a transformation of the religious services on offer as well as for changes in the professionalization and credentialing of chaplains.

What is common across the various remaining differences among chaplains and their religious affiliations and inclinations in the United States today is the centrality of a religious practice that addresses the suffering of the human person in a very basic, almost naively precultural, way. Prohibited from appearing to favor one's own or to proselytize either formally by law or, more informally, by the political and existential situation of religious diversity and competition, but also because of the illegibility of traditional religious practices to a fragmented and unchurched population, many chaplains in the United States in many different kinds of settings today are practicing what they call a "ministry of presence."[1] This practice is a minimalist, almost ephemeral, form of empathic spiritual care that is, at the same time, deeply rooted in religious histories and suffused with religious references for those who can read them.[2] It is religion stripped to the basics. Religion naturalized. Religion without code, cult, or community. Religion without metaphysics. It is religion for a state of uncertainty. As is typical of American religion, it both resists specific theological elaboration and is deeply rooted in a specifically Christian theology of the Incarnation.

A ministry of presence has become commonplace in a breathtakingly short space of time. It has moved well beyond its Christian roots; the phrase, a ministry of presence, is used by chaplains from a wide spectrum of religious traditions in a range of institutional settings to denominate their work. The language of presence is also the language that the government and other institutions often use to describe what chaplains do. Ed Waggoner, a theologian at Yale, writes to describe the various resonances of a ministry of presence in his wife's practice as an Episcopal priest: "it signals a refusal to proselytize; it stresses 'authentic' interpersonal relationships—perhaps less formal—in which the minister is conscious of representing the divine, but also fully present as a human individual with her own life experiences and personality and hopes and fears and joys."[3] It is particularly salient, he suggests, in a military setting: "Soldiers are afraid that killing threatens their own humanity. There is an explicit hope (on the part of soldiers and on the part of the Pentagon as an institution) that the chaplain will be a sentinel guarding the human-ness of those who, in the name of their country or of freedom or of whatever, must do violence against fellow humans."[4] A ministry of presence acknowledges religious pluralism, diffusely represents the divine, and guards the humanness of its participants, chaplain and client, while tacitly acknowledging the violence that "must" be done.

Sometimes an entire ministry is described as a ministry of presence; sometimes presence is one of a number of possible specialized ministries performed by chaplains. One army chaplain summarized his experience being rotated into Bosnia in 1996: "I went to some of the base camps but I did a lot out of Tuzla. It was a base camp ministry, Bible Studies . . . Wor-

---

1. It was Cynthia Lindner, director of ministry studies at the University of Chicago Divinity School, who first called my attention to the centrality of the ministry of presence to the work of chaplains.

2. See, e.g., Stella Rock, "Editorial," *Religion, State and Society* 39 (2011): 1–8.

3. Personal communication from Ed Waggoner, lecturer in theology, Yale Divinity School (October 27, 2011).

4. Ibid.

ship services, seeing the people, and a ministry of presence."[5] The navy, in its recruitment materials, uses the phrase to describe what their chaplains do: "regardless of denomination, the job of a Navy Chaplain is to minister to all. To care for all. To be there for all in those moments of need. Listening. Understanding. Supporting. It's the essence of a ministry of presence."[6] The army, too: "an army chaplain has to have what we call a ministry of presence."[7] Chaplains in hospitals, prisons, and universities also describe their work in these words.

It is difficult to tell a single story about the history and practice of the ministry of presence—even of the linguistic origins of the phrase. Ministry of presence has a range of semantic and cultural references. That is part of its elusive power. In some contexts for some people, presence can be reassuringly immanent and down to earth, empty of formal doctrinal content, comfortingly abstracted from tradition, but in and for others, it can specifically evoke highly elaborated theological understandings and rituals that acknowledge and pay homage to the presence of the divine in very insistent ways, cutting across Catholic and Protestant spiritual practices. The sayings of Brother Lawrence of the Resurrection, a discalced Carmelite monk who lived in Paris in the seventeenth century, collected in *The Practice of the Presence of God*, form a point of reference for some who practice this ministry.[8] John Wesley, founder of Methodism, among many others, was influenced by Brother Lawrence.

If one listens to current users of the concept, a ministry of presence may seem to refer to the simple physical presence of the minister—the minister's or chaplain's willingness simply to "sit with" a client without anxious expectation. It may refer to the actual presence of an undefined spirit, or, more thickly, by way of reference to specific religious and social doctrines and histories including the notion of Eucharistic presence in the Catholic traditions, the felt presence of Jesus in Protestant pietist traditions, the distinctive understanding of the presence of the divine in Jewish teaching, psychotherapeutic notions of transference, or the usually more broadly humanistic language of such traditions as the hospice movement. A Jewish

---

5. Kenneth E. Lawson, "Faith and Hope in a War-Torn Land: The US Army Chaplaincy in the Balkans, 1995–2005" (Fort Leavenworth, KS: Combat Studies Institute Press, 2006).

6. http://www.navy.com/careers/chaplain-support/notes-from-the-field/anonymous-chaplain .html (accessed February 8, 2013).

7. http://www.goarmy.com/chaplain/profiles/joel-panzer.html (accessed February 8, 2013); Pauletta Otis, "An Overview of the U.S. Military Chaplaincy": 4; see also Hansen, *Military Chaplains and Religious Diversity*, 19.

8. Thank you to Bernard McGinn for this reference.

chaplain, speaking of the response of the chaplain in the context of disaster relief, summarizes this distinctive orientation of pastoral care:

> Words do not have to be said—giving a bottle of water to a thirsty person speaks volumes about not being forgotten. Maintaining a calm presence at the bedside does not remove fear; it lessens isolation. To be with a person at a time of need is to honor the survivor's humanity, the inherent dignity endowed by the Creator. Teaching others how to be present, and how to listen to those in distress is a divine-like intervention that spreads the safety net of care and concern.[9]

As continues to be typical in the United States, Protestant, Catholic, and Jewish tropes dominate even when the effort—and even the practice—is broadly intended to be ecumenical or what is called multifaith.

In a recent article in the *Washington Post*, an American army chaplain, Rabbi Arnold E. Resnicoff, responding to the hiring of the first Hindu chaplain and the design of a new insignia for that person, argued that it is time to stop having separate insignia for chaplains from different religious traditions, and rather to institute a single symbol, the shepherd's crook, to denote all military chaplains: "During hard times the insignia has been a silent reminder that a chaplain is present. A 'ministry of presence' begins with an awareness of presence, and we must recapture the power of the chaplain's symbol to broadcast the message that he or she is present, part of the team."[10] Presence implies not just the presence of the individual chaplain, Resnicoff insists, but the presence of the whole host of military chaplains and the unified power symbolized in the shepherd's staff of their no-longer-different religious orientations.

In the contemporary moment, presence also seems to be a practice that is defined and takes place in opposition to a range of possible secular and sectarian modes of human interaction that are seen as undesirable or impossible. It might be read as a form of resistance—or, even, as a movement of insurrection, in Foucault's words.[11] The chaplain, whether in a hospital or prison or military setting, is not a doctor or a guard or a soldier or a government agent. He or she is not a priest or a rabbi. He is not trying to improve or constrain your life, but rather simply to be there, to listen, if asked to, to

---

9. Myrna Matsa, "Jewish Theology of Disaster and Recovery," *Journal of Jewish Spiritual Care* 10, no. 1 (2010): 20–31.

10. Arnold E. Resnicoff, "A New Symbol for America's Military Chaplains," *Washington Post*, August 9, 2011. (Thank you to Dianne Avery for this reference.)

11. Foucault, *Security, Territory, Population*, 227ff.

witness, to be with . . . you, whoever and wherever you are. If the chaplain does not, in the encounter, positively identify himself with a religious tradition, or demand that his client does so, the assumption is that he cannot be accused of imposition or proselytization, either morally or legally. But there is more. She can empower you through her receptive empathetic presence, empower you in handling the sometimes overwhelming demands on the modern self.[12]

Presence also works as a place of resistance to instrumentalist approaches to religion and spirituality. The ministry of presence refuses interpretation and explanation. While in some ways highly immanentist, even secularist in a strong disenchanting sense, presence can refuse to be made part of a system—to be measured and quantified and offered as a means to an end. It is the end. The ministry of presence respects loss. Presence, in other words, means or implies—or attempts to encompass—both presence and absence.

This chapter will look more closely at the ministry of presence and how it is described and defended today by those who practice it, with a view toward understanding it as, in part, a production of a recent religious politics. As is typical of American religion, one sees a mixing not only of religious traditions, but also of modes of religious or spiritual practice that are mystical, pietist, moralist, ritualistic, patriotic, instrumental, or just plain kitsch. As is also typical of American religion, the metaphysical implications are left underdefined, a condition that can be read at the same time as naively ignorant of its imposition or as a genuine reach for liberation.

Defining Presence

The principal reference work for ministers, chaplains, and other practitioners of pastoral care, a religious form of professional personal counseling, is the *Dictionary for Pastoral Care and Counseling*, a fifteen-hundred-page work defining and bringing together in alliance terms from medical, psychological, and theological lexicons of relevance to those who practice this form of ministry across many different denominations and religious communities. "Pastoral care," according to the dictionary, "derives from the biblical image of shepherd and refers to the solicitous concern expressed within the religious community for persons in trouble or distress . . . pastoral care is in

12. See Nikolas Rose, *Governing the Soul: Shaping the Private Self*, 2nd ed. (Free Association Books, 1999).

the cure-of-souls tradition."[13] The article goes on over some eight double-columned pages to distinguish various branches of the Christian churches in their approach to the cure of souls.

The entry on ministry of presence in the *Dictionary for Pastoral Care and Counseling* explains the deliberate self-abnegation characterizing the practice:

> The ministry of presence has come to mean a form of servanthood (*diakonia*, ministry) characterized by suffering, alongside of the hurt and the oppressed—a *being*, rather than a doing or a telling. The articulation or celebration of faith goes on within the individual or community that chooses these circumstances, but does so in the form of *disciplina arcani*, the "hidden discipline," with no program of external testimony.[14]

"A *being*, rather than a doing or a telling." The soldier, the patient, the prisoner, the worker is imagined here as in need of companionship not of a shared formal articulation of a specified theory of the purpose or end of the life that is supported. For each person, there is a hidden discipline that does that work. (*Disciplina arcani*, perhaps anachronously here, finds its meaning historically in the practice of early Christians who deliberately withheld knowledge of the "sacred mysteries" from the uninitiated.) The dictionary goes on explicitly to claim its Christian premise:

> The ministry of Christian presence is grounded in the doctrine of the Incarnation, sometimes in its kenotic form, and/or the doctrine of Atonement, especially the priestly office. The identification of the ministrant with the condition of those in need is viewed as a continuation of the ministry of Christ who "emptied himself, taking the form of a servant . . . and became obedient unto death" (Phil. 2:7a–8a).[15]

The word "presence" does the double work of suggesting nonimposition of a particular religious perspective while also expressing a very Christian understanding of the significance of suffering in the economy of salvation. For those who know the theology of the Incarnation, who have a commit-

---

13. Rodney J. Hunter, ed., *Dictionary for Pastoral Care and Counseling* (Nashville, TN: Abingdon Press, 1990), 836–44; See also Myers-Shirk, *Helping the Good Shepherd*, delineating the similarities and differences among liberal and conservative Christian approaches to pastoral counseling.

14. *Dictionary for Pastoral Care and Counseling*, 950–51.

15. Ibid.

ment to the "real presence" of Christ's body and blood in the Eucharist, and who aspire to live a life in imitation of Christ, being is doing. Overall, the dictionary entry on ministry of presence reflects the often contradictory motives, practices, and religious sourcing that are included in this ministry today, one that does not overtly proclaim its allegiances, but which is deeply inflected by Christian forms of knowing and doing. The entry also notes the importance of the strategic use of this form of ministry in secular lay contexts: "Here Christian presence refers to the exercise of ministry by the people of God in the secular world, preeminently the workplace, horizontally rather than hierarchically."[16]

The life and work of Charles de Foucauld is often mentioned, in the *Dictionary for Pastoral Care and Counseling* and elsewhere, as the privileged model for the ministry of presence today. Charles de Foucauld (beatified at the Vatican in 2005) was a French army officer who served in Algeria and Morocco at the end of the nineteenth century.[17] In the 1890s, he left the French army and entered a Trappist monastery, afterward becoming a hermit and ascetic, first in Palestine and then in southern Algeria among the Tuareg. De Foucauld was killed in 1916 while living as a solitary Christian ascetic. He made no converts or disciples during his lifetime and apparently made no effort to do so. In the thirties, however, groups of dedicated Christians were formed in Algeria known as the Little Brothers of Jesus and the Little Sisters of Jesus, inspired by his ideas and example. Members of these groups live today in small communities among the poor. They make no explicit attempt to convert their neighbors. Their declared purpose is simply to live among them as Christians.[18] There is also a group of regular priests, known as Jesus Caritas, who model their spirituality on the witness of de Foucauld. While we know from his writings that his own practice was explicitly infused with classic French Catholic Eucharistic piety, de Foucauld is venerated today as advocating and modeling respect for Islam, a hero to those who preach interfaith tolerance.[19]

Understanding the nature of the presence of Christ in the Eucharist, the meal and worship service memorializing the Last Supper, has been

16. Ibid.

17. De Foucauld's spiritual writings are collected in Robert Ellsberg, ed., *Charles de Foucauld* (New York: Orbis Books, 1999).

18. I am indebted to Fr. Donald Senior of the Catholic Theological Union for directing me to the work of these followers of de Foucauld.

19. For a Muslim reading of de Foucauld's life, see Ali Merad, *Christian Hermit in an Islamic World: A Muslim's View of Charles de Foucauld*, trans. Zoe Hersov (Mahwah, NJ: Paulist Press, 2000). See also *Des Hommes et des Dieux*, a French film directed by Xavier Beauvois about a group of French monks living in the Atlas Mountains in Algeria who were assassinated in 1996.

the object of a great deal of theological work and devotional attention by Christians. Reflecting on what exactly Jesus meant in what are known as the words of institution, "this is my body, this is my blood, do this in memory of me,"[20] has occupied the work of many thousands of theologians but also has formed the basis for devotional practices, particularly in the high-liturgical traditions. In the medieval church, images of Christ, meditation on the host, monstrances, liturgical processions—but most importantly the words and actions of the Mass—were designed to awaken in the devotee an experience of the real presence, the continued life of Christ in the world. They were also connected to displays of religio-political power. Such practices, as well as more popular forms of devotion, continue to characterize the sacramentalism of the inheritors of the traditions of the medieval church. In that context, the meaning of presence as a religious practice is shaped in relation to a particular church-defined orthodoxy.

Since the fourth century when a doctrinal definition of the Mass first crystallized, there have been differences about how exactly to understand and express Christian confidence in the continued presence of Christ, and many reformations. Redefinition was occasioned, for example, by the many changes to the churches during the breakup of the Roman monopoly of the sixteenth and seventeenth centuries. Each of the Christian communities has developed articulations of and practices of the Incarnation. Rejecting what they took to be a tendency toward superstitious and nonbiblical idolatry in the church of the Middle Ages, presence in the low-church pietist traditions, for example, articulated in the eighteenth and nineteenth centuries, a dominant tradition in the United States, tends to be more associated with the believer's personal experience of the presence of God or Jesus. As the gospel hymn has it:

> And He walks with me, and He talks with me,
> And He tells me I am His own;
> And the joy we share as we tarry there,
> None other has ever known.[21]

There is a sense in which in the United States these two forms of piety, Catholic Eucharistic devotion and evangelical Protestant pietism, have been largely opaque to one another across this divide until quite recently. In the last few decades, the gap has narrowed and the two traditions have con-

---

20. As reported in the various gospels: Matthew 26:25–29; Mark 14:21–25; Luke 22:18–21.
21. C. Austin Miles, "In the Garden," RCA Victor Records catalog number LSP-1885.

verged as evangelicals have discovered the medieval liturgy and Catholics have discovered Bible reading. The definitional ambiguity of the expression "ministry of presence" helps to enable that convergence while also opening to a more general spiritual presence embracing religious practices beyond Christianity.

Real Presence

Presence can be understood then to be the straightforward invocation of the Christian doctrine of the Incarnation. If Eucharistic presence implies a certain understanding of the continued presence of Jesus in the world after his death in the ritual commemoration of the Last Supper, incarnation also gestures toward the moment of his birth. Incarnation is the process of a god taking on the body of a human—of the enfleshment of a god. For Christians, the Incarnation, as a theological doctrine, refers to the Christian god having become a human with the event of the conception of Jesus, as announced to Mary by the angel.[22] In the words of the fourth-century Nicene Creed, "We believe in one God . . . who for us men, and for our salvation, came down and was incarnate and was made man." God made flesh. Christian theology interprets this event as God's taking on of the burden of humanity in order to redeem it. There is for Christians in the Incarnation a simultaneous making available of a future life for humans with the taking on of a body for the god. Incarnation is not an exclusively Christian religious idea, however. Both the enfleshment of gods and the desire to escape the body are present in many traditions.

Incarnation is not just central to many religious traditions and important for any multifaith ministry for that reason; its ubiquity in writing about chaplaincy in particular reflects a persistent concern with the double embodiedness of the chaplain's work—in the church and in the world. Chaplains work in hospitals, on battlefields, on the docks and in factories, and in prisons, among many other places; notwithstanding its claim to be a practice of *spiritual* care, the work of chaplains is profoundly attentive to bodies—to being there. The chaplain understands herself as incarnating God's presence within her flock, particularly in times of suffering and death.

John Brinsfield, in his history of the US Army chaplaincy since Vietnam, emphasizes the intense identification of military chaplains with the gritty lives of soldiers. In a chapter describing the role of chaplains in Operation Desert Shield, "Ministry of Presence: Go Where Soldiers Go," Brinsfield

22. Luke 1:28–30.

assembles a pastiche of reminiscences about the chaplains' experiences, extolling the integration of chaplains with the lives of the soldiers. As he explains, "For many chaplains, ministry during Desert Shield did not begin at the time of arrival in Saudi Arabia, but from the moment the troop unit was alerted . . . . During the flights chaplains walked the aisles of the aircraft and talked and joked with their people. Upon arrival, of course, the chaplains went wherever the soldiers did." He quotes Jeffrey Phillips, author of a memoir about the first Gulf War, who was there: "When the 1st Cavalry Division arrived at Dhahran, they emerged into suffocating heat, . . . they were flooded with sensations: the first sight of an Arab in red and white checked headdress; from nowhere, a band playing . . . the first drop of sweat trickling down the small of their backs." Quoting from one of his many interviews with former army chaplains who were there at Dharam: "'We couldn't wait to get out of there,' Chaplain Sanford recalled, 'but we were busy every minute listening to the soldiers' gripes, concerns and complaints.'"[23] Robert J. Phillips, a retired navy Chaplain agrees: "The unit chaplain is not imbedded with that unit. He or she is *incarnate* with that unit."[24]

The chaplain lives the physical life of the soldier. He is present in that sense, but he also incarnates, one might say, the legal and ethical ambiguities of his many roles. He physically suffers the life of the soldier, but he also suffers the impossible contradictions of his own suspension at the center of so many demands. Phillips optimistically invokes this notion of presence in his description of the chaplain's work:

> As a point person for the free exercise of religion for all personnel, *as a [sic] incarnate presence* in nurturing the human worth and needs of service members, as a "helpful bystander" in settings of potential moral disengagement, and as a caring bridge-builder for the combat veteran's spiritual and emotional reentry into the larger world, the military chaplain can offer the armed forces a unique and indispensable service without betraying the integrity of the faith group *ethos* that has endorsed him or her to serve.[25]

Speaking with a former navy chaplain who served for more than two decades, I asked her whether what I was calling in-betweenness properly characterized the chaplain's role. She responded quickly and emphatically that the chaplain could not be effective if she was in-between. She must fully enter

23. Brinsfield, *Encouraging Faith*, pt. 2, 92–93.
24. Phillips, "The Military Chaplaincy of the 21st Century," 5.
25. Ibid, 9.

into the life of the marine—into the muddiness and danger and ennui. She would only be trusted if she was one of them.[26] Presence is a deeply physical experience, but it is also, as chaplains keep saying, a "suffering with."

It is not just the American army. Joanne Benham Rennick explains how Canadian military chaplains, facing "a threefold challenge in carrying out traditional religious ministry: increasing pluralism, deinstitutionalized beliefs and the loss of moral consensus," have also developed a "ministry of presence." Rennick explains that a ministry of presence involves participating in and being vulnerable to the world of the soldier, and—when necessary—suffering alongside them. She notes that "the [Canadian] Department of National Defence defines the Ministry of Presence as, 'being available to, and known by, the soldier, being available for a comforting chat, developing a relationship with the members of the unit, and participation in unit life. . . . [This ministry] makes the chaplaincy an outward and visible sign of the church who cares and consoles.'"[27] Canadian prison chaplains also speak of incarnation: "[Presence] can be determined by checking the sign-in sheet at the front gate . . . visible presence is something less concrete . . . refers to the theological concept of incarnating the divine in the ministry and pastoral services offered."[28] These are the words of a sacramental ministry.

Hospital chaplains also speak this way, as Wendy Cadge explains: "What chaplains most offer in hospitals is their presence. 'Just somebody who walks in, takes them [the patient or family] as they are, listens to their stories, shares their concerns . . . somebody who takes them the way they are, who has no expectations.' . . . There's a challenge to put words to what we do . . . it is about presence, about being present for whatever happens."[29] This incarnational aspect of chaplaincy work—of the ministry of presence—also finds a historical resonance with the priests who joined the labor movement. For example, in an article remembering the work of George Higgins, a Catholic priest labor activist, William Bole comments, "He often referred to his work in the labor movement as simply a 'ministry of presence.' When he was asked in a 1994 interview to list two or three of his greatest

26. Personal conversation with Joan Miller (February 8, 2013). Quoted with permission. Joan Miller served for over twenty years as a navy chaplain in both active and reserve components. She also emphasized in our conversation that a chaplain must be "wholly absorbed in the life of one's faith tradition as well."

27. Department of National Defence, Canada, "Chaplains: What They Do,"; Joanne Benham Rennick, "The Ministry of Presence and Operational Stress," *Journal of Military and Strategic Studies* 7 (Spring 2005).

28. "National Chaplaincy Evaluation: Pastoral Care" Evaluation and Review Branch. Chaplaincy Branch NHQ File # 394-2-026.

29. Cadge, *Paging God*, 93.

accomplishments with labor, he said, 'I tend not to think in those terms. I've always felt that my role, a limited role, was . . . just to be there, to be present, to give them support.'"[30] Lacking specific doctrinal content, presence gains the specificity of its content from the shared life experience, as a way of overcoming the alienation—and the absence—of modern ways of living. A well-known Jewish chaplain explaining the work of the chaplain says that "the third resource is the concept of 'non-anxious presence,' which is how many chaplains might speak about the 'ministry of presence.'"[31]

Another frequently mentioned exemplar for the ministry of presence is Henri Nouwen, a Dutch Catholic priest and widely read and revered spiritual teacher. He lived at the L'Arche community for the intellectually disabled in Toronto for the last ten years of his life until his death in 1996. He spoke of his incarnational ministry to the mentally disabled as a ministry of presence: "More and more, the desire grows in me simply to walk around, greet people, enter their homes, sit on their doorsteps, play ball, throw water, and be known as someone who wants to live with them. It is a privilege to have the time to practice this simple ministry of presence."[32] A ministry of presence means living the life of the person who is being cared for, suffering with them and very specifically undergoing the same living and working conditions, to "be known as someone who wants to live with them."

Like those who teach clinical pastoral education, Nouwen's writing emphasized the value of this ministry for the minister as well as for those who are ministered to. The need in the ministry of presence is not simply that of the soldier, the prisoner, or the patient. Each of the testimonies in this book also reveals a yearning on the part of the chaplain. Wendy Cadge comments on the desire of chaplains to be able to record their visits on hospital charts. What she describes is almost like the motive for tagging graffiti: I was here.[33] In a simple sense, it is about not being alone. The chaplain offers herself as a sacrifice to the suffering brought on by a myriad of seemingly intractable modern ills and the prevalence of a sense of abandonment, including her own. But she also seeks to be in relationship, not just with the divine, but

30. William Bole, "The Ministry of Presence," U.S. Catholic Historian, 19, no. 4 (2001): 3–10; "Social Catholicism: Essays in Honor of Monsignor George Higgins," U.S. Catholic Historian 19, no. 4 (2001): 3–10. See also Jerry Filteau, "Monsignor George Higgins: Labor Priest; A Success Story Par Excellence," National Institute for the Revival of the Priesthood, http://www.jknirp.com/higgins2.htm (accessed February 8, 2013).

31. Edwin H. Friedman, From Generation to Generation: Family Process in Church and Synagogue (New York: Guilford Press, 2011), 208–10.

32. Henri Nouwen, Gracias: A Latin American Journal (New York: Harper & Row, 1983), 147.

33. Cadge, Paging God, 180.

also with the client. As Constance Furey says, "What makes religious relationships—relationships construed in relation to divine as well as human beings—especially intriguing is the particular nuance and intensity of the way they combine the extraordinary and the ordinary, the normative and the transcendent."[34] Likewise, Robert Orsi affirms the ongoing importance of practices of presence, even in the face of centuries of insistence on the absence of God.[35] Christopher Swift gives the example of a chaplain entering a hospital room in which all the patient wished to talk about was the failure of the hospital staff; all she wanted was for him to listen to her and take her concerns seriously.[36] Summarizing his work for hospice, one chaplain interviewed by the *New York Times* simply said, "We are there to be there."[37]

The Science of Presence

How is it that a ministry of presence can be the appropriate prescription in a world characterized by all the measuring and quantifying of spiritual assessment today? How can something as naively intuitive and apparently nonrational as presence be the answer to poor spiritual health in a scientific age? The ministry of presence seems to depend on a deliberate rejection of utilitarian action, a rejection that at its strongest might even be seen as a witness to the apocalyptic. Yet, in our evidence-based, data-driven era, there is a constant pressure on chaplains to justify their work in biomedical and quantitative terms. Even as simple and apparently nonutilitarian a practice as presence demands proof of efficacy and causal explanation. A Houston-based health-care chaplaincy explicitly includes science in its review of all of the various religious approaches comprehended in their ministry, citing "a recent study [in which] scientists found that hospital patients who had someone sit with them a few hours a week, as opposed to those who did not, had changes in brain chemistry which indicate that they are less likely

34. Constance Furey, "Body, Society, and Subjectivity in Religious Studies," *Journal of the American Academy of Religion* 80 (2012): 7–33.

35. Robert Orsi, "Real Presences: Catholic Prayer as Intersubjectivity: From Practices of Presence to Sacred Absence; Theoretical Context," posted in *Reverberations: New Directions in the Study of Prayer*, March 18, 2013, http://forums.ssrc.org/ndsp/2013/03/18/from-practices-of-presence-to-sacred-absence/.

36. Swift, *Hospital Chaplaincy*, 109–10. The importance of simply listening is constantly mentioned by chaplains. J. L. Cedarleaf traces the emphasis on listening in pastoral care to Richard Cabot and Russell Dicks's early influential work, *The Art of Ministering to the Sick* (New York: Macmillan, 1936). S. V. "Listening" in *Dictionary of Pastoral Care and Counseling*.

37. Paul Vitello, "Hospice Chaplains Take Up Bedside Counseling," *New York Times*, October 29, 2008.

to become depressed." Research journals are replete with studies that seek to explain and show the value of presence in healing.

The partnership between Christian ministry and psychology is an old one, as has been noted. The value of presence is testified to in that literature as well. Claire Badarocco writes of America's long-standing faith in "healing presence" and the power of positive thinking on health.[38] Christopher White, in his history of spirituality and science, tells of Edwin Starbuck, a nineteenth-century Canadian psychologist, and his idea of the value of "infusing Presence."[39] One finds a continuity both with explicitly religious traditions of healing and an effort in the scientific community to account for the apparent value of companionship, natural and supernatural, to recovery. Chaplains offer themselves as expert in presence—as practitioners, perhaps, of an eclectic applied psychotheology.[40]

Seeking to find an empirical basis for the ministry of presence, one British hospice chaplain undertook empirical research in a hospital in the United Kingdom.[41] Bringing together contemporary Christian teaching, psychotherapy, Heidegger, Levinas, and a variety of social scientific research methods, he concluded, after interviewing a group of British chaplains who work with dying patients, that

> working with their patients' transferential projections—positive or negative—
> to the point of being accepted as an accompanier; demonstrating their prepared-
> ness to stay-with their patient no-matter-what; attending to their patient's
> soul by sharing something of their experience, containing and surviving it: in
> these ways chaplains may comfort (*confortare*) their patients and may conse-
> quently support them to be hopeful, not now so much concerned with the
> future of desire unfulfilled, but to be a being towards life, open to connected-
> ness and possibility—their hope reconfigured to "hope in the present."[42]

Sociologist Erving Goffmann described what he called copresence as the experience of face-to-face interaction.[43] In one essay on what he called face-

38. Claire Badarocco, *Prescribing Faith: Medicine, Media, and Religion in American Culture* (Waco, TX: Baylor University Press, 2007), 114. See also Candy Brown, *Healing Gods*.

39. White, *Unsettled Minds*, 156–57.

40. See Eric Santner, *On the Psychotheology of Everyday Life: Reflection on Freud and Rosenzweig* (Chicago: University of Chicago Press, 2001).

41. Steve Nolan, "Hope Beyond (Redundant) Hope: How Chaplains Work with Dying Patients," *Palliative Medicine* 25 (2011): 21.

42. Ibid., 25.

43. Erving Goffman, *Interaction Ritual: Essays in Face-to-Face Behavior* (Chicago: Aldine Publishing Company, 1967).

work, Goffman analyzed the dyad of the modern encounter between two persons:

> Many Gods have been done away with, but the individual himself stubbornly remains a deity of considerable importance. He walks with dignity and is the recipient of many little offerings. He is jealous of the worship due him, yet, approached in the right spirit, he is ready to forgive those who may have offended him. Because of their status relative to his, some persons will find him contaminating while others will find they contaminate him, in either case finding that they must treat him with ritual care. Perhaps the individual is so viable a god because he can actually understand the ceremonial significance of the way he is treated, and quite on his own can respond dramatically to what is proffered him. In contacts between such deities there is no need for middlemen; each of these gods is able to serve as his own priest.[44]

Chaplains offer themselves as everyman's dyadic companion, with the possibilty of a triad left ambiguous.

Politics of Presence

It is very hard to escape the idea that the ministry of presence is a profoundly Christian practice in most American contexts, whatever the intention, even in its anonymous generalized form, and yet it also gains credibility in part from its ability to enable cross-religious communication. Like other efforts at coping with the social fact of religious multiplicity, it seems always to be both/and, both Christian and secular or neutral.

In a familiar interfaith comparative move, the Houston-based healthcare chaplaincy mentioned above explains on their website how the ministry of presence is common to all world religions, naming them one by one, and in the process slowly erasing their differences, merging them all into a universal ministry of presence.[45] From Judaism is taken creation and scripture: "In Jewish theology, presence begins with God's hands-on creation of humanity and understanding that it is not good for a human to be alone in the world. . . . The idea of humans companioning each other through life's suffering is poignantly depicted in the Book of Job. . . . Job is not alone; the community is supporting him through the presence of his three companions." From Christianity, the Incarnation: "The idea of presence is grounded

---

44. Ibid., 95.
45. www.interfaithcarepartners.org (accessed July 22, 2013).

in the theology of the incarnation of Jesus Christ. Christians are charged to show and be the love of God (in our imperfect way) to others, just as Jesus Christ was love incarnate." Presence is understood to be the will of Allah, as exemplified by the Prophet: "For Muslims, being present to the sick and elderly is considered a command of Allah as exemplified by the Prophet Muhammad, who taught that the community should visit the sick." And "the worldview in Eastern traditions includes suffering as a given of life's existence." The fusing of these religious narratives and ideas, an effort that draws confirmation from a certain irenic comparative approach to the study of religion, authenticates and authorizes the work of the chaplain.[46]

The Houston chaplaincy, too, returns, however, to the example of the French mystics. "They are experts at 'being present,'" the Houston folks insist, citing the words of another Frenchman, the seventeenth-century theologian François Fénelon:

> Speak little; listen much; think far more of understanding hearts and of adapting yourself to their needs than of saying clever things to them. Show that you have an open mind, and let everyone see by experience that there is safety and consolation in opening his mind to you. Avoid extreme severity, and reprove, where necessary, with caution and gentleness. Never say more than is needed, but let whatever you say be said with entire frankness. Let no one fear to be deceived by trusting you.[47]

Fénelon was a Roman Catholic theologian, churchman, and tutor to the son of Louis XIV of France, a man who occupied a complicated place between religious tolerance and religious proselytization, between the monarchy and the aristocracy, and between advocacy on behalf of religious innovators within the Catholic Church and obedience to authority. A prolific writer, bits and pieces of his writings circulate as Christian wisdom today.[48] The phenomenology of presence resonates with strains within contemporary French philosophical theology as well, including Jean-Luc Marion's notion of the saturated phenomenon,[49] while that tradition also feels alien to the practiced resistance of American religion to such metaphysical articulation.

---

46. The drawing of a common practice from comparison across traditions can be seen in the writings of Mircea Eliade, Joseph Campbell, and Huston Smith.

47. http://www.healthcarechaplaincy.org/about-us/finding-meaning-bringing-comfort.html (accessed July 21, 2013).

48. As a quick Google search will reveal! He was also read in the nineteenth century as any reader of nineteenth-century English novels will know.

49. See, e.g., Kevin Hart, ed., *Jean-Luc Marion: The Essential Writings* (New York: Fordham

Can a ministry of presence ever actually overcome structures of difference—and injustice? Labor priests and others have used the ministry as a form of leftist political action. A powerful example of such ministry is provided in the extraordinary Canadian novel *Such Is My Beloved* by Morley Callaghan.[50] Challenged by his bishop to explain why he has taken to hanging out at night in the flat of a couple of young prostitutes in 1930s Depression-era Toronto, Father Dowling explains that his is a ministry of presence. The lack of an explicit articulation of what presence is and how it works can allow the minister to focus on the object of the ministry without focusing on the source of suffering. It can be a way of avoiding both the theology and the politics of the ministry of presence—of both the problem of theodicy, as Hauerwas notes, and the possibility of political critique of the secular authority responsible for the suffering.

There remains an unresolved tension between a presence that leads to trust and an ongoing need to account to yourself, your religious masters, and the institution that employs you—as to the value of what you do—a tension that makes politics difficult. Theologian John Cobb worries about this aspect of the ministry of presence: "The pastor's task is to be present with and to hear the sufferer, to let the parishioner know that expressing fear, anger, and loneliness is acceptable . . . but to treat it only that way fails to take the questioner with full seriousness as a human being. A pastor who has not reflected about the question, who has nothing to say, has a truncated ministry."[51] In the military context, for example, it could be seen as a way of avoiding conflict over the morality of war.

Army Chaplain Timothy Bedsole tells of a sermon he gave to explain this aspect of the ministry of presence:

> Several years ago I was invited by a group of students to speak at an anti-war "preach-in." . . . I titled my sermon "Buying the Field," using a text from the book of Jeremiah. . . . Jeremiah is told by God to purchase land during a time when Israel was under siege and he was confined in the king's courtyard in Jerusalem. . . . He bought the field with silver and recorded the deed even though he would never be able to see the land or utilize it . . . military chaplains serve in an organization where they do not vote on war but rather serve

University Press, 2013).

50. Morley Callaghan, *Such Is My Beloved* (New York: Charles Scribner's Sons, 1934).

51. J. B. Cobb Jr., "The Problem of Evil and the Task of Ministry," in *Encountering Evil: Live Options in Theodicy*, 2nd ed., ed. Stephen T. Davis (Louisville, KY: Westminster John Knox Press, 2001), 181.

the warriors by providing a "ministry of presence" in the organization—that is, chaplains "buy into the field" of ministry in the military.[52]

They buy it on faith, like Jeremiah. Bedsole's idea is that the purpose of being a military chaplain is untranslatable. You do it because you are compelled to be there for the soldiers. But Bedsole does not leave it there. He also says that you do it in support of an American idea of freedom: "Those serving in the U.S. military are dedicated to the protection of the freedom that allowed them to gather and protest against the war. . . . Just as Jeremiah felt compelled by God to buy the field no matter his opinion of the circumstances, military chaplains feel compelled by God and country to serve members of the military."[53] Like Jeremiah, they serve a political reality as well as a divine one. A similar point about the usefulness of the ministry of presence to the military is made in an article about American operations in Kosovo: "Individual chaplains having the same faith as indigenous religious groups were solicited to build goodwill among the local populace through the ministry of presence. . . . In Kosovo an Orthodox US Army chaplain interacted with local Orthodox clergy to promote understanding and confidence toward US military operations."[54] Many critics of the provision of spiritual care through government chaplaincies think that the problem is too much overt proselytizing, that is, they worry about the coerciveness and Christian-ness of a "metaphysics of presence," but the bigger problem may be rather a naive service of whatever project is at hand.

Christopher Swift persuasively insists that, for all of this, a ministry of presence is the necessary work of a highly skilled professional:

In a culture where the production of new knowledge and skill is paramount, the chaplains are vulnerable to a creeping sense of occupational inferiority. However, I would contend that being alive to the ambiguities and "emptiness" of spirituality in the face of suffering is in itself a vocational skill that has value. . . . Standing in the place where there are no answers, no quick exits to open, does not require the gifts of those whose hands are full. It is a situation that calls for great patience, compassion and faithfulness to the value of the human being in front of you. While some might assume that this kind of

52. Bedsole, "The World Religions Chaplain."
53. Ibid.
54. William Sean Lee, Christopher J. Burke, and Zonna M. Crayne, *Military Chaplains as Peace Builders: Embracing Indigenous Religions in Stability Operations* (Maxwell Air Force Base, AL: Air University Press, 2005).

availability is simple, I would contend that it is fact the product of considerable preparation, maturity and deep personal self-knowledge.[55]

For Swift, the work is important in itself.

A ministry of presence, whatever else it may do, does seem to solve the US constitutional problem. Avoiding naming the particularist narratives that might be invoked in support of the work of chaplains allows the employers and the chaplains—and the judges—to make the claim that this is a necessary ministry that has a neutral scientific basis and that serves all without discriminatory imposition. Politically and theologically speaking, it affirms the real presence—incarnation—without hierarchy.

Minimalism

Haunting the ministry of presence is the absence to which the ministry of presence is apparently responding, an absence that, for many, is at the heart of religious mystical reflection and practice. The minimalist movement in art is understood by some to spiritualize something that is termed "empty presence." In an article about this work, art historian Anna Chave considers the spirituality depicted by minimalist artists, including an art installation in New Mexico by minimalist artist Walter de Maria entitled *Lightning Field*, an installation of poles evenly distributed across a stretch of desert:

> Just as the *Field*'s spiked, steely poles impose the ubiquitous, tyrannical regularity of the grid on the randomness of nature, nature simultaneously imposes its own insistent randomness over the regularity of the grid: De Maria's perfectionist demand that "the plane of the tips" should "evenly support an imaginary sheet of glass" necessitated strictly differentiating all those apparently identical poles, making each a singular height, ranging all the way from 15 feet to 26 feet 9 inches, to accommodate—while, as it were, canceling—the randomness of terrain chosen in part for its seeming flatness.[56]

At its best, a ministry of presence might seem to be understood to be a similar expression of the irresolvability of nature and culture.

---

55. Swift, *Hospital Chaplaincy*, 175.

56. Anna Chave, "Revaluing Minimalism. Patronage, Aura, and Place," *Art Bulletin* 90 (2008): 466–86.

AFTERWORD

Let us return now to Kate Braestrup, chaplain to the Maine Warden Service, whom we met in the preface. The Maine Warden Service is one of thousands of law enforcement and other public service agencies in the United States that employ a chaplain. Those chaplains, like chaplains in the other institutions of contemporary society, those in hospitals, the military, prisons, and the workplace, receive their education and training from American colleges, universities, and seminaries that have different histories and different constituencies, but whose curricula are increasingly founded in an understanding of religion as a natural attribute of human beings, human beings who are understood to be constitutionally entitled to freely exercise a universal need.[1]

US chaplains identify with and are endorsed by many different American religious communities, mostly varieties of Christianity, but not exclusively so; increasingly they regard the objects of their solicitude as sharing not their particular religious commitments but rather a more generalized spirituality as well as a right, and need, to have the space to develop and exercise that faculty. As with Reverend Braestrup, the professional work of these chaplains takes place outside of conventional church spaces and moves across the diverse religious terrain of the United States—and abroad—where Americans find themselves, manifesting itself broadly in what is called a ministry of presence, a spiritual ministry understood to be essential but

1. I mean here to include a very wide spectrum of Americans from those who self-locate within historic religious communities through the very disparate claims to confidence in an essential spirituality to human life on a variety of grounds. There is, of course, a small, but vocal, atheist minority in the United States, who resist this description. Their resistance depends on an understanding of religion that is much narrower.

nonproselytizing and noncoercive. As with hers as well, the work of these chaplains reflects a particular interdependence of religion and law in the twenty-first-century United States, an interdependence that we might call governance through spiritual care. Law is present in the constitutional structuring of our understanding of what constitutes legal religion in the United States, in the regulation of the education and training Reverend Braestrup received, and in the secular employment setting in which she plies her trade. Law in a broader sense, religious and secular, is also present in the normative frame and background cosmology and anthropology of her religious training and commitments. At the same time, religion and ideas about religion inflect her work and the way her work is apprehended by US law. Her work is an instantiation of US law and religion.

In some ways, a warden service may seem an odd place to find the French contemplative religious practice that is the ministry of presence. The combination of backwoods country, high-tech space-age law enforcement, and crisis management she describes may seem a strange place for any kind of religion. And, in some ways, it is the very unlikeliness of such a location that characterizes this form of ministry, whether it takes place on a battlefield, in a hospital room, in a prison cell, or on the Brooklyn docks. That is one of the attractions of this kind of work for those who do it. But a close look at any of these sites of ministry can also connect that place to a longer history of religion—as we have seen with hospitals and armies.

In the case of the Maine Warden Service, one could tell a story of the continuity of Braestrup's work with the religion of the frontier and with nature religion in the United States more generally, including the story of the founding of the national park system. One could also connect the religion of the Maine woods, the ritualized ways of man and moose and crow, to the very long history of hunting religions, especially in the northern hunting cultures in the Americas and in Eurasia.[2] The practice of universal spirituality, while bland and nonspecific on the surface, collects a whole history of religion. It justifies itself with its capacity to hold that history together, even recreate it, using the resources of the European study of religion, including such work as that of Mircea Eliade, and the long history of perennialist philosophy, as well as that of contemporary Christian spirituality. The sacralizing capacity of universal spirituality also reflects the work of religious studies scholars who are trained to pull on any thread of social fact and

2. See Laurie F. Maffly-Kipp, *Religion and Society in Frontier California* (New Haven, CT: Yale University Press, 1994); Catherine Albanese, *Nature Religion in America: From the Algonkian Indians to the New Age* (Chicago: University of Chicago Press, 1991).

follow it to a story of religion. The compelling reliability of universal spirituality underlying the effort is what justifies such scholarship, one that is complicit in the work of resacralization today, not only through the work of individual scholars but also through the institutionalization of religious studies, in religion departments, in the American Academy of Religion, and elsewhere.

The Maine Warden Service is more than a hundred and thirty years old. It dates its history from the day of its first arrest for poaching, March 12, 1880.[3] The mission of the Maine Warden Service is conservation; it is charged with protecting moose and deer from people, or, rather, perhaps, in the tradition of hunting religions, with controlling and ritualizing the killing of moose and deer by people. In 2013, the service boasts certified personnel and up-to-date equipment to assist in a comprehensive monitoring of game and of lawbreakers, as proudly described in its official history:

> The Maine Warden Service is a modern, professional, highly effective law enforcement agency. Members are certified law enforcement officers who use state-of-the-art equipment, including four-wheel drive trucks, boats, snowmobiles, ATV's, personal computers, a two-way radio repeater network, portable radios, GPS, forensic mapping equipment, fixed wing aircraft, and night vision equipment, in carrying out their responsibilities. In addition, the service maintains its own forensic laboratory, Dive team, K-9 unit, Firearms Team, Forensic Mapping Team, ERT Team, and aircraft division. These aircraft enable Wardens to patrol remote sections of their assigned districts, effectively respond to emergency situations, participate in fish stocking, conduct angler surveys, and oversee boating activity.[4]

Wardens also have a spiritual life. Chaplain Braestrup accompanies the wardens on their work protecting moose and deer and coyotes and fish, rescuing small children, and arresting scofflaws, all the while sacralizing their mission and delivering pastoral care through her ministry of presence.

The chaplain today, then, is perhaps best understood not just as the left-over descendant of the religious specialists of the medieval church but rather as an indispensable part of a very contemporary religious situation: the very person needed to make it all work today. The chaplain extends the religious community to minister to people where they are. The chaplain allows the host institution to outsource questions of meaning and

---

3. http://www.maine.gov/ifw/warden_service/history.html (accessed July 11, 2013).
4. Ibid.

purpose . . . and to deal with suffering and death. Chaplaincy is also an avoidance or escape from the religious marketplace for the chaplain—a way to have your establishment and eat it too! Through the ambiguous but insistent practice of the ministry of presence, chaplains honor the right of their flock to exercise their rights to religious freedom and claim there is no imposition or coercion even while they witness to their own religious commitments, structure that of others through their practice, and legitimate the purposes of their employers.

In the United States, the deregulated field of religion mostly disperses the tight unity of church and state, even as a memory, that concerned Foucault. It is difficult to believe that Kate Braestrup, or most of the other chaplains we have met, is an instrument of pastoral care in the statist European sense. While American chaplains use the image of the shepherd and the shepherd's crook to symbolize their work, one might imagine not one shepherd and one crook with one flock but, widening the lens and pulling back from the scene, a Monty Pythonesque scene in which there are many, many shepherds, and other odd anachronistic characters plying their trades while the sheep wander around choosing a shepherd, or doing something entirely different as they themselves wish.[5] It is also possible to imagine that some of the shepherds and some of the sheep are refusing to follow the rules of voluntarism and toleration. Some on the right and the left are engaged in what Foucault termed "revolts of conduct."[6] Some of them are wolves in sheep's clothing—or wolves in shepherd's clothing.

There are at least two parallel legal discourses about religion and religious freedom at work domestically today in the United States. Law increasingly appropriates a universalizing language about religion, one produced both by the academic study of religion and its popular offspring, one that speaks of religion or spirituality as being common to all humans and as being necessary for human flourishing, seeing divisive exclusive religion as simply aberrant.[7] Law also bends at times to an attempted reassertion of religious

---

5. I am here thinking of the *Life of Brian* crucifixion scene, "Always Look on the Bright Side of Life."

6. For a thoughtful portrait of some American religionists who refused the mid-twentieth-century consensus, see Jason Bivins, *The Fracture of Good Order: Christian Anti-Liberalism and the Challenge to Postwar American Politics* (Chapel Hill: University of North Carolina Press, 2003).

7. On August 7, 2013, US Secretary of State John Kerry said, in a speech celebrating the creation of the new State Department Office of Faith-Based Community Initiatives, that if he were to return to college today he would major in religious studies. It was tempting to cheer. For those of us in religious studies, though, I think the context of this announcement should give us real concern. Indeed the context should suggest that in some important ways, religious studies

authority by defenders of traditional hierarchies and radical separatists who sharply distinguish between religion and un-religion, between the right kind of religion and the wrong kind of religion. The two religious discourses, universal and particular, depend on each other and implicate law in interesting ways. The universalizing language of religious studies, understanding itself as authorized itself in part by First Amendment orthodoxies, depends for its legitimacy on and continually returns to the messy particularities of actual historical traditions, even while it abstracts from them and helps to remake them.[8] Advocates for religious liberty, too, while employing the universalism of human rights talk, defend the rights of members of living religious communities bound to theologies that are often far from bulwarks of human rights. Meanwhile, traditional religious authorities link their cause to that of human rights advocacy in the vain hope that their own abuses will be overlooked in the name of religious liberty and that their particular charisms will not be lost in the universalizing maw. Chaplains negotiate the interface of these tensive oppositions.

The legal regulation of this negotiation exemplifies primarily a horizontal, bureaucratic management of religion, rather than a top-down church-state constitutional settlement, notwithstanding effects that sometimes reinforce nationalist projects.[9] What this study of chaplains reveals is something

---

has failed in its objective to serve as a nontheological and apolitical discourse about religion. Speaking of humans as properly "safe guarders of God's creation," Kerry spoke of his belief that, in spite of religious diversity, "there is much more that unites us, and should unite us, than divides us. . . . All of these faiths are virtuous and they are in fact, most of them, tied together by the golden rule, as well as fundamental concerns about the human condition, about poverty, about relationships between people, our responsibilities each to each other. And they all come from the same human heart." Kerry affirmed the commitment of the State Department to work in partnerships with religious "leaders" and with religious "communities" to defeat extremists, neatly separating bad religion from good religion. Describing religion as a collective endeavor led by inspired religious leaders such as Gandhi, Kerry finished with a quote from scripture: "For even the Son of Man did not come to be served, but to serve, and to give his life as a ransom for the many."

Sixteenth-century versions of religious universalism are described in Carlo Ginzburg, *The Cheese and the Worms: The Cosmos of a Sixteenth Century Miller*, trans. John and Anne Tedeschi (Baltimore: Johns Hopkins University Press, 1980), and in Stuart B. Schwartz, *All Can Be Saved: Religious Tolerance and Salvation in the Iberian Atlantic World* (New Haven, CT: Yale University Press, 2009).

8. For a discussion of how and why US religious studies scholars justify their presence in public universities by evoking the US Supreme Court's decision in Abingdon v. Schempp, 374 U.S. 203 (1963), see Imhoff "The Creation Story."

9. One of the most interesting studies of the bureaucratic regulation of religion in a modernizing society is Franklin Presler's longitudinal study of the administration of the Hindu temples of south India, both by the British colonial administration and then by the postcolonial state. Presler describes first the precolonial exchange between kings and temples that served both to

otherwise difficult to see. The new way of regulating religion in the United States results less from a standoff between church and state on the pre-modern model or from a top-down regulatory model more common outside the United States and more from a horizontal negotiation operating in a decentered form in various places. In this negotiation, orthodoxy—or what counts as legal religion—is decided neither by church officials nor government officials but by private-public interactions at the middle-management level.[10] This form of religious regulation might be compared to what is sometimes called the new governance, understood by political scientists to be innovative forms of regulation that move beyond reliance on a command-and-control style of state regulation dependent on experts toward a post–New Deal form of regulation more suited to a complex and interdependent global world.[11] Whether such horizontal law can be held accountable to constitutional standards and whether the adversarial legalism of the United States can tolerate such governance remain questions.

Military chaplaincies are rapidly adjusting to this newly complex religious configuration. The Department of Defense has recently issued a directive concerning what they are calling RMPs (religious ministry professionals). An RMP must be willing to function in a pluralist environment and meet advanced educational and leadership qualifications. An RMP must also be

legitimate the king and maintain the orthodoxy and regular administration of the temples, but in which each was largely independent. This system was replaced by successive bureaucracies whose goal rather was extraction of tax revenues, proper accounting practices, tidiness, and regularization of services. Presler shows how over time, this horizontal regulation resulted in the invention of new kinds of Hindu practice, one characterized by a more bourgeois form of religion, one that served the Indian state in a new way. These bureaucracies whose mandate it was to manage tax revenues, land ownership, and charitable endowments also transformed religion. Under bureaucracy, Presler says, temple religion changed. While like their early modern royal predecessors, Indian politicians today continue to seek public approval through association with the temples and seek to influence temple management, what is paramount in the administration of the temples is bureaucratic concern for efficiency, good fiscal policy, standardization, equal access, and qualified staff. Religion was universalized and law sacralized. Franklin A. Presler, *Religion under Bureaucracy: Policy and Administration for Hindu Temples in South Asia* (Cambridge: Cambridge University Press, 1987). See also Arjun Appadurai, *Worship and Conflict under Colonial Rule: A South Indian Case* (Cambridge: Cambridge University Press, 1981) and, for a careful reconstruction of the discourses of religious freedom in pre-independence India, see C. S. Adcock, *The Limits of Tolerance: Indian Secularism and the Politics of Religious Freedom* (Oxford: Oxford University Press, 2013).

10. For an introduction to such horizontal governance, see Jody Freeman, "The Private Role in Public Governance," *New York University Law Review* 75 (2000): 543–675.

11. For discussions of the new governance, see Orly Lobel, "The Renew Deal: The Fall of Regulation and the Rise of Governance in Contemporary Legal Thought?," *Minnesota Law Review* 89 (2004): 342–470; Jason M. Solomon, "Law and Governance in the 21st Century Regulatory State," *Texas Law Review* 86 (2008): 819–56.

endorsed by a government-approved ecclesiastical endorser. An RMP is expected to minister to everyone, regardless of personal religious affiliation, and provide a model for universal spiritual care.[12]

A recent article describing the new position of world religions chaplain in the army explains this from a practitioner's perspective:

> The U.S. Army Chaplaincy's motto is *Pro Deo Et Patria*, for God and country. The motto reflects the tension of the dual mandate of serving both state and faith. Being *for* God and *for* country are not necessarily opposing goals; indeed, when pursued wisely these goals can often be complementary. The chaplaincy as a whole seeks to embody this ethos in word and deed, and the role of a World Religions Chaplain is no different. Providing advice to the commanders of the U.S. military on the dynamic influences of religion and religious beliefs means buying into the field of service to both God and government. There are few easy answers, and tensions will likely persist—but chaplains have no choice but to work to ensure that these tensions are constructive rather than destructive of the greater good.[13]

Reaching always for another abstraction, here, under the banner of "the greater good," chaplains are once more being asked to do the messy work.

The VA has recently amended its rules concerning the placement of religious symbols on government-provided headstones. The definitions section of the new rules struggle to define an increasingly uneasy and fuzzy boundary between religious and secular and the embracing of an inclusivity that is supposed to suggest the universality of religion:

(1) Affiliated organization refers to an organization that practices the system of beliefs that were held by a deceased eligible individual and that has a religious purpose. The term "religious purpose" includes a purpose that appears to be secular, but which nevertheless assumes the functional significance of a religious purpose. This term does not refer to any organization representing or affiliated with social, cultural, ethnic, fraternal, trade, professional, or military groups.

(2) Belief system refers to a genuine and non-frivolous group of religious opinions, doctrines, and/or principles believed or accepted as true by a group of

---

12. But see Tim Townsend, "Military Chaplains Are Faith Mismatch for Personnel They Serve," *St. Louis Post-Dispatch*, January 9, 2011, http://www.stltoday.com/lifestyles/faith-and-values/military-chaplains-are-faith-mismatch-for-personnel-they-serve/article_19c66ee6-82b8-59f7-b3d5-fd3cc05bc538.html (accessed July 12, 2013).

13. Bedsole. "The World Religions Chaplain."

persons. This term includes a belief system that appears to be secular, but which nevertheless assumes the functional significance of a religion in the lives of a group of persons.

(3) Emblem of belief refers to an emblem that represents the belief system of the decedent. It does not include social, cultural, ethnic, fraternal, trade, professional, or military emblems, or any emblem that is obscene or would have an adverse impact on the dignity and solemnity of cemeteries honoring those who served the Nation.[14]

This is an astonishingly opaque and confusing summary of the nature of religion today: "The term 'religious purpose' includes a purpose that appears to be secular, but which nevertheless assumes the functional significance of a religious purpose." But "this term emphatically does not refer to any organization representing or affiliated with social, cultural, ethnic, fraternal, trade, professional, or military groups." Organizations with religious purposes, those whose members are entitled to have their membership memorialized on a headstone by the VA, include only those that are religious or that appear secular but are nevertheless functionally religious, as long as their beliefs are genuine and nonfrivolous, not obscene or antipatriotic, and specifically not social, cultural, or fraternal. Such a mainstreaming garble of sociological and anthropological ideas about religion can be seen across the spectrum of government management of religion today.[15] It also under-

14. Headstone and Marker Application Process. 38 CFR Part 38. *Federal Regular* 72 (2007): 2480–84.

15. In his concurring opinion in *Hosanna-Tabor*, Justice Alito, troubled by the exclusivity of the language of church and minister in the majority opinion, attempted a functional expansion of the ministerial exemption. Citing the *Oxford English Dictionary*, the *New Catholic Encyclopedia*, and the *Encyclopedia of Religion*, Alito says, "The term 'minister' is commonly used by many Protestant denominations to refer to members of their clergy, but the term is rarely if ever used in this way by Catholics, Jews, Muslims, Hindus, or Buddhists." For this reason, he advises that "Because virtually every religion in the world is represented in the population of the United States, it would be a mistake if the term 'minister' or the concept of ordination were viewed as central to the important issue of religious autonomy that is presented in cases like this one. Instead, courts should focus on the function performed by persons who work for religious bodies." Confident that such a functional approach will be possible, he recommends a reading of the First Amendment that protects the autonomy of all religions: "The First Amendment protects the freedom of religious groups to engage in certain key religious activities, including the conducting of worship services and other religious ceremonies and rituals, as well as the critical process of communicating the faith. Accordingly, religious groups must be free to choose the personnel who are essential to the performance of these functions. The 'ministerial' exception should be tailored to this purpose. It should apply to any 'employee' who leads a religious organization, conducts worship services or important religious ceremonies or rituals, or serves as a messenger or teacher of its faith. If a religious group believes that the ability of such an employee to perform these key functions has been compromised, then the constitutional guarantee of

writes the practices of chaplains. The practice of chaplains today depends on an abstraction of religion, one that is justified by the belief that, in the words of a leading scholar of pastoral theology, "both the symbolic truth of traditional religious language and the truth of philosophical and scientific critiques of religious language [can] be held together in a conjunctive style of faith."

This universalist ideal and its incomplete realization in practice are both interestingly evident in a recent book by Army Chaplain William McCoy, *Under Orders: A Spiritual Handbook for Military Personnel*,[16] endorsed by General David Petraeus. Even while evidencing a clear Christian prejudice, McCoy makes a strong case that everyone is spiritual and that all religions are valuable. "You can be any religion you want, that is your choice," McCoy advises. He refers readers to a footnote for further reading: "Read Joseph Campbell's works on *Religion and Culture*; Mircea Eliade, *The Myth of the Eternal Return*; Paul Ricoeur, *Symbolism of Evil* and *Time and Narrative*; Reinhold Niebuhr, *Christ and Culture*." But the book begins with the Roman centurion who decided to follow Jesus and ends with this exhortation: "It is a time for a change in the way we understand faith in our world. It is time we begin emphasizing the good news over 'some' generic news. The Gospel liberates people from the sin of religious regime, boredom, routine, sectarianism and legalism."[17]

While much of the new spiritual establishment is broadly inclusive, there is, to be sure, still excluded, disfavored, religion under this new legal regime, but the arbiter is no longer the court. Religion is being neutralized and naturalized—de-constitutionalized, formally. Now it is the government procurer or private contractor who decides which religious bidder offers the best hope of promoting social welfare and the individual chaplain who determines what constitutes spiritual health. And it is private regulation and politics, not the Constitution, that determine whether the individual chaplain should be given a job. It is difficult for the separationist litigators to keep up. The Supreme Court seems to be uninterested in whether incorporating religion into social services is constitutional. In various ways, it is becoming more difficult to challenge that incorporation. Individuals will be negotiating their own religious lives in the workplace, in the hospital, in

religious freedom protects the group's right to remove the employee from his or her position." Hosanna-Tabor v. EEOC, Alitto, J., dissenting. Slip Opinion p 2.

16. William McCoy, *Under Orders: A Spiritual Handbook for Military Personnel* (Ozark, AL: ACW Press, 2006).

17. Ibid., 218.

prison, in school, although it is clear that implementation of the normalization of religion on an egalitarian basis is far from being realized.

The religion that is desired by many in the United States today is one that will produce pious—but not too pious—law-abiding, healthy-minded, and productive citizens. Formal legal administration of governmental and quasi-governmental chaplaincies in the United States combined with the private law of professional associations and educational institutions is arguably producing a new religious establishment of sorts in the United States. This establishment is both new and old. It is old in the sense that American religion, notwithstanding its formal disestablishment and an ideology of separation, has always provided, and been understood by Americans to provide, the training of the moral citizens necessary to a democratic society, and has been enabled through various governmental privileges, formal and informal. The new establishment is not entirely unlike what is known as the de facto Protestant establishment of the nineteenth and early twentieth centuries. But it is new in the sense that it is no longer wholly Protestant, and it has been deeply influenced by a commitment to equality and equivalence among religious traditions imported from the new centrality of the equal protection clause of the Fourteenth Amendment. Another aspect of its "newness" is the impact of a curious amalgam of scientist and therapeutic understandings of the human person including the new interest in the nature of consciousness. The new establishment has as a normative goal the ensuring of professional spiritual treatment that is nondiscriminatory and voluntary. The assumption is that everyone needs it and that it is not about religion in any divisive sense.[18]

18. For a particularly thoughtful effort to describe religion today, see "A Discussion between Hubert Knoblauch (from the Technical University of Berlin) and Detlef Pollack (from the University Viadrina in Frankfurt an der Oder) about the Supposed Return of Religion," http://www .goethe.de/ges/phi/dos/her/mod/en2404205.htm (accessed January 19, 2013).

Armed Forces Chaplains Board Endorsers

(JANUARY 2013)

Administrative Agents/Organizations

Reverend Dr. Floyd C. Chapman Jr.
AMERICAN COUNCIL OF CHRISTIAN CHURCHES (ACCC)

James F. Poe, CAPT, CHC, USN, Ret.
ASSOCIATED GOSPEL CHURCHES

Dr. Klon K. Kitchen Jr.
CHAPLAINCY FULL GOSPEL CHURCHES

Reverend David B. Plummer
COALITION OF SPIRIT-FILLED CHURCHES INC.

Rear Admiral Harold L. Robinsin, CHC, USN-Ret.
NATIONAL JEWISH WELFARE BOARD

Chaplain David Cyr, Brigadier General, USAF (Ret.)
NATIONAL ASSOCIATION OF EVANGELICALS (NAE)

Chaplain (BG) Douglas E. Lee, USA-Ret.
PRESBYTERIAN AND REFORMED COMMISSION ON CHAPLAINS
AND MILITARY PERSONNEL (PRCC)

Chaplain, Colonel Edward T. Brogan, USAF-Ret.
THE PRESBYTERIAN COUNCIL FOR CHAPLAINS AND MILITARY PERSONNEL (PC)

Very Reverend Luke Uhl
STANDING CONFERENCE OF CANONICAL ORTHODOX BISHOPS IN THE AMERICAS (SCOBA)

Ecclesiastical Endorsing Agents

The Reverend Ronald S. Bezanson Jr.
ADVENT CHRISTIAN GENERAL CONFERENCE

Bishop Reginald T. Jackson
AFRICAN METHODIST EPISCOPAL CHURCH

Reverend Dr. W. Robert Johnson III
AFRICAN METHODIST EPISCOPAL ZION CHURCH

Reverend Christopher T. Copeland
ALLIANCE OF BAPTISTS, INCORPORATED

Reverend Richard T. Day
AMERICAN ASSOCIATION OF LUTHERAN CHURCHES, THE

Chaplain (Colonel) Herbert E. Kitchens, USA (Ret.)
AMERICAN BAPTIST ASSOCIATION

The Reverend Paul E. Clark
AMERICAN BAPTIST CHURCHES IN THE U.S.A.

Reverend Frank P. Miloro
AMERICAN CARPATHO-RUSSIAN ORTHODOX GREEK CATHOLIC CHURCH IN THE
U.S.A. (SCOBA)

Bryce Bartruff
INFAITH

Mr. Qaseem A. Uqdah
AMERICAN MUSLIM ARMED FORCES AND VETERANS AFFAIRS COUNCIL

Bishop Sanjay Thakore
ANGLICAN CHURCH, THE

The Rt. Rev. D. Presley Hutchens
ANGLICAN CATHOLIC CHURCH, THE

Chaplain (Colonel) Alan M. Koller, USA (Ret.)
ANGLICAN CHURCH IN AMERICA, THE

Archbishop Michael B. Simmons
ANGLICAN CHURCH OF THE AMERICAS, THE

The Very Rev. David B. Fucci
ANGLICAN MISSION IN AMERICA CHAPLAINCY

The Venerable HG Miller
ANGLICAN MISSION IN THE AMERICAS, THE

Most Reverend Metropolitan Philip Saliba
ANTIOCHIAN ORTHODOX CHRISTIAN ARCHDIOCESE OF NORTH AMERICA

The Most Reverend Diana C. Dale
APOSTOLIC CATHOLIC ORTHODOX CHURCH

Chaplain (Colonel) Scott McChrystal, USA (Ret.)
ASSEMBLIES OF GOD, GENERAL COUNCIL OF

Reverend Dr. Theodore A. Lanes
ASSEMBLIES OF GOD, INTERNATIONAL FELLOWSHIP (CFGC)
ENDORSING EXECUTIVE: Dr. Klon K. Kitchen Jr.

Reverend Gordon A. Taylor
ASSOCIATION OF REFORMED BAPTIST CHURCHES OF AMERICA (ARBCA)

The Reverend C. Ronald Beard
ASSOCIATE REFORMED PRESBYTERIAN CHURCH (PC)
ENDORSING EXECUTIVE: Chaplain Douglas E. Lee

Mr. Mike Weldon
ASSOCIATION OF INDEPENDENT METHODISTS, THE

Reverend Hazel A. Rayl
ASSOCIATION OF INTERNATIONAL GOSPEL ASSEMBLIES, INC. (CFGC)
ENDORSING EXECUTIVE: Dr. Klon K. Kitchen Jr.

Rev. Lenae C. Rasmussen
AUGSBURG LUTHERAN CHURCHES

Reverend James G. Smith
BAPTIST BIBLE FELLOWSHIP INTERNATIONAL

David B. Kennedy
BAPTIST GENERAL CONFERENCE

Mr. Bobby R. Smith
BAPTIST GENERAL CONVENTION OF TEXAS

Mr. David R. Norvell
BAPTIST MISSIONARY ASSOCIATION OF AMERICA

Mr. Frank VanCampen
BEREAN FUNDAMENTAL CHURCH COUNCIL, INC.

Reverend Donald Horath
BETHEL MINISTERIAL ASSOCIATION, INC.

Reverend Dennis M. Cahill
BIBLE FELLOWSHIP CHURCH

Elder Philip Resnick
BIBLE PRESBYTERIAN CHURCH (GENERAL SYNOD)

Mr. Joseph E. Hanna
BRETHREN CHURCH, INC., THE (ASHLAND, OHIO)
ENDORSING EXECUTIVE: Chaplain David Cyr, Brigadier General, USAF (Ret.)

Rev. Kodo Umezu
BUDDHIST CHURCHES OF AMERICA

Dr. Robbie Morrison
CALVARY BAPTIST CHURCH (ALL POINTS BAPTIST MISSION)

Pastor Jon Rogers
CALVARY CHAPEL OF COSTA MESA

Mr. Bernard M. Sloan
CALVARY CHAPEL MIRA MESA

Most Reverend Andre J. W. Queen
CATHOLIC APOSTOLIC NATIONAL CHURCH

Rabbi David S. Goldstein
CENTRAL CONFERENCE OF AMERICAN RABBIS (JWB)
ENDORSING EXECUTIVE: Rear Admiral Harold L. Robinson, CHC, USN-Ret.

Archbishop Craig Bates
CHARISMATIC EPISCOPAL CHURCH OF NORTH AMERICA

Dr. Apparao Mukkamala
CHINMAYA MISSION WEST

Reverend Dr. Jonpatrick S. Anderson
CHRIST-IMMANUEL MINISTERIAL ASSOCIATION (CFGC)
ENDORSING EXECUTIVE: Dr. Klon K. Kitchen Jr.

Reverend Robert W. Collins II
CHRISTIAN AND MISSIONARY ALLIANCE, THE

The Reverend Steven B. Doan
CHRISTIAN CHURCH (DISCIPLES OF CHRIST)

Rev. David Plummer
CHRISTIAN CHURCH OF NORTH AMERICA

Mr. John D. Craycraft
CHRISTIAN CHURCHES AND CHURCHES OF CHRIST

Reverend Dr. Gary R. Moncher
CHRISTIAN EVANGELICAL CHURCHES OF AMERICA, INC.

Bishop Paul A. Stewart
CHRISTIAN METHODIST EPISCOPAL CHURCH

Reverend Ron Klimp
CHRISTIAN REFORMED CHURCH IN NORTH AMERICA

Chaplain (COL) Donald Taylor, USA (Ret.)
CHURCH OF CHRIST

Reverend Richard David Erb
CHURCH OF GOD MINISTRIES

Reverend Richard L. Pace
CHURCH OF GOD (CLEVELAND, TENNESSEE)

Dr. David Krogh
CHURCH OF GOD, GENERAL CONFERENCE

Mr. Jack R. Smith
CHURCH OF GOD (HOLINESS) (NAE)
ENDORSING EXECUTIVE: Chaplain David Cyr, Brigadier General, USAF (Ret.)

Chaplain Samuel F. Morgan
CHURCH OF GOD IN CHRIST, INC.

Reverend Dr. Douglas R. Stephenson
CHURCH OF GOD OF PROPHECY

Mr. Frank W. Clawson
CHURCH OF JESUS CHRIST OF LATTER-DAY SAINTS, THE (LDS)

Mr. Robert Terry Jr.
CHURCH OF OUR LORD JESUS CHRIST OF THE APOSTOLIC FAITH

Reverend Joel R. Egge
CHURCH OF THE LUTHERAN BRETHREN

Chaplain Dwight C. Jennings
CHURCH OF THE NAZARENE

Bishop Ronald R. Ramsey
CHURCH OF THE UNITED BRETHREN IN CHRIST

Dr. Lawrence Kennedy
CHURCH ON THE ROCK, INTERNATIONAL (CFGC)
ENDORSING EXECUTIVE: Dr. Klon K. Kitchen Jr.

Reverend Ralph Hux
CHURCHES OF CHRIST IN CHRISTIAN UNION

Dr. Thomas L. Lucas
CHURCHES OF GOD, GENERAL CONFERENCE

The Rt. Rev. Dr. Steven Raulerson
COMMUNION OF CONVERGENCE CHURCHES

Mr. Ronald Runyon
COMMUNITY CHURCH OF GREENWOOD, INC.

Mr. Steven Albert McCrosson
COMMUNITY OF CHRIST

The Reverend Samuel T. Tialavea Sr.
CONGREGATIONAL CHRISTIAN CHURCH IN AMERICAN SAMOA, THE

Reverend Dr. D. Elizabeth Mauro
CONGREGATIONAL CHRISTIAN CHURCHES, NATIONAL ASSOCIATION OF

Reverend Cregg Puckett
CONGREGATIONAL METHODIST CHURCH, THE

The Reverend Allen E. Russell
CONSERVATIVE BAPTIST ASSOCIATION OF AMERICA

Reverend Dr. Robert G. Leroe
CONSERVATIVE CONGREGATIONAL CHRISTIAN CONFERENCE

Reverend James Elmore
CONSERVATIVE LUTHERAN ASSOCIATION

The Right Reverend Derek S. Jones
CONVOCATION OF ANGLICANS IN NORTH AMERICA

Mr. George C. Pickle
COOPERATIVE BAPTIST FELLOWSHIP, INC.

Dr. Jeff Burnsed
CORAL RIDGE CHRISTIAN FELLOWSHIP

The Reverend Robert D. Rush
CUMBERLAND PRESBYTERIAN CHURCH, THE (PC)
ENDORSING EXECUTIVE: Chaplain, Colonel Edward T. Brogan, USAF-Ret.

Michael Sharpe
CUMBERLAND PRESBYTERIAN CHURCH IN AMERICA (PC)
ENDORSING EXECUTIVE: Chaplain, Colonel Edward T. Brogan, USAF-Ret.

Joe Jansen
ELIM FELLOWSHIP, INC. (NAE)

The Rt. Reverend James B. Magness
EPISCOPAL CHURCH, THE

Rt. Reverend William W. Millsaps
EPISCOPAL MISSIONARY CHURCH, THE

Bishop Houston Miles
EVANGEL FELLOWSHIP INTERNATIONAL (CFGC)
ENDORSING EXECUTIVE: Dr. Klon K. Kitchen Jr.

Reverend Dr. George L. Miller
EVANGELICAL CHURCH ALLIANCE

Reverend William J. McEllroy Jr.
EVANGELICAL CONGREGATIONAL CHURCH

Reverend Mark A. Novak
EVANGELICAL COVENANT CHURCH, THE

Ms. Emily A. Grider
EVANGELICAL EPISCOPAL CHURCH, THE

The Most Reverend Russell T. McClanahan
EVANGELICAL EPISCOPAL CHURCHES, THE COMMUNION OF

Dr. Roy L. Bebee
EVANGELICAL FREE CHURCH OF AMERICA

Reverend L. Randall Heckert
EVANGELICAL FRIENDS CHURCH INTERNATIONAL (NAE)
ENDORSING EXECUTIVE: Chaplain David Cyr, Brigadier General, USAF (Ret.)

Dr. Henry A. Harbuck
EVANGELICAL GOSPEL ASSEMBLIES MINISTRIES INTERNATIONAL, INC., ASSOCIATION OF

The Reverend Franklin Eric Wester
EVANGELICAL LUTHERAN CHURCH IN AMERICA

The Reverend Russell N. Burr
EVANGELICAL LUTHERAN CONFERENCE AND MINISTERIUM

CH (COL) Brian C. Donley, Ret.
EVANGELICAL METHODIST CHURCH, THE

Reverend Mark S. Ingles
EVANGELICAL PRESBYTERIAN CHURCH

Mrs. Pat G. Harrison
FAITH CHRISTIAN FELLOWSHIP INT'L CHURCH, INC. (CFGC)
ENDORSING EXECUTIVE: Dr. Klon K. Kitchen Jr.

Most Reverend John T. Kelly
FEDERATED ORTHODOX CATHOLIC CHURCHES INTERNATIONAL

Dr. Klon K. Kitchen Jr.
FELLOWSHIP OF CHURCHES AND MINISTERS INTERNATIONAL (CFGC)
ENDORSING EXECUTIVE: Dr. Klon K. Kitchen Jr.

Ms. Janet Y. Horton
FIRST CHURCH OF CHRIST, SCIENTIST, THE

Reverend Timothy K. Skramstad
FREE LUTHERAN CONGREGATION, ASSOCIATION OF (NAE)
ENDORSING EXECUTIVE: Chaplain David Cyr, Brigadier General, USAF (Ret.)

Chaplain Rex E. Carpenter
FREE METHODIST CHURCH OF NORTH AMERICA

Reverend Larry A. Powell
FREE WILL BAPTISTS, NATIONAL ASSOCIATION OF

Reverend Robert M. Green
FULL GOSPEL FELLOWSHIP OF CHURCHES AND MINISTERS INTERNATIONAL

Bishop A. A. Wells, PhD
FULL GOSPEL PENTECOSTAL CHURCH

Dr. John C. Vaughn
FUNDAMENTAL BAPTIST FELLOWSHIP INT'L

Franklin Dumond
GENERAL BAPTISTS, GENERAL ASSOCIATION OF

Reverend George D. McCurdy
GENERAL CHURCH OF THE NEW JERUSALEM, THE

Reverend John W. Schumacher
GRACE BRETHREN CHURCHES, THE FELLOWSHIP OF

CH (COL-RET) Ronald A. Crews
GRACE CHURCHES INTERNATIONAL

Reverend Traynor F. Hansen Jr.
GRACE GOSPEL FELLOWSHIP (NAE)

Mr. Clayton S. Peck
GRACE PLACE

Father James Robinson
GREEK ORTHODOX ARCHDIOCESE OF VASILOUPOLIS

Mr. James K. Anderson
HARVEST NETWORK INTERNATIONAL (CFGC)
ENDORSING EXECUTIVE: Dr. Klon K. Kitchen Jr.

Tyler Hendricks
HOLY SPIRIT ASSOCIATION FOR THE UNIFICATION OF WORLD CHRISTIANITY

Chaplain Robert J. Meyer
IFCA INTERNATIONAL

Lizzette Gabriel
IGLESIA METODISTA DE PUERTO RICO

Elder Rudy Leutzinger
INDEPENDENCE BRANCH, THE

Bishop John Reid
ORTHODOX CATHOLIC DIOCESE OF LOS ANGELES

Rev. Daniel J. Tyler
INTERNATIONAL CHRISTIAN CHURCH

Chaplain (COL) USA, Ret. Daniel A. Miller
INTERNATIONAL CHURCH OF THE FOURSQUARE GOSPEL

Mr. Dennis M. Burke
INTERNATIONAL CONVENTION OF FAITH MINISTRIES, INC. (CFGC)
ENDORSING EXECUTIVE: Dr. Klon K. Kitchen Jr.

Rev. Donald Ashmall
INTERNATIONAL COUNCIL OF COMMUNITY CHURCHES

Reverend Ron A. Brovold
INTERNATIONAL MINISTERIAL FELLOWSHIP

Safaa Zarzour
ISLAMIC SOCIETY OF NORTH AMERICA

Dr. William Jenkins
KINGSWAY FELLOWSHIP INTERNATIONAL (CFGC)
ENDORSING EXECUTIVE: Dr. Klon K. Kitchen Jr.

Reverend Seonjung Kim
KOREAN-AMERICAN PRESBYTERIAN CHURCH (PRJC)
ENDORSING EXECUTIVE: Chaplain (BG) Douglas E. Lee, USA-ret.

Reverend Samuel Jang
KOREAN EVANGELICAL CHURCH OF AMERICA

Mr. Bong Hwan Cho
KOREAN PRESBYTERIAN CHURCH OF AMERICA (PRJC)
ENDORSING EXECUTIVE: Chaplain (BG) Douglas E. Lee, Usa-ret.

The Rt. Reverend Dr. Robert S. McGinnis Jr.
LIBERAL CATHOLIC CHURCH

Dr. Charles N. Davidson
LIBERTY BAPTIST FELLOWSHIP FOR CHURCH PLANTING, INC.

Dr. Klon K. Kitchen Jr.
LIBERTY FELLOWSHIP OF CHURCHES AND MINISTERS, INC. (CFGC)
ENDORSING EXECUTIVE: Dr. Klon K. Kitchen Jr.

Chaplain Mark J. Schreiber
LUTHERAN CHURCH–MISSOURI SYNOD, THE

Reverend Tim White
LUTHERAN CONGREGATIONS IN MISSION FOR CHRIST

Rabbi Barney Kasdan
MESSIANIC JEWISH CONGREGATIONS, UNION OF

Dr. William Hessler
MISSIONARY CHURCH, INC. (NAE)
ENDORSING EXECUTIVE: Chaplain David Cyr, Brigadier General, USAF (Ret.)

The Reverend David Guthrie
MORAVIAN CHURCH IN AMERICA

Reverend Jerry Wm. Dailey
NATIONAL BAPTIST CONVENTION OF AMERICA, INC.

Dr. Charles F. Thomas
NATIONAL BAPTIST CONVENTION, USA, INC.

Reverend Dr. C. D. Sammons
NATIONAL MISSIONARY BAPTIST CONVENTION OF AMERICA

Pastor Garry L. Thompson
NEW TESTAMENT ASSOCIATION OF INDEPENDENT BAPTIST CHURCHES

Reverend Ray W. Hinsch
NORTH AMERICAN BAPTIST CONFERENCE

The Most Reverend Thomas E. Nesbitt
THE OLD HOLY CATHOLIC CHURCH USA & THE CANADIAN DISCIPLES OF OLD
CATHOLICISM IN NORTH AMERICA

Chaplain (RADM) Robert F. Burt (Ret.)
OPEN BIBLE STANDARD CHURCHES

CH (COL) Harry C. Grubbs, USAR (Ret.)
ORIGINAL FREE WILL BAPTISTS CONVENTION

Most Reverend Archbishop Scott McLaughlin
ORTHODOX ANGLICAN CHURCH

Metropolitan Jonah (Paffhausen)
ORTHODOX CHURCH IN AMERICA, THE

Reverend Donald J. Duff
ORTHODOX PRESBYTERIAN CHURCH (PRJC)
ENDORSING EXECUTIVE: Chaplain (BG) Douglas E. Lee, USA-ret.

Ms. Roxanne McDaniels
PENTECOSTAL ASSEMBLIES OF THE WORLD, INC.

District Elder Norman Allen II
PENTECOSTAL CHURCHES OF THE APOSTOLIC FAITH ASSN.

Reverend Dr. Lemuel M. Boyles
PENTECOSTAL CHURCH OF GOD, INC.

Dr. Hugh H. Morgan
PENTECOSTAL HOLINESS CHURCH, INTERNATIONAL

Reverend Fr. Michael A. Green
MILITARY VICARIATE FOR THE OLD ROMAN CATHOLIC CHURCH

Rabbi Fishel Todd
PIRCHEI SHOSHANIM

Dr. Kenneth V. Botton
PLYMOUTH BRETHREN

Most Reverend Robert M. Nemkovich
POLISH NATIONAL CATHOLIC CHURCH OF AMERICA

Chaplain (BG) Douglas E. Lee, USA-Ret.
PRESBYTERIAN CHURCH IN AMERICA, THE

The Reverend Clifton Kirkpatrick
PRESBYTERIAN CHURCH (U.S.A.), THE (PC)
ENDORSING EXECUTIVE: Chaplain, Colonel Edward T. Brogan, USAF-ret.

Reverend Robert Jemerson
PROGRESSIVE NATIONAL BAPTIST CONVENTION, INC.

Rabbi Joel H. Meyers
RABBINICAL ASSEMBLY (CONSERVATIVE), THE (JWB)
ENDORSING EXECUTIVE: Rear Admiral Harold L. Robinson, CHC, USN-ret.

Rabbi Basil Herring
RABBINICAL COUNCIL OF AMERICA (ORTHODOX) (JWB)
ENDORSING EXECUTIVE: Rear Admiral Harold L. Robinson, CHC, USN-ret.

Daniel J. Groen, COL, USA (Ret.)
REFORMED CHURCH IN AMERICA

Rt. Reverend Royal U. Grote Jr.
REFORMED EPISCOPAL CHURCH

Mr. James K. McFarland
REFORMED PRESBYTERIAN CHURCH OF NORTH AMERICA (PRJC)
ENDORSING EXECUTIVE: Chaplain (BG) Douglas E. Lee, USA-ret.

Reverend Dr. John B. Murdoch
REGULAR BAPTIST CHURCHES, GENERAL ASSOCIATION OF

Reverend Kenneth W. Hagin
RHEMA BIBLE CHURCH (CFGC)
ENDORSING EXECUTIVE: Dr. Klon K. Kitchen Jr.

Archbishop Timothy P. Broglio
ROMAN CATHOLIC CHURCH, THE

Bishop Peter (Loukianoff)
RUSSIAN ORTHODOX CHURCH OUTSIDE RUSSIA

Colonel William Harfoot
SALVATION ARMY, THE

Chaplain (Colonel) Gary R. Councell, US Army Retired
SEVENTH DAY ADVENTISTS–UNITED STATES, GENERAL CONFERENCE OF

Reverend Gordon P. Lawton
SEVENTH DAY BAPTIST GENERAL CONFERENCE U.S.A. AND CANADA

Rabbi Sanford L. Dresin
SHUL, THE

Mr. Keith Travis
SOUTHERN BAPTIST CONVENTION

Reverend Dr. John T. Hucks Jr.
SOUTHERN METHODIST CHURCH, THE

Dr. Ronald W. Shinkle
SOVEREIGN GRACE BAPTIST ASSOCIATION OF CHURCHES

Reverend Richard L. Tafel
SWEDENBORGIAN CHURCH, THE

The Most Reverend Bishop Jerome Bernard
SYRIAN EASTERN ORTHODOX EXARCHATE IN AMERICA

Dr. Klon K. Kitchen Jr.
TRINITY FULL GOSPEL FELLOWSHIP (CFGC)

Archbishop Antony (Scharba)
UKRAINIAN ORTHODOX CHURCH OF THE U.S.A.

Dr. Ronald L. Tottingham
UNAFFILIATED BAPTIST CHURCHES OF AMERICA

Reverend Sarah K. Lammert
UNITARIAN UNIVERSALIST ASSOCIATION, THE

Most Reverend Gregory A. Francisco
UNITED CATHOLIC CHURCH OF AMERICA

Rev. Stephen Boyd
UNITED CHURCH OF CHRIST

The Rev. T. J. Bradshaw
UNITED EPISCOPAL CHURCH OF NORTH AMERICA, THE

Mr. Robert B. Fort
UNITED EVANGELICAL CHURCHES (CFGC)
ENDORSING EXECUTIVE: Dr. Klon K. Kitchen Jr.

Dr. Maston Love Jr.
UNITED FULL GOSPEL CHURCH (CFGC)
ENDORSING EXECUTIVE: Dr. Klon K. Kitchen Jr.

Bishop Woodie White
UNITED METHODIST CHURCH, THE

Reverend Daniel E. Batchelor
UNITED PENTECOSTAL CHURCH INTERNATIONAL

Reverend Marjorie Brach
UNITY CHURCHES, ASSOCIATION OF

Reverend Billy Joe Daugherty
VICTORY CHRISTIAN CENTER (CFGC)
ENDORSING EXECUTIVE: Dr. Klon K. Kitchen Jr.

Reverend Thomas J. Cooley
VINEYARD CHRISTIAN FELLOWSHIP CHURCH OF COBB COUNTY, INC.

Reverend Russ Gunsalus
WESLEYAN CHURCH, THE

Reverend Kenneth R. Mitchell
WESTSIDE CHRISTIAN FAMILY CHAPEL (NAE)
ENDORSING EXECUTIVE: Chaplain David Cyr, Brigadier General, USAF (Ret.)

Reverend Thomas M. Raley
WORLD BAPTIST FELLOWSHIP, INC.

Reverend Dr. John Lupoli
WORLD COUNCIL OF INDEPENDENT CHRISTIAN CHURCHES, THE

The Most Reverend David Scott
COMMUNION OF EVANGELICAL EPISCOPAL CHURCHES

Rev. George C. Paul
CONVERGE WORLDWIDE

SELECTED BIBLIOGRAPHY

LEGAL CASES

Adair v. England, 417 F. Supp. 2d 1 (D.D.C. 2006).

American Guidance Foundation, Inc. v. United States, 490 F. Supp. 304, 306 n.2 (D.D.C. 1980).

Arizona Christian School Tuition Organization v. Winn, 131 S. Ct. 1436 (2011).

Baz v. Walters, 782 F.2d 701 (1986).

Bob Jones University v. United States, 461 U.S. 574 (1983).

Boerne v. Flores, 521 U.S. 507 (1997).

Carter v. Broadlawns Medical Center, 857 F.2d 448 (1988).

Chaplaincy of Full Gospel Churches v. England, 454 F.3d 290 (D.C. Cir. 2006).

Chappell v. Wallace, 462 U.S. 296 (1983).

Cruz v. Beto, 405 U.S. 319, 322 (1972).

Cutter v. Wilkinson, 544 U.S. 709 (2005).

Employment Division v. Smith, 494 U.S. 872, 890 (1990).

Flast v. Cohen, 392 U.S. 83 (1968).

Foundation of Human Understanding v. U.S., 614 F.3d 1383 (2010).

Freedom from Religion Foundation v. Nicholson, 469 F. Supp. 2d 609 (W.D. Wis. 2007), *vacated and remanded*, 536 F.3d 730 (7th Cir. 2008).

Frothingham v. Mellon, 262 U.S. 447 (1923).

Garcetti v. Ceballos, 547 U.S. 410 (2006).

Gonzales v. Roman Catholic Archbishop of Manila, 280 U.S. 1 (1910).

HEB Ministries, Inc. v. Texas Higher Educ. Coordinating Bd., 235 S.W.3d 627 (2007).

Hein v. FFRF, 551 U.S. 587 (2007).

Hinrichs v. Speaker of the House of Representatives of the Indiana General Assembly, 506 F.3d 584, 598 (7th Cir. 2007).

Hosanna-Tabor Evangelical Lutheran Church and School v. EEOC, 132 S. Ct. 694 (2012).

In re England, 375 F.3d 1169 (D.C. Cir. 2004), *cert. denied*, 543 U.S. 1152 (2005).

Katcoff v. Marsh, 582 F. Supp. 463, 464–65 (1984), *affirmed* 755 F.2d 223 (2d Cir. 1985).

Kerr v. Farrey, 95 F.3d 472 (7th Cir. 1996).

Larsen v. U.S. Navy, 486 F. Supp. 2d 11 (D.D.C. 2007).

Lemon v. Kurtzman, 403 U.S. 602 (1971).

Locke v. Davey, 540 U.S. 712 (2004).

Lynch v. Donnelly, 465 U.S. 668 (1984).

Marsh v. Chambers, 463 U.S. 783 (1983).

Murphy v. Derwinski, 990 F.2d 540 (1993).

New Jersey State Bd. of Education v. Bd. of Directors of Shelton College, 90 N.J. 470 (1982).

R. v. The Governing Body of JFS, 2009 UKSC 15.

Rasul v. District of Columbia, 680 F. Supp. 436, 442 (D.D.C. 1988). Tennessee *ex rel.* McLemore v. Clarksville School of Theology, 636 S.W.2d 706 (Tenn. 1982).

Townshend v. Gray, 62 Vt. 373 (1890).

Trustees of Dartmouth College v. Woodward, 17 U.S. (4 Wheat.) 518 (1819).

U.S. v. Seeger 380 U.S. 163 (1965).

Valley Forge Christian College v. Americans United for the Separation of Church and State, 454 U.S. 464 (1982).

Veitch v. England, 471 F.3d 124 (2006).

Warner v. Orange County Dept. of Probation, 115 F.3d 1068 (2nd Cir. 1997).

Wilkins v. U.S., 2005 U.S. Dist. LEXIS 41268 (S.D. Cal. 2003).

Zorach v. Clauson, 343 U.S. 306 (1952).

BOOKS AND ARTICLES

Abbott, Andrew. *The System of Professions: An Essay on the Division of Expert Labor.* Chicago: University of Chicago Press, 1988.

Abernethy, Bob. "Martin Marty: Extended Interview." *Religion and Ethics Newsweekly* May 9, 2002. http://www.pbs.org/wnet/religionandethics/2002/05/03/may-3-2002-martin -marty-extended-interview/11648/ (accessed September 30, 2013).

Adams, George. "Chaplains as Liaisons with Religious Leaders: Lessons from Iraq and Afghanistan." *Peaceworks* 56 (2006).

Adcock, C. S. *The Limits of Tolerance: Indian Secularism and the Politics of Religious Freedom.* Oxford: Oxford University Press, 2013.

Aden, Leroy, and J. Harold Ellens, eds. *Turning Points in Pastoral Care: The Legacy of Anton Boisen and Seward Hiltner.* Grand Rapids, MI: Baker Books, 1990.

Aden, Steven H. "The Navy's Perfect Storm: Has a Military Chaplaincy Forfeited Its Con-stitutional Legitimacy by Establishing Denominational Preferences?" *Western State University Law Review* 31, no. 2 (2004): 185–238.

Adler, Amy B., Carl Andrew Castro, and Thomas W. Britt, eds. *Military Life: The Psychology of Serving in Peace and Combat.* Westport, CN: Praeger Security International, 2006.

Albanese, Catherine. *Nature Religion in America: From the Algonkian Indians to the New Age.* Chicago: University of Chicago Press, 1991.

Aleshire, Daniel O. *Earthen Vessels: Hopeful Reflections on the Work and Future of Theological Schools.* Grand Rapids, MI: Eerdmans, 2008.

Alonzo, Ana María. "The Politics of Space, Time and Substance: State Formation, Nation-alism, and Ethnicity." *Annual Review of Anthropology* 23 (1994): 379–405.

Anandarajah, Gowri, and Ellen Hight. "Spirituality and Medical Practice: Using the HOPE Questions as a Practical Tool for Spiritual Assessment." *American Family Physician* 63, no. 1 (2001): 81–88.

Anidjar, Gil. "The Idea of an Anthropology of Christianity." *Interventions* 11 (2011): 367–93.
———. "Secularism." *Critical Inquiry* 33 (2006): 52–77.

Appadurai, Arjun. *Worship and Conflict under Colonial Rule: A South Indian Case.* Cambridge: Cambridge University Press, 1981.

Appelquist, A. Ray, ed. *Church, State and Chaplaincy: Essays and Statements on the American Chaplaincy System*. Washington, DC: General Commission on Chaplains and Armed Services Personnel, 1969.

Areen, Judith. "Accreditation Reconsidered." *Iowa Law Review* 96 (2011): 1471–94.

Army and Navy Chaplain: A Professional Journal for Chaplains and Religious Workers 12, no. 3 (January–February 1942).

Asad, Talal. *Formations of the Secular: Christianity, Islam, Modernity*. Stanford, CA: Stanford University Press, 2003.

———. "Response to Gil Anidjar." *interventions* 11, no. 3 (2009): 394–99.

———. "Thinking about Religion, Belief and Politics." Foerster Lecture. University of California, Berkeley. October 2, 2008. Accessed July 12, 2013. http://blogs.ssrc.org/tif/2009/01/13/talal-asad-on-religion-belief-and-politics/.

Asimov, Nanette. "Stanford Gets a Chaplain for Atheists." *San Francisco Chronicle*. December 22, 2012. Accessed January 29, 2013. www.sfgate.com/news/article/Stanford-gets-a-chaplain-for-atheists-4139991.php.

Association for Clinical Pastoral Education. *Standards and Manuals: Definitions of Terms*. Decatur, GA: ASCP, 2010.

Association of Theological Schools, "Basic Programs Oriented Toward Ministerial Leadership," Association of Theological Schools, Commission on Accrediting, http://www.ats.edu/memberschools/pages/degrees.aspx?pf=1 (accessed February 5, 2013).

———. "2010–11 Annual Data Tables," Association of Theological Schools, Commission on Accrediting, http://www.ats.edu/Resources/Pages/AnnualDataTablesFactBooks.aspx (accessed February 5, 2013).

———. *Theological Education in the 1970s: A Report of the Resources Planning Commission* (1968).

Astuti, Rita, and Maurice Bloch. "Are Ancestors Dead?" In *Companion to the Anthropology of Religion*, edited by Janice Boddy and Michael Lambek. West Sussex: Wiley Blackwell, 2012.

Bachrach, David S. "The Medieval Military Chaplain and His Duties." In *The Sword of the Lord: Military Chaplains from the First to the Twenty-First Century*, edited by Doris L. Bergen. Notre Dame, IN: University of Notre Dame Press, 2004.

Badarocco, Claire Hoertz. *Prescribing Faith: Medicine, Media, and Religion in American Culture*. Waco, TX: Baylor University Press, 2007.

Bailey, Beth. *America's Army: Making the All-Volunteer Force*. Cambridge, MA: Harvard University Press, 2009.

Banerjee, Neela. "Indiana, Faced with Suit, Takes Chaplain Off Payroll." *New York Times*, September 28, 2007.

Bartell, Rich. "USARAF Chaplains Teach Resiliency in Africa." US Army Africa Public Affairs Office, Kinshasa, Democratic Republic of the Congo. February 29, 2012. http://www.usaraf.army.mil/NEWS/NEWS_120229_CHAPS_DRC.html.

Baubérot, Jean, and Séverine Mathieu. *Religion, modernité et culture au Royaume-Uni et en France, 1800–1914*. Paris: Seuil Points Histoire, 2002.

Beauvois, Xavier. *Des Hommes et des Dieux*. 2010.

Beckford, James, and Sophie Gilliat-Ray. *Religion in Prison: Equal Rites in a Multi Faith Society*. Cambridge: Cambridge University Press, 1998.

Bedsole, Timothy K., Sr. "The World Religions Chaplain: A Practitioner's Perspective." *Review of Faith & International Affairs* 7, no. 4 (2009): 63–69.

Bellah, Robert, et al. *Habits of the Heart*. 3rd ed. Berkeley: University of California Press, 2007.

Bender, Courtney. *The New Metaphysics: Spirituality and the American Religious Imagination*. Chicago: University of Chicago Press, 2010.

———. "Pluralism and Secularism." In *Religion on the Edge: New Directions in the Sociology of Religion*, edited by Courtney Bender, Wendy Cadge, Peggy Levitt, and David Smilde. Oxford University Press, 2013.

Bender, Courtney, Wendy Cadge, Peggy Levitt, and David Smilde, eds. *Religion on the Edge: De-centering and Re-centering the Sociology of Religion*. New York: Oxford University Press, 2013.

Bender, Courtney, and Pamela Klassen, eds. *After Pluralism: Reimagining Religious Engagement*. New York: Columbia University Press, 2010.

Bender, Courtney, and Omar McRoberts, "Mapping a Field: Why and How to Study Spirituality." Social Science Research Council website, October 2012. http://blogs.ssrc .org/tif/wp-content/uploads/2010/05/Why-and-How-to-Study-Spirtuality.pdf (accessed January 26, 2013).

Bergen, Doris, ed. *The Sword of the Lord: Military Chaplains from the First to the Twenty-First Century*. Notre Dame, IN: University of Notre Dame Press, 2004.

Berger, Benjamin. "Law's Aesthetics." In *Varieties of Religious Establishment*, edited by Winnifred Fallers Sullivan and Lori Beaman. London: Ashgate, 2013.

Berman, Alex, and Michael A. Flannery. *America's Botanico-Medical Movements: Vox Populi*. Binghampton, NY: Haworth Press, 2001.

Berman, Harold. *Law and Revolution: The Formation of the Western Legal Tradition*. Cambridge, MA: Harvard University Press, 1983.

Bindon, Emilie Kraft. "Entangled Choices: Selecting Chaplains for the United States Armed Forces." *Alabama Law Review* 56, no. 1 (2004): 247–83.

Bivins, Jason. *The Fracture of Good Order: Christian Anti-Liberalism and the Challenge to Postwar American Politics*. Chapel Hill: University of North Carolina Press, 2003.

Boison, Anton T. *Out of the Depths: An Autobiographical Study of Mental Disorders and Religious Experience*. New York: Harper, 1960.

Bole, William. "The Ministry of Presence" and "Social Catholicism: Essays in Honor of Monsignor George Higgins." *U.S. Catholic Historian* 19, no. 4 (2001): 3–10.

Boone, Joseph F. "The Roles of the Church of Jesus Christ of Latter-Day Saints in Relation to the United States Military, 1900–1975." PhD diss., Brigham Young University, 1975.

Bossy, John. "The Social History of Confession in the Age of the Reformation." *Transactions of the Royal Historical Society*, 5th ser., 25 (1975): 21–38.

Boyarin, Daniel. "Rethinking Jewish Christianity: An Argument for Dismantling a Dubious Category (to Which Is Appended a Correction of My Border Lines)." *Jewish Quarterly Review* 99 (2009): 7–36.

Boyce, Nathan M. "From Rubik's Cube to Checkers: Determining Church Status Is Not as Hard as You Think." *Exempt Organization Tax Review* 68, no. 1 (2011): 27.

Boyer, Pascal. *Religion Explained: The Evolutionary Foundations of Religious Belief*. New York: Basic Books, 2001.

Braestrup, Kate. "Blessing the Moose: Praying for Good News, Planning for Bad; True Stories from the Chaplain of the Maine Warden Service." *Boston Globe*, September 23, 2007.

———. *Here If You Need Me*. Boston: Little Brown, 2007.

———. "Presence in the Wild." Chapter 11 from *Here If You Need Me*. Accessed July 12, 2013. http://being.publicradio.org/programs/braestrup/chapter11.shtml.

Brassey, Paul. "Eliminate Endorsement." *Plain Views* 6, no. 4 (2009): n.p.

Brinsfield, John W. "The Army Chaplaincy and World Religions: From Individual Ministries to Chaplain Corps Doctrine." *Army Chaplaincy* (2009): 11–18.

———. *Encouraging Faith, Supporting Soldiers: The United States Army Chaplaincy, 1975–1995.* Washington, DC: Office of the Chief of Chaplains, Department of the Army, 1997.

———. "The U.S. Military Chaplaincy, Then and Now." *Review of Faith & International Affairs* 7, no. 4 (2009): 17–24.

Brodman, James W. "Religion and Discipline in the Hospitals of Thirteenth-Century France." In *The Medieval Hospital and Medical Practice*, edited by Barbara S. Bowers. Burlington, VT: Ashgate, 2007.

Brown, Candy Gunther. *Healing Gods.* Oxford: Oxford University Press, 2013.

Brudnick, Ida A. "House and Senate Chaplains: An Overview." Congressional Research Service, May 26, 2011.

Budd, Richard. *Serving Two Masters: The Development of American Military Chaplaincy, 1860–1920.* Lincoln: University of Nebraska Press, 2002.

Bumiller, Elisabeth. "A Day Job Waiting for a Kill Shot a World Away." *New York Times*, July 29, 2012.

Burns, Robert. *Kafka's Revenge.* Chicago: University of Chicago Press, forthcoming.

———. *A Theory of the Trial.* Princeton, NJ: Princeton University Press, 2001.

Cabot, Richard. *Adventures on the Borderlands of Ethics.* New York: Harper & Bros., 1926.

Cabot, Richard, and Russell Dicks, *The Art of Ministering to the Sick.* New York: Macmillan, 1936.

Cadge, Wendy. *Paging God: Religion in the Halls of Medicine.* Chicago: University of Chicago Press, 2012.

———. "Saying Your Prayers, Constructing Your Religions: Medical Studies of Intercessory Prayer." *Journal of Religion* 89 (2009): 299–327.

Cadge, Wendy, and Emily Sigalow. "Negotiating Religious Differences: The Strategies of Interfaith Chaplains in Healthcare." *Journal for the Scientific Study of Religion* 52, no. 1 (2013): 146–58.

Cadge, Wendy, Jeremy Freese, and Nikolas A. Christakis. "The Provision of Hospital Chaplaincy in the United States: A National Overview." *Southern Medical Journal* 101, no. 6 (2008): 626–30.

Cahners, Nancy. "What Does a Hospital Chaplain Do Again? Trying to Explain the Meaning of Making Meaning in the World of Medical Ethics." In *Medical Ethics in Health Care Chaplaincy*, edited by Walter Moczynski, Hille Haker, and Katrin Bentele. Berlin: Lit Verlag 2009.

Callaghan, Morley. *Such Is My Beloved.* New York: Charles Scribner's Sons, 1934.

Carlson, John. "Cashing in on Religion's Currency? Ethical Challenges for a Post-secular Military." *Review of Faith and International Affairs* 7, no. 4 (2009): 51–62.

Carrette, Jeremy, and Richard King. *Selling Spirituality: The Silent Takeover of Religion.* New York: Routledge 2005.

Carroll, Chris. "Military's First Hindu Chaplain Brings a Diverse Background." *Stars and Stripes*, June 2, 2011.

Casanova, José. *Public Religions in the Modern World.* Chicago: University of Chicago Press, 1995.

Case, Mary Anne. "The Peculiar Stake U.S. Protestants Have in the Question of State Recognition of Same-Sex Marriage." In *After Secular Law*, edited by Winnifred Fallers Sullivan, Robert A. Yelle, and Mateo Taussig-Rubbo, 302–21. Stanford, CA: Stanford University Press, 2011.

Catechism of the Catholic Church. http://www.vatican.va/archive/ENG0015/__P2U.HTM (accessed June 27, 2013).

A Catechism of Christian Doctrine, Prepared and Enjoined by Order of the Third Council of Baltimore. 1865.

Chave, Anna. "Revaluing Minimalism: Patronage, Aura, and Place." *Art Bulletin* 90 (2008): 466–86.

Chaves, Mark. *American Religion: Contemporary Trends.* Princeton, NJ: Princeton University Press, 2011.

———. "SSSR Presidential Address: Rain Dances in the Dry Season; Overcoming the Religious Congruence Fallacy." *Journal for the Scientific Study of Religion* 49, no. 1 (2010): 1–14.

Chaves, Mark, and Bob Wineburg. "Did the Faith-Based Initiative Change Congregations?" *Nonprofit and Voluntary Sector Quarterly* 39 (2010): 343–55.

The Chicago Council on Global Affairs. "Engaging Religious Communities Abroad: A New Imperative for U.S. Foreign Policy." R. Scott Appleby and Richard Cizik, cochairs; Thomas Wright, project director. 2010.

Cobb, J. B., Jr. "The Problem of Evil and the Task of Ministry." In *Encountering Evil: Live Options in Theodicy,* 2nd ed., edited by Stephen T. Davis, 181–90. Louisville, KY: Westminster John Knox Press, 2001.

Comaroff, John. "Reflections on the Rise of Legal Theology: Law and Religion in the 21st Century." *Social Analysis* 53 no. 1 (2009): 193–216.

Cohen, Andrew. "At Louisiana's Most Notorious Prison, a Clash of Testament." *Atlantic,* October 11, 2013. http://www.theatlantic.com/national/archive/2013/10/at-louisianas -most-notorious-prison-a-clash-of-testament/280414/ (accessed October 27, 2013).

Contreras, Alan L. "The Legal Basis for Degree-Granting Authority in the United States." Unpublished manuscript, on file with State Higher Education Executive Officers. Accessed July 12, 2013. http://www.sheeo.org/govern/Contreras2009-10-LegalDegree Granting.pdf.

Cover, Robert. "Foreword: *Nomos* and Narrative." *Harvard Law Review* (1983): 4–68.

Coxe, Matson. "Here Is the Church, Where Is the Steeple? *Foundation of Human Understanding v. U.S.*" *North Carolina Law Review* 89 (2011): 1248–72.

Day, Matthew. "The Sacred Contagion: John Trenchard, Natural History, and the Effluvial Politics of Religion." *History of Religions* 50 (2010): 144–61.

Dempsey, Terry A. "Asymmetric Threats to the United States Army Chaplaincy in the 21st Century." USAWC Strategy Research Report. US Army War College. April 10, 2000.

Department of the Army. "Spiritual Fitness." Department of the Army Pamphlet 600-63-12. 1987.

Department of Defense, Statement of Hon. Charles S. Abell, Principal Deputy Under Secretary for Personnel and Readiness. *Hearing before the Subcommittee on Terrorism, Technology and Homeland Security of the Committee on the Judiciary,* 108th Cong. 43–49 (2003).

Devji, Faisal. *The Terrorist in Search of the Humanity: Militant Islam and Global Politics.* New York: Columbia University Press, 2008.

DeVries, Raymond, Nancy Berlinger, and Wendy Cadge, "Lost in Translation: The Chaplain's Role in Health Care." *Hastings Report,* November–December 2008.

DiMaggio, Paul J., and Walter W. Powell. "The Iron Cage Revisited: Institutional Isomorphism and Collective Rationality in Organizational Fields." *American Sociological Review* 48 (1983): 147–60.

Dolan, Jay. *In Search of an American Catholicism: A History of Religion and Culture in Tension.* Oxford: Oxford University Press, 2003.

Dolan, Mary Jean. "Government-Sponsored Chaplains and Crisis: Walking the Fine Line in Disaster Response and Daily Life." *Hastings Constitutional Law Quarterly* 35 (2008): 505–46.

Douzinas, Costas, and Lynda Nead. *Law and the Image: The Authority of Art and the Aesthetics of Law.* Chicago: University of Chicago Press, 1999.

Drazin, Israel, and Cecil B. Currey. *For God and Country: The History of a Constitutional Challenge to the Army Chaplaincy.* Hoboken, NJ: KTAV Publishing House, 1995.

Dubler, Joshua. *Down in the Chapel: Religious Life in an American Prison.* New York: Farrar, Straus and Giroux, 2013.

Ebel, Jonathan. *Faith in the Fight: Religion and the American Soldier in the Great War.* Princeton, NJ: Princeton University Press, 2010.

Eckholm, Erik. "Bible College Helps Some at Louisiana Prison Find Peace." *New York Times*, October 6, 2013, A15.

Edgell, Penny, Joseph Gerteis, and Douglas Hartmann. "Atheists as 'Other': Moral Boundaries and Cultural Membership in American Society." *American Sociological Review* 71 (2006): 211–34.

Ellsberg, Robert, ed. *Charles de Foucauld.* New York: Orbis Books, 1999.

Epstein, Greg M. "Military Needs Chaplains for Humanists, Atheists." *Washington Post*, July 25, 2008. Accessed January 29, 2013. http://newsweek.washingtonpost.com /onfaith/panelists/greg_m_epstein/2008/07/us_military_needs_chaplains_fo.html.

Fanning, William H. "Chaplain." In *Catholic Encyclopedia*, edited by Robert C. Broderick. New York: Thomas Nelson, 1990.

Fenn, Richard K. *Liturgies and Trials: The Secularization of Religious Language.* London: Blackwell, 1984.

Fessenden, Tracy. *Culture and Redemption: Religion, the Secular, and American Religion.* Princeton, NJ: Princeton University Press, 2007.

Filteau, Jerry. "Monsignor George Higgins: Labor Priest; A Success Story Par Excellence." National Institute for the Revival of the Priesthood. http://www.jknirp.com/higgins2 .htm (accessed February 8, 2013).

Fitchett, George. *Assessing Spiritual Needs: A Guide for Caregivers.* Minneapolis: Augsburg Fortress, 1993.

Fitzkee, David E., and Linell A. Letendre. "Religion in the Military: Navigating the Channel between the Religion Clauses." *Air Force Law Review* 59 (2007): 1–71.

Fitzpatrick, Peter. *The Mythology of Modern Law.* New York: Routledge, 1992.

Foucault, Michel. *Security, Territory, Population: Lectures at the Collège de France, 1977–78.* Translated by Graham Burchell. New York: Picador, 2007.

Fowler, James W. *Stages of Faith: The Psychology of Human Development and the Quest for Meaning.* San Francisco: Harper & Row, 1981.

Freedom from Religion Foundation. "FFRF Calls for Halt to Army 'Spiritual Fitness' Survey," December 29, 2010. http://www.ffrf.org/news/releases/ffrf-calls-for-halt-to -army-spiritual-fitness-survey/ (accessed January 27, 2013).

Freeman, Jody. "The Private Role in Public Governance." *New York University Law Review* 75 (2000): 543–675.

Friedman, Edwin H. *From Generation to Generation: Family Process in Church and Synagogue.* New York: Guilford Press, 2011.

Friedman, Milton. *Capitalism and Freedom.* Chicago: University of Chicago Press, 1962.

Furey, Constance. "Body, Society, and Subjectivity in Religious Studies." *Journal of the American Academy of Religion* 80 (2012): 7–33.

Garland, David. *The Culture of Control: Crime and Social Order in Contemporary Society.* Chicago: University of Chicago Press, 2001.

———. *Mass Imprisonment: Social Causes and Consequences.* London: Sage, 2001.

Garland, Diana, Ellen Netting, and Mary Katherine O'Connor. "Belief Systems in Faith-Based Human Service Programs." *Journal of Religion & Spirituality in Social Work: Social Thought* 25, nos. 3–4 (2006): 261–86 .

Garvin, David A. "Making the Case: Professional Education for the World of Practice," *Harvard Magazine*, July–August 2013.

Gaubatz, Derek L. "RLUIPA at Four: Evaluating the Success and Constitutionality of RLUIPA's Prisoner Provisions." *Harvard Journal of Law and Public Policy* 28 (2005): 501–607.

Gey, Steven G. "Religious Coercion and the Establishment Clause." *University of Illinois Law Review* 463 (1994): 467–72.

Gibson, William. *A Social History of the Domestic Chaplain: 1530–1840.* London: Leicester University Press, 1997.

Gilliat-Ray, Sophie. "Being There: Shadowing a British Muslim Hospital Chaplain." *Culture and Religion* 11, no. 4 (2010): 413–32.

———. "From 'Chapel' to 'Prayer Room': The Production, Use, and Politics of Sacred Space in Public Institutions." *Culture and Religion* 6, no. 2 (2005): 287–308.

———. "Nursing, Professionalism, and Spirituality." *Journal of Contemporary Religion* 18, no. 3 (2003): 335–49.

———. *Religion in Higher Education: The Politics of the Multi-faith Campus.* London: Ashgate, 2000.

———. "'Sacralising' Sacred Space in Public Institutions: A Case Study of the Prayer Space at the Millennium Dome." *Journal of Contemporary Religion* 20, no. 3 (2005): 357–72.

Ginzburg, Carlo. *The Cheese and the Worms: The Cosmos of a Sixteenth Century Miller*, translated by John and Anne Tedeschi. Baltimore: Johns Hopkins University Press, 1980.

Goffman, Erving. *Interaction Ritual: Essays in Face-to-Face Behavior.* Chicago: Aldine Publishing Company, 1967.

Gollin, George, Emily Lawrence, and Alan Contreras, "Complexities in Legislative Suppression of Diploma Mills." *Stanford Law and Policy Review* 21 (2010): 1–32.

Goodrich, Peter. *Oedipus Lex.* Berkeley: University of California Press, 1995.

Gordon, Sarah Barringer. *Spirit of the Law: Religious Voices and the Constitution in Modern America.* Cambridge, MA: Harvard University Press, 2010.

Gorski, Philip. *The Disciplinary Revolution: Calvinism and the Rise of the State in Early Modern Europe.* Chicago: University of Chicago Press, 2003.

Grant, Don, Kathleen O'Neill, and Laura Stephens. "Spirituality in the Workplace: New Empirical Directions in the Study of the Sacred." *Sociology of Religion* 65, no. 3 (2004): 265–83.

Green, Steven K. "The Slow, Tragic Demise of Standing in Establishment Clause Challenges." *American Constitution Society*, September 2011.

Greenawalt, Kent. *Religion and the Constitution.* Vol. 2, *Establishment and Fairness.* Princeton, NJ: Princeton University Press, 2008.

Haefeli, Evan. "Toleration and Empire: The Origins of American Religious Diversity." In *Oxford History of the British Empire*, supplemental volume. Oxford: Oxford University Press, forthcoming.

Halliday, Terence. "Knowledge Mandates: Collective Influence by Scientific, Normative and Syncretic Professions." *British Journal of Sociology* 36, no. 3 (1985): 477–95.

Hamburger, Philip. *Separation of Church and State.* Cambridge, MA: Harvard University Press, 2000.

Hann, Chris, and Mathijs Pelkmans. "Realigning Religion and Power in Central Asia: Islam, Nation-State and (Post)Socialism." *Europe-Asia Studies* 61 (2009): 1517–41.

Hansen, Kim Philip. *Military Chaplains and Religious Diversity.* New York: Palgrave, 2012.

Harcourt, Bernard. *The Illusion of Free Markets: Punishment and the Myth of Natural Order.* Cambridge, MA: Harvard University Press, 2011.

Harrington, Peter J. "Civil and Canon Law Issues Affecting American Catholic Higher Education 1948–1998: An Overview and the ACCU Perspective." *Journal of College and University Law* 26 (1999): 67–106.

Harrison, Peter. *"Religion" and the Religions in the English Enlightenment.* Cambridge: Cambridge University Press, 1990.

Hart, Kevin, ed. *Jean-Luc Marion: The Essential Writings.* New York: Fordham University Press, 2013.

Hastings Center. "Can We Measure Good Chaplaincy? A New Professional Identity Is Tied to Quality Improvement." *Hastings Center Report* 38 no. 6 (2008).

Hauerwas, Stanley. *God, Medicine and Suffering.* Grand Rapids, MI: Eerdmans, 1994.

Hefner, Robert. "Religious Resurgence in Contemporary Asia: Southeast Asian Perspectives on Capitalism, the State, and the New Piety." *Journal of Asian Studies* 69, no. 4 (2010): 1031–47.

Herberg, Will. *Protestant, Catholic, Jew: An Essay in American Religious Sociology.* Garden City, NY: Doubleday, 1955.

Hester, Richard L. "Toward Professionalism or Voluntarism in Pastoral Care." *Pastoral Psychology* 24 (1976): 305–16.

Hicks, Allison. "Role Fusion: The Occupational Socialization of Prison Chaplains." *Symbolic Interaction* 31, no. 4 (2008:): 400–421.

Hillinger, Charles. "Ministry Reaches the Great Outdoors: Chaplains: Student Ministers Preach at National Parks in Spare Time, Offering Religious Services for Tourists." *Los Angeles Times*, February 1, 1992. Accessed July 12, 2013. http://articles.latimes .com/1992-02-.

Hobbins, Daniel. *The Trial of Joan of Arc.* Cambridge, MA: Harvard University Press, 2007.

Holifield, E. Brooks. *God's Ambassadors: A History of the Christian Clergy in America.* Grand Rapids, MI: Eerdmans, 2007.

———. *A History of Pastoral Care in America: From Salvation to Self-Realization.* Nashville: Abingdon Press, 1983.

Howe, Mark deWolfe. *The Garden and the Wilderness: Religion and Government in American Constitutional History.* Chicago: University of Chicago Press, 1967.

Hunter, Charlotte E. "The Ethics of Military Sponsored Prayer." Defense Equal Opportunity Management Institute. http://isme.tamu.edu/ISME07/Hunter07.html (accessed July 12, 2013).

Hurd, Elizabeth Shakman. *The Politics of Secularism in International Relations.* Princeton, NJ: Princeton University Press, 2007.

———. *Secular Establishment: Religion, Law, and Authority in International Politics.* Forthcoming.

Ignatieff, Michael. *A Just Measure of Pain: The Penitentiary in the Industrial Revolution, 1750–1850.* London: Penguin Books, 1970.

Jakobsen, Janet, and Ann Pellegrini. *Love the Sin: Sexual Regulation and the Limits of Religious Tolerance.* New York: New York University Press, 2003.

———. eds. *Secularisms.* Durham, NC: Duke University Press, 2008.

James, William. *Varieties of Religious Experience.* New York: Longmans and Green, 1902.

Johnson, Creola. "Credentialism and the Proliferation of Fake Degrees: The Employer Pretends to Need a Degree; The Employee Pretends to Have One." *Hofstra Labor and Employment Law Journal* 23 (2006): 269–343.

———. "Degrees of Deception: Are Consumers and Employers Being Duped by Online Universities and Diploma Mills?" *Journal of College & University Law* 32 (2006): 411–90.

Johnson, Greg. "Varieties of Native Hawaiian Establishment: Recognized Voices, Routinized Charisma, and Church Desecration." In *Varieties of Religious Establishment,* ed. Winnifred Fallers Sullivan and Lori Beaman. London: Ashgate, 2013.

Johnson, Paul C. "An Atlantic Genealogy of 'Spirit Possession.'" *Comparative Studies in Society and History* 53, no. 2 (2011): 393–425.

Johnston, Douglas M. "U.S. Military Chaplains: Redirecting a Critical Asset." *Review of Faith & International Affairs* 7 (2009): 25–32.

Joint Commission on Accreditation of Healthcare Organizations. *The Source* 3, no. 2 (February 2005).

Jones, Michael T. "The Air Force Chaplain: Clergy or Officer?" A Research Report Submitted to the Faculty in Fulfillment of the Curriculum Requirement. USAF Air War College Air University, 1996.

Jost, Timothy Stoltzfus. "Medicare and the Joint Commission on Accreditation of Healthcare Organizations: A Healthy Relationship?" *Law and Contemporary Problems* 57 (1994): 15–45.

Kafka, Franz. *The Trial.* Translated Willa and Edwin Muir. New York: Alfred A. Knopf, 1937.

Kahn, Paul W. *The Cultural Study of Law: Reconstructing Legal Scholarship.* Chicago: University of Chicago Press, 2000.

Kantorowicz, Ernst. *The King's Two Bodies: A Study in Mediaeval Political Theology.* Princeton, NJ: Princeton University Press, 1957.

Kaplan, Benjamin. *Divided by Faith: Religious Conflict and the Practice of Toleration in Early Modern Europe.* Cambridge, MA: Harvard University Press, 2007.

Keane, Webb. *Christian Moderns: Freedom and Fetish in the Missionary Encounter.* Berkeley: University of California Press, 2007.

Klassen, Pamela. *Spirits of Protestantism: Medicine, Healing, and Liberal Christianity.* Berkeley: University of California Press, 2011.

Kmiec, Douglas. "Standing Still—Did the Roberts Court Narrow, but Not Overrule, *Flast* to Allow Time to Re-think Establishment Clause Jurisprudence." *Pepperdine Law Review* 35 (2008): 509–22.

Koenig, Harold G. "Does God Wear a White Coat?" *Inside Duke University Medical Center Employee Newsletter* 13, no. 20 (2004).

———. "Religion, Spirituality, and Medicine: Research Findings and Implications for Clinical Practice." *Southern Medical Journal* 97, no. 12 (2004): 1194–1200.

Konefsky, Alfred S. "The Accidental Legal Historian: Herman Melville and the History of American Law." *Buffalo Law Review* 52 (2005): 1179–1276.

Koppelman, Andrew. 'Secular Purpose." *Virginia Law Review* 88 (2002): 87–166

Laborde, Cécile. "Political Liberalism and Religion: On Separation and Establishment." *Journal of Political Philosophy* 21 (2013): 67–86.

Lambert, Lake, III. *Spirituality Inc.: Religion in the American Workplace.* New York: New York University Press, 2009.

LaRocca-Pitts, Mark. "In FACT Chaplains Have a Spiritual Assessment Tool." *Australian Journal of Pastoral Care and Health* 3 (2009): 8–15.

Latham, Stephen R. "Law Students File Suit against Army: Charge Funding of Chaplaincy Is Unconstitutional." *The Crimson*, November 30, 1979.

Latterell, Justin. "Secular Purpose Tests, 1815–2012: The Moral Logics of Separating Civil and Religious Law in U.S. Courts." Dissertation in progress, Emory University.

Lawson, Kenneth E. *Faith and Hope in a War-Torn Land: The US Army Chaplaincy in the Balkans, 1995–2005.* Fort Leavenworth, KS: Combat Studies Institute Press, 2006.

Lee, William Sean, Christopher J. Burke, and Zonna M. Crayne. *Military Chaplains as Peace Builders: Embracing Indigenous Religions in Stability Operations.* Maxwell Air Force Base, AL: Air University Press, 2005.

Lehrich, Christopher, ed. *On Teaching Religion: Essays by Jonathan Z. Smith.* Oxford: Oxford University Press, 2012.

Leiter, Brian. "American Legal Realism." In *Blackwell Guide to the Philosophy of Law and Legal Theory*, edited by Martin P. Golding and William A. Edmundson, 50–66. Oxford: Blackwell, 2006.

Lincoln, Bruce. *Authority: Construction and Corrosion.* Chicago: University of Chicago Press, 1994.

———. *Gods and Demons, Priests and Scholars: Critical Explorations in the History of Religions.* Chicago: University of Chicago Press, 2012.

Lobel, Orly. "The Renew Deal: The Fall of Regulation and the Rise of Governance in Contemporary Legal Thought?" *Minnesota Law Review* 89 (2004): 342–470.

Loveland, Anne C. *American Evangelicals and the U.S. Military 1942–1993.* Baton Rouge: Louisiana State University Press, 1996.

———. "From Morale Builders to Moral Advocates: U.S. Army Chaplains in the Second Half of the Twentieth Century." In *The Sword of the Lord: Military Chaplains from the First to the Twenty-First Century*, edited by Doris L. Bergen. Notre Dame, IN: Notre Dame University Press, 2008.

Lupu, Ira C., and Robert W. Tuttle. "Ball on a Needle: *Hein v. Freedom from Religion Foundation, Inc.* and the Future of Establishment Clause Adjudication." *Brigham Young University Law Review* (2008): 115–226.

———. "The Forms and Limits of Religious Accommodation: The Case of RLUIPA." *Cardozo Law Review* 32 (2011): 1907–36.

———. "Instruments of Accommodation: The Military Chaplaincy and the Constitution." *West Virginia Law Review* 110 (2007): 89–166.

———. "The State of the Law 2008: A Cumulative Report on Legal Developments Affecting Government Partnerships with Faith-Based Organizations." The Roundtable of Religion and Social Policy, Rockefeller Institute of Government.

Lynn, Elizabeth, and Barbara G. Wheeler. "Missing Connections: Public Perceptions of Theological Education and Religious Leadership." *Auburn Studies* 6 (1999): 1–32.

Madison, James. "Detached Memoranda," ca. 1817. In *The Founders' Constitution*, Vol. 5, Amendment I (Religion), Document 64. Chicago: University of Chicago Press, 1987.

Maffly-Kipp, Laurie F. *Religion and Society in Frontier California.* New Haven, CT: Yale University Press, 1994.

Mahmood, Saba. *Politics of Piety: The Islamic Revival and the Feminist Subject.* Princeton, NJ: Princeton University Press, 2005.

———. "Religious Freedom, the Minority Question, and Geopolitics in the Middle East." *Comparative Studies in Society and History* 54, no. 2 (2012): 418–46.

———. "Sectarian Conflict and Family Law in Egypt." *American Ethnologist* 39 (2012): 54–62.

———. "Secularism, Hermeneutics, and Empire: The Politics of Islamic Reformation." *Public Culture* 18 (2006): 323–47.

Mallory, Jeremy G. "'An Officer of the House Which Chooses Him, and Nothing More': How Should *Marsh v. Chambers* Apply to Rotating Chaplains?" *University of Chicago Law Review* 73 (2006): 1421–53.

Marshall, William P., and Gene R. Nichol. "Not a *Winn*-Win: Misconstruing Standing and the Establishment Clause." *Supreme Court Review* (2011): 215–52.

Martin, Jeffrey C. "Recent Developments Concerning Accrediting Agencies in Postsecondary Education." *Law and Contemporary Problems* 57 (1994): 121–50.Masuzawa, Tomoko. *The Invention of World Religions, or How European Universalism Was Preserved in the Language of Pluralism.* Chicago: University of Chicago Press, 2005.

———. "The University and the Advent of the Academic Secular: The State's Management of Public Instruction." In *After Secular Law*, edited by Winnifred Fallers Sullivan, Robert A. Yelle, and Mateo Taussig-Rubbo, 119–39. Stanford, CA: Stanford University Press, 2011.

Matsa, Myrna. "Jewish Theology of Disaster and Recovery." *Journal of Jewish Spiritual Care* 10, no. 1 (2010): 20–31.

McConnell, Michael. "Reflections on Hosanna-Tabor." *Harvard Journal of Law & Public Policy* 35 (2012): 821–37.

McCoy, William. *Under Orders: A Spiritual Handbook for Military Personnel.* Ozark, AL: ACW Press, 2006.

McCutcheon, Russell. *Critics Not Caretakers: Redescribing the Public Study of Religion.* Albany: State University of New York Press, 2001.

McGreevy, John. *Catholicism and American Freedom: A History.* New York: Norton, 2004.

McLaughlin, Paul. "The Chaplain's Evolving Role in Peace and Humanitarian Relief Operations." *Peaceworks* 46 (2002).

McNair, Van, Jr. *Chaplain on the Waterfront: The Story of Father Saunders.* New York: Seabury Press, 1963.

Mead, Sidney. *The Lively Experiment: The Shaping of Christianity in America.* New York: Harper & Row, 1963.

Melville, Herman. *Billy Budd, Sailor (An Inside Narrative).* Edited by Harrison Hayford and Merton M. Sealts Jr. Chicago: University of Chicago Press, 1962.

Merad, Ali. *Christian Hermit in an Islamic World: A Muslim's View of Charles de Foucauld.* Translated by Zoe Hersov. Mahwah, NJ: Paulist Press, 2000.Mertz, Elizabeth, William Ford, and Gregory Matoesian, eds. *Translating the Social World for Law.* New York: Oxford University Press, 2013.

Mirkay, Nicholas A. "Losing Our Religion: Reevaluating the Section 501(C)(3) Exemption of Religious Organizations that Discriminate." *William & Mary Bill of Rights Journal* 17, no. 3 (2009): 715–64.

Mode, Daniel L. *The Grunt Padre: Father Vincent Robert Capodanno, Vietnam, 1966–1967.* Oak Lawn, IL: CMJ Marian Publishers, 2000.

Modern, John Lardas. "Ghosts of Sing Sing; or, The Metaphysics of Secularism." *Journal of the American Academy of Religion* 75 (2007): 615–50.

———. *Secularism in Antebellum America.* Chicago: University of Chicago Press, 2011.

Morris, Norval, and David Rothman, eds. *The Oxford History of the Prison*. Oxford: Oxford University Press, 1995.

Moyn, Samuel. "From Communist to Muslim: Religious Liberty in European Human Rights Law." *South Atlantic Quarterly* 113 (Winter 2014).

———. *The Last Utopia: Human Rights in History*. Cambridge, MA: Harvard University Press, 2010.

Myers-Shirk, Susan E. *Helping the Good Shepherd: Pastoral Counselors in a Psychotherapeutic Culture: 1925–1975*. Baltimore: Johns Hopkins University Press, 2009.

Nay, Robert. "The Operational, Social, and Religious Influences upon the Army Chaplain Field Manual, 1926–1952." Master of military art and science thesis, US Army Command and General Staff College, 2008.

Nolan, Steve. "Hope Beyond (Redundant) Hope: How Chaplains Work with Dying Patients." *Palliative Medicine* 25, no. 1 (2011):): 21–25.

Noll, Mark. "Jefferson's America? From 1789 to 1815, in Gordon Wood's Telling." *Christianity Today*, December 17, 2009.

Norwood, Frances. "The Ambivalent Chaplain: Negotiating Structural and Ideological Difference on the Margins of Modern-Day Hospital Medicine." *Medical Anthropology* 25, no. 1 (2006): 1–29.

Nouwen, Henri. *Gracias: A Latin American Journal*. New York: Harper & Row, 1983.

Novak, William. "The American Law of Association: The Legal-Political Construction of Civil Society." *Studies in American Political Development* 15 (2001): 163–88.

———. "The Myth of the 'Weak' American State." *American Historical Review* 113 (2008): 752–72.

O'Connor, Daniel. *The Chaplains of the East India Company 1601–1858*. New York: Continuum, 2012.

O'Donnell, Joseph F. "Clergy in the Military, Vietnam and After: One Chaplain's Reflections." In *The Sword of the Lord: Military Chaplains from the First to the Twenty-First Century*, edited by Doris L. Bergen. Notre Dame, IN: Notre Dame University Press, 2008.

Office of the Inspector General of the Department of Justice. *A Review of the Bureau of Prisons' Selection of Muslim Religious Services Providers*. 2004.

Oliver, Ian. "In Coffin's Pulpit: Yale's Protestant Chaplain Then and Now" (forthcoming).

O'Neill, Kevin. "The Reckless Will: Prison Chaplaincy and the Problem of Mara Salvatrucha." *Public Culture* 22, no. 1 (2010): 67–88.

Oppenheimer, Mark. "At 'Occupy' Protests, Bearing Christian Witness without Preaching." *New York Times*, November 11, 2011.

———. "The Rise of the Corporate Chaplain." *Bloomberg Businessweek*, August 23, 2012, 58–61.

Orsi, Robert. "Real Presences: Catholic Prayer as Intersubjectivity: From Practices of Presence to Sacred Absence; Theoretical Context." Posted on *Reverberations: New Directions in the Study of Prayer*, March 18, 2013. http://forums.ssrc.org/ndsp/2013/03/18/from-practices-of-presence-to-sacred-absence/.

Otis, Pauletta. "An Overview of the U.S. Military Chaplaincy: A Ministry of Presence and Practice." *Review of Faith & International Affairs* 7 (2009): 3–15.

Pargament, Kenneth, and Patrick Sweeney. "Building Spiritual Fitness in the Army: An Innovative Approach to a Vital Aspect of Human Development." *American Psychologist* 66 (2011): 58–64.

Peters, Jeremy W. "Give Us This Day, Our Daily Senate Scolding: Senate Chaplain Shows His Disapproval during Morning Prayer." *New York Times*, October 6, 2013, A1.

Phillips, Robert J. "The Military Chaplaincy of the 21st Century: *Cui Bono?*" Paper presented at the International Society for Military Ethics Conference on Religion and the Military and the Military and Codes of Ethics, Springfield, VA, January 25–26, 2009.

Pilgrim, M. Sgt. Eric B. "Spiritual Fitness: What Is It, Can We Train It, and If So, How?" http://www.hooah4usa.com/spirit/FHPspirit.htm (accessed January 27, 2013).

Plummer, David B. "Chaplaincy: The Greatest Story Never Told." *Journal of Pastoral Care* 50 (1996): 1–12.

Pressler, Franklin A. *Religion under Bureaucracy: Policy and Administration for Hindu Temples in South Asia.* Cambridge: Cambridge University Press, 1987.

Putnam, Robert D., and David E. Campbell. *American Grace: How American Religion Divides and Unites Us.* New York: Simon & Schuster, 2012.

Rabinow, Paul. "Foucault's Untimely Struggle: Toward a Form of Spirituality." *Theory Culture Society* 26 (2009): 25–45.

Rahdert, Mark C. "Forks Taken and Roads Not Taken: Standing to Challenge Faith-Based Spending." *Cardozo Law Review* 32 (2011): 1009–97.

Rennick, Joanne Benham. "The Ministry of Presence and Operational Stress." *Journal of Military and Strategic Studies.* 7, no. 4 (2005): n.p.

Resnicoff, Arnold E. "A New Symbol for America's Military Chaplains." *Washington Post*, August 9, 2011.

Rieff, Philip. *The Triumph of the Therapeutic: Uses of Faith after Freud.* Chicago: University of Chicago Press, 1966.

Risse, Guenter B. *Mending Bodies, Saving Souls: A History of Hospitals.* Oxford: Oxford University Press, 1999.

Rivers, Julian. *The Law of Organized Religions: Between Establishment and Secularism.* Oxford: Oxford University Press, 2010.

Roberts, John H., and James Turner. *The Sacred and Secular University.* Princeton, NJ: Princeton University Press, 2000.

Rock, Stella. "Editorial." *Religion, State and Society* 39 (2011): 1–8.

Rose, Nikolas. *Governing the Soul: Shaping the Private Self.* 2nd ed. London: Free Association Books, 1999.

Rosen, Richard D. "*Katcoff v. Marsh* at Twenty-Two: The Military Chaplaincy and the Separation of Church and State." *University of Toledo Law Review* 38 (2007): 1137–78.

Rudnyckyj, Daromir. "Spiritual Economies: Islam and Neoliberalism in Contemporary Indonesia." *Cultural Anthropology* 24 (2009): 104–14.

Sakurai, Michele L. "Ministry of Presence: Naming What Chaplains Do at the Bedside." PhD diss., San Francisco Theological Seminary, 2005.

Sanderson, Ward. "War in the Chaplain Corps." *Stars and Stripes*, November 23, 2003.

Santner, Eric. *On the Psychotheology of Everyday Life: Reflection on Freud and Rosenzweig.* Chicago: University of Chicago Press, 2001.

Schaffer, Susanne M. "School for Chaplains Dedicated at Fort Jackson." Associated Press, May 6, 2010.

Schmidt, Leigh. *Restless Souls: The Making of American Spirituality.* San Francisco: Harper, 2005.

Schragger, Richard. "The Relative Irrelevance of the Establishment Clause." *Texas Law Review* 89 (2011): 583–649.

Schulz, Kevin. *Tri-Faith America: How Catholics and Jews Held Postwar America to Its Protestant Promise.* Oxford: Oxford University Press, 2013.

Schwartz, Stuart B. *All Can Be Saved: Religious Tolerance and Salvation in the Iberian Atlantic World.* New Haven, CT: Yale University Press, 2008.

Sehat, David. *The Myth of American Religious Freedom.* Oxford: Oxford University Press, 2011.

Seiple, Chris. "Ready . . . or Not? Equipping the U.S. Military Chaplain for Interreligious Liaison." *Review of Faith & International Affairs* 7, no. 4 (2009): 43–49.

Seligman, Martin. *Flourish: A Visionary New Understanding of Happiness and Well-Being.* New York: Free Press, 2011.

Seritella, James, et al., eds. *Religious Organizations in the United States: A Study of Identity, Liberty, and the Law.* Durham, NC: Carolina Academic Press, 2004.

Sheehan, Jonathan. "What Was Disenchantment? History and the Secular Age." *Varieties of Secularism in a Secular Age,* edited by Michael Warner, Jonathan VanAntwerpen, and Craig Calhoun, 217–42. Cambridge, MA: Harvard University Press, 2010.

Smith, Jonathan Z. *Imagining Religion: From Babylon to Jonestown.* Chicago: University of Chicago Press, 1982.

Solie, Stacey. "For Scientologists Divorce Is No Simple Matter." *New York Times,* July 8, 2012.

Solomon, Jason M. "Law and Governance in the 21st Century Regulatory State." *Texas Law Review* 86 (2008): 819–56.

Stahl, Ronit Y. "God, War, and Politics: The American Military Chaplaincy and the Making of Modern American Religion." PhD diss., University of Michigan, 2014.

Staudt, Nancy C. "Taxpayers in Court: A Systematic Study of a (Misunderstood) Standing Doctrine." *Emory Law Journal* 52 (2003): 771–848.

Stokes, Alison. *Ministry after Freud.* Cleveland, OH: Pilgrim Press, 1985.

Stout, Taylor G. "The Costs of Religious Accommodation in Prisons." *Virginia Law Review* 96 (2010): 1201–39.

Sundt, Jody L., and Francis T. Cullen. "The Correctional Ideology of Prison Chaplains: A National Survey." *Journal of Criminal Justice* 30 (2002): 365–85.

Sullivan, Karen. *The Interrogation of Joan of Arc.* Minneapolis: University of Minnesota Press, 1999.

Sullivan, Winnifred Fallers. "The Church." *The Immanent Frame,* January 31, 2012. http://blogs.ssrc.org/tif/2012/01/31/the-church/ (accessed January 26, 2013).

———. *The Impossibility of Religious Freedom.* Princeton, NJ: Princeton University Press, 2005.

———. "Neutralizing Religion, or What Is the Opposite of 'Faith-Based?'" *History of Religions Journal* 41, no. 4 (2002): 369–90. Reprinted in *Religion: Beyond a Concept,* edited by Hent deVries, 563–79. New York: Fordham University Press, 2008.

———. *Paying the Words Extra: Religious Discourse in the Supreme Court of the United States.* Cambridge, MA: Harvard Center for the Study of World Religions, 1995.

———. *Prison Religion: Faith-Based Reform and the Constitution.* Princeton, NJ: Princeton University Press, 2009.

———. "The Religious Expert in American Courts." In "Expertise publique et religion," special issue, *Archives des Sciences Sociales des Religions* 155 (2011): 41–60.

Sullivan, Winnifred Fallers, and Lori Beaman, eds. *Varieties of Religious Establishment.* London: Ashgate, 2013.

Sullivan, Winnifred Fallers, Elizabeth Shakman Hurd, Saba Mahmood, and Peter Danchin, eds. *After Religious Freedom.* Chicago: University of Chicago Press, forthcoming.

Sullivan, Winnifred Fallers, and Christopher Swift. "The Chaplain: Physician of the Soul in a Secular Age." In *A World of Work,* edited by Ilana Gershon. Ithaca: Cornell University Press, forthcoming.

Sullivan, Winnifred Fallers, Robert Yelle, and Mateo Taussig-Rubbo, eds. *After Secular Law.* Stanford, CA: Stanford University Press, 2011.

Sundt, Jody L., and Francis T. Cullen, "The Correctional Ideology of Prison Chaplains: A National Survey." *Journal of Criminal Justice* 30 (2002): 365–85.

The Supreme Court of the United States: Hearings and Reports on Successful and Unsuccessful Nominations of Supreme Court Justices by the Senate Judiciary Committee, 1916–.

Swift, Christopher. *Hospital Chaplaincy in the Twenty-First Century.* Farnham, UK: Ashgate, 2009.

———. "Speaking of the Same Things Differently." In *Spirituality in Health Care Contexts,* edited by Helen Orchard. London: Jessica Kingsley Publishers, 2001.

Tabak, Robert. "The Emergence of Jewish Health-Care Chaplaincy: The Professionalization of Spiritual Care." *American Jewish Archives Journal* 62, no. 2 (2010): 89–109.

Taussig-Rubbo, Mateo. "Outsourcing Sacrifice: The Labor of Private Military Contractors." *Yale Journal of Law & the Humanities* 21, no. 1 (2009): 105–70.

Taves, Ann. *Fits, Trances and Visions: Experiencing Religion and Explaining Experience from Wesley to James.* Princeton, NJ: Princeton University Press, 1999.

———. *Religious Experience Reconsidered: A Building Block Approach to the Study of Religion and Other Special Things.* Princeton, NJ: Princeton University Press, 2009.

Taylor, Charles. *A Secular Age.* Cambridge, MA: Harvard University Press, 2005.

Townsend, Tim. "Military Chaplains Are Faith Mismatch for Personnel They Serve." *St Louis Post-Dispatch,* January 9, 2011. Accessed July 12, 2013. http://www.stltoday.com/lifestyles/faith-and-values/military-chaplains-are-faith-mismatch-for-personnel-they-serve/article_19c66ee6–82b8–59f7-b3d5-fd3cc05bc538.html.

US Air Force. "Report of the Headquarters Review Group concerning Religious Climate at the U.S. Air Force Academy." 2005.

US Army Chaplain Corps. "The Army Chaplaincy Strategic Plan, 2009–2014." http://www.chapnet.army.mil/pdf/strategic_map.pdf (accessed January 27, 2013).

US Department of Veteran Affairs. "History of VA Chaplaincy." Available at http://www.va.gov/CHAPLAIN/components/History_of_VA_Chaplaincy.asp (accessed January 19, 2013).

US Joint Chiefs of Staff. "Religious Support in Joint Operations." Joint Publication 1-05. 2004.

VandeCreek, Larry, and Lance Burton, eds. "Professional Chaplaincy: Its Role and Importance in Healthcare." *Journal of Pastoral Care* 55, no. 1 (2001): 81–97.

Vitello, Paul. "Hospice Chaplains Take Up Bedside Counseling." *New York Times,* October 29, 2008.

Wagoner, Walter D. *The Seminary: Protestant and Catholic.* New York: Sheed and Ward, 1966.

Warner, Michael, Jonathan van Antwerpen, and Craig Calhoun. *Varieties of Secularism in a Secular Age.* Cambridge, MA: Harvard University Press, 2010.

Weil, Rachel. *A Plague of Informers.* New Haven, CT: Yale University Press, forthcoming.

Wheeler, Barbara G. "Is There a Problem: Theological Students and Religious Leadership for the Future." *Auburn Studies* 8 (2001): 1–28.

Wheeler, Barbara G., Sharon L. Miller, and Daniel O. Aleshire. "How Are We Doing: The Effectiveness of Theological Schools as Measured by the Vocations and Views of Graduates." *Auburn Studies* 13 (2007).

White, Christopher G. *Unsettled Minds: Psychology and the American Search for Spiritual Assurance, 1830–1940.* Berkeley: University of California Press, 2009.

White, Joseph M. *The Diocesan Seminary in the United States: A History from the 1870s to the Present.* Notre Dame, IN: University of Notre Dame Press, 1989.

Whitehouse, Harvey. *Modes of Religiosity: A Cognitive Theory of Religious Transmission.* Lanham, MD: AltaMira Press, 2004.

Whitman, James Q. *Harsh Justice: Criminal Punishment and the Widening Divide between America and Europe.* Oxford: Oxford University Press, 2003.

———. "Separating Church and State: The Atlantic Divide." *Historical Reflections/Réflexions historiques* 34, no. 3 (2008): 86–104.

Wildhack, William A., III. "Navy Chaplains at the Crossroads: Navigating the Intersection of Free Speech, Free Exercise, Establishment, and Equal Protection." *Naval Law Review* 51 (2005): 217–51.

Williams, Roger. *The Hireling Ministry None of Christ's.* London, 1652.

Wuthnow, Robert. *After Heaven: Spirituality in America since the 1950s.* Berkeley: University of California Press, 1998.

———. *The God Problem: Expressing Faith and Being Reasonable.* Berkeley: University of California Press, 2012.

———. *The Restructuring of American Religion: Society and Faith since World War II.* Princeton, NJ: Princeton University Press, 1988.

Yates, Julian E. "Armed for Combat." *Army and Navy Chaplain* 12 (1942): 3–4.

Yelle, Robert. *The Language of Disenchantment: Protestant Literalism and Colonial Discourse in British India.* Oxford: Oxford University Press, 2013.

Young, S. David. *The Rule of Experts: Occupational Licensing in America.* Washington, DC: Cato Institute, 1987.

pastoral care (*cont.*)
and IRS regulations, 134; Jewish, 89,
176; legislative, 64, 150; and listening,
185n36; and MDiv, 111; and Michel
Foucault, 14, 20; Pentecostal, 131n78;
and presence, 177, 195; Protestant,
112; in seminaries, 117; theologies of,
44n64; by VA, 45, 46, 49
pastoral power, 19–22, 31, 51
paternalism (European), 21
patients, 11, 37–50, 54, 84–85, 87, 102–3,
124–27, 136, 150, 154–58, 173, 185–86
patriotic modes of religious practice, 177
patriotic purposes, 14
Paul, Saint, 169
Pearl Harbor, 6
Pentagon, 174
Pentecostal chaplain. *See* chaplain(s)
Pentecostal Christianity, 125
Pentecostal churches, 131
Pentecostal minister, 156
Pentecostals, 129, 133, 160; neo-
Pentecostal, 81; Protestant, 104
Perry, Rick, 35
personal law jurisdictions, 169
Petraeus, David, 201
Pew Foundation, 92
Pew Research Center, 8n12, 22n9
phenomenology of religion, 18, 51, 134,
165, 168, 188
Philadelphia, x, 83, 89
Philippines, 61n20
Phillips, Jeffrey, 182
Phillips, Roger J., 74n60
philosophy, 22; Buddhist, 111; of CPE,
154; of life, 47; natural, 46; perennialist,
194; personal, 128n73; of religion, 122;
stoic, 27
phrenology, 32
physicians, 87n107, 89–90. *See also*
doctor(s)
Piaget, Jean, 44
piety, 54, 96, 179, 180
Pledge of Allegiance, 35
pluralism (minimal vs. maximal), 160
pluralism (religious), 13, 143, 149n36,
161, 174
police, 137, 154
Poling, Clark V., 69n43
political authority. *See* authority
political discourse, 15

political partisanship, 11
political science, 8, 198
political theology, 16
politics, 9, 80, 165, 169; of fear, xi; religious, 12, 21, 63, 72, 77, 140, 153, 168,
171, 173, 177, 187–89
pope, 21, 59
Pope Pius XII, 101
popular sovereignty, 21
populist America, 57
populist ethos of credentialing, 105
populist faith in local management, 140
populist religion, 137
positive thinking, 186
positivism, 51
postcolonial administrations, 21
postcolonial countries, 10n22
postcolonial state, 197n9
posttraumatic stress disorder (PTSD), 44
poverty, 197n7
Practice of the Presence of God, The (Brother
Lawrence), 175
practices (of care), 20
prayer, 24, 35, 44, 47–48, 75, 85, 100,
132, 136n87, 142, 146, 150–53, 160,
167nn97–98
preaching, 4, 53, 56, 59, 60–62, 107, 109,
112, 149, 156, 158, 179, 189
prejudice, 159, 201
Presbyterian(s), 113
Presbyterian minister, 151
presence: divine, 62, 174, 175, 176, 183,
184, 185, 190; Eucharistic, 175, 179,
181; healing, 186; infusing, 186; physical, 175
priest, ix, 5, 47, 53, 58n13, 65, 71, 86, 158,
176; Catholic, ix, xii, 59, 60, 128, 157,
164, 179, 183–84; chaplains, x n6; Old
Testament, 66–67; of the secular, 3, 87
priesthood of all believers, 61, 112
priestly role of the chaplain, 67, 72, 150,
154, 178
priest-penitent privilege, 58n13
prison(s), 36, 86; chaplains in, x, xv, 4,
13, 18, 53, 61, 64, 65, 77, 78, 95n127,
101, 130n76, 137, 150, 155, 175, 176,
193, 194; in Kafka's *The Trial*, 5; prison
chaplains (*see* chaplain[s]); religion in,
79, 80, 89, 148, 202; self-help literature
in, 44n64; Victorian, 90
prisoner(s), 6, 54, 150, 173, 178, 181, 184